Madness at Home

MEDICINE AND SOCIETY

Andrew Scull, Editor

This series examines the development of medical knowledge and psychiatric practice from historical and sociological perspectives. The books contribute to a scholarly and critical reflection on the nature and role of medicine and psychiatry in modern societies.

1. *The Regulation of Madness: Origins of Incarceration in France,* by Robert Castel, translated by W. D. Halls
2. *Stubborn Children: Controlling Delinquency in the United States, 1640–1981,* by John R. Sutton
3. *Social Order/Mental Disorder: Anglo-American Psychiatry in Historical Perspective,* by Andrew Scull
4. *Inheriting Madness: Professionalization and Psychiatric Knowledge in Nineteenth-Century France,* by Ian R. Dowbiggin
5. *Madness and Social Representations: Living with the Mad in One French Community,* by Denise Jodelet, translated by Tim Pownall, edited by Gerard Duveen
6. *Inventing the Feeble Mind: A History of Mental Retardation in the United States,* by James W. Trent, Jr.
7. *Impure Science: AIDS, Activism, and the Politics of Knowledge,* by Steven G. Epstein
8. *Mental Ills and Bodily Cures: Psychiatric Treatment in the First Half of the Twentieth Century,* by Joel Braslow
9. *Mind Games: American Culture and the Birth of Psychotherapy,* by Eric Caplan
10. *Imperial Bedlam: Institutions of Madness in Colonial Southwest Nigeria,* by Jonathan Sadowsky
11. *Undertaker of the Mind: John Monro and Mad-Doctoring in Eighteenth-Century England,* by Jonathan Andrews and Andrew Scull
12. *Customers and Patrons of the Mad Trade: The Management of Lunacy in Eighteenth-Century London, with the Complete Text of John Monro's 1766 Case Book,* by Jonathan Andrews and Andrew Scull
13. *Madness at Home: The Psychiatrist, the Patient, and the Family in England, 1820–1860,* by Akihito Suzuki

Madness at Home

THE PSYCHIATRIST, THE PATIENT, AND THE FAMILY IN ENGLAND, 1820–1860

Akihito Suzuki

UNIVERSITY OF CALIFORNIA PRESS
BERKELEY LOS ANGELES LONDON

University of California Press, one of the most distinguished university presses in the United States, enriches lives around the world by advancing scholarship in the humanities, social sciences, and natural sciences. Its activities are supported by the UC Press Foundation and by philanthropic contributions from individuals and institutions. For more information, visit www.ucpress.edu.

University of California Press
Berkeley and Los Angeles, California

University of California Press, Ltd.
London, England

Library of Congress Cataloging-in-Publication Data

Suzuki, Akihito, 1963–.
Madness at home : the psychiatrist, the patient, and the family in England, 1820–1860 / Akihito Suzuki.
p. ; cm. — (Medicine and society ; 13)
Includes bibliographical references and index.
ISBN 0-520-24580-6 (cloth : alk. paper)
1. Mentally ill—Care—England—History—19th century. 2. Mentally ill—Home care—England—History—19th century. 3. Mentally ill—England—Family relationships—History—19th century. 4. Mental health laws—England—History—19th century. 5. Psychiatry—England—History—19th century.
[DNLM: 1. England. 2. Psychiatry—history. 3. History of Medicine, 19th Cent. 4. Mental Disorders—history. WM 11 FE5 S968m 2006]
I. Title: Psychiatrist, the patient, and the family in England, 1820–1860. II. Title. III. Series.

RC450.G7S89 2006
616.89'00942'09034—dc22 2005010547

Manufactured in Canada

15 14 13 12 11 10 09 08 07 06
10 9 8 7 6 5 4 3 2 1

This book is printed on New Leaf EcoBook 60, containing 60% post-consumer waste, processed chlorine free; 30% de-inked recycled fiber, elemental chlorine free; and 10% FSC-certified virgin fiber, totally chlorine free. EcoBook 60 is acid-free and meets the minimum requirements of ANSI/ASTM D5634–01 (*Permanence of Paper*).

To Mika and Kanako

CONTENTS

ILLUSTRATIONS

FIGURES

TABLES

ACKNOWLEDGMENTS

This book has been written over a long period spanning my years in Britain and in Japan, and it has incurred a large number of debts across the globe.

At the Wellcome Institute for the History of Medicine in London, I was lucky to meet Jonathan Andrews, Peter Bartlett, Cheryce Kramer, Sonu Shamdasani, and Philip Wilson. Their help, encouragement, and lasting friendship were invaluable. The Institute's teaching staff, particularly Bill Bynum, Chris Lawrence, and Michael Neve, were constantly supportive. My brief stay in Aberdeen, Scotland, was rewarded by a warm friendship with Clark Lawlor. David Wright has continued to inspire my research, first from Oxford and then from Canada. From California, Andrew Scull has provided unflagging support throughout the years I have been struggling to write this book.

I will remain most deeply indebted to the late Roy Porter, who has changed my life since he supervised my thesis. His intellectual vigor, generosity with eye-opening suggestions, and infectious enthusiasm for new perspectives are the model I have tried to emulate. I can only hope this book is not a travesty of Porter's social history of medicine.

Back in Japan, my colleagues at Keio University have provided a congenial working atmosphere. My thanks go particularly to Ken'ichi Tomobe, Takeshi Nagashima, Kentaro Saito, Junko Kitanaka, Hayato Kosuge, and Hiroshi Muto. At the library of Keio University, Kazuhiko Kinoshita, Maya Yamada, Masako Yamada, Makiko Ueoka, Yasuko Hanai, and Emiri

Kon'nai have efficiently dealt with an insane number of requests. My research assistants, Kaoriko Yokozawa, Yoko Yogo, Chikako Maruta, and Chiemi Iwamoto, have been both cheerful and unfailingly reliable. I should also like to express deep gratitude to Jacqueline Volin and Randy Heyman at the University of California Press for their immense help, and to Madeleine Adams and Caroline Knapp for copy editing and proofreading.

Now, at the very last, the time has come to thank my family, Mika and Kanako. Mika has lived with this book now for almost a decade, the memory of which I cherish. But for her patience and love, this book would never exist. Kanako had to spend countless hours both at home and abroad with a father who had to work on a PC. Even before she can read, she has acquired the skill to be cheerful and supportive of her father. Only they know how much they are in this book. It is a pure joy to thank them and tell them that it is finished.

Introduction

Psychiatry in the Private and the Public Spheres

THIS BOOK EXAMINES THE SOCIAL history of madness from the perspective of the family. I have chosen the family as my main subject for two reasons—first, because family members historically have been important actors in psychiatric decision making, and second, because they are now assuming vital roles in social policies for the mentally ill in many developed countries. Mental diseases, particularly in their more severe forms, impair the sufferer's ability to make proper decisions for and by him- or herself. The patient often fails or refuses to realize the very fact that he or she is ill. Therefore, recognizing the existence of the disease often has fallen to those who live with the patient, usually his or her family. Because patients frequently cannot take actions that are conducive to their own welfare, their families assume the responsibility for arranging treatment or custody. Because the family has historically performed a vital function by judging a sick person's state, transforming him or her into a "patient," and providing or seeking the assistance they regard as necessary, the family has been, arguably, the real agent in psychiatric treatment and care.

The social policies for the mentally ill that are now widely applied in Western Europe and North America have called the family back to center stage. From the 1960s on, quite a few countries have pursued the policy of decarceration: the number of patients hospitalized on a long-term basis has been drastically reduced, and these patients have been returned to their families or accommodated in neighborhood hostels. Historical examination of the role of the family in the care of the mentally ill therefore is highly relevant for contemporary concerns.

In the scholarship on the history of psychiatry in nineteenth-century England, however, family has not been given due attention until quite recently. This neglect is mainly because historians have focused on asylums, which brought about enormous changes in the structure of the care and control of the mentally ill during the nineteenth century. Indeed, historians of psychiatry have characterized the nineteenth century by two interrelated features: the rise of the asylum and the advent of the psychiatric profession.[1] Specialist institutions took the insane away from home, assuming the responsibility of their treatment and custody. Medically qualified men, many of whom specialized in the treatment of mental diseases, gradually replaced the patient's family as the major decision makers regarding the patient's treatment. This portrayal of nineteenth-century psychiatry in England is basically correct: asylums multiplied; their medical superintendents were well established; psychiatrists' professional status was slowly, if not fully, becoming recognized; and the number of lunatics taken care of in medical institutions increased. Although considerable nuances have been added and many important revisions have been made to the chronology, dynamics, and causes of this momentous change, none has refuted the core thesis of the rise of the asylum and psychiatry in Victorian England. Nor do I intend to dispute it. It is true that the family became less frequently the locus of care for those recognized as suffering from mental disease, and the family's role in providing care and in organizing a therapeutic or controlling regime diminished during the course of the nineteenth century.[2]

Caution is necessary, however. Historians have not so much verified as assumed the diminishing role of the family vis-à-vis that of the asylum and the psychiatric profession. Between the asylum and psychiatrists and the home and families, a kind of zero-sum game is tacitly assumed, in which the gain of the asylum and the psychiatric profession was the loss of the home and the family. No historical study has actually evaluated whether this model is applicable to nineteenth-century psychiatry as a whole.[3]

Our knowledge of the relationship between the family and the institution is therefore one-sided: although scholarly attention has been lavished on psychiatry in institutions, surprisingly little is known about how lunatics were treated in their own homes, as James Moran has pointed out in his pioneering work on the domestic management of the insane in antebellum America.[4] The major goal of this book is to fill that gap in historical scholarship and to explore the domestic side of the social history of insanity. In so doing, I will show that a set of behaviors that can be called "domestic psychiatry" existed, and even flourished, during the Victorian period. The rise of psychiatry certainly affected, but did not destroy, this well-established set of behaviors toward lunatics in their own families. Actually, some evidence suggests that institutional psychiatry and domestic psychiatry reinforced each other. During the rise of professional psychiatry, the family did *not* lose its cultural framework for understanding madness. Indeed, there are reasons to believe that the framework of domestic psychiatry became more established and better articulated in the early nineteenth century. On the other hand, domestic psychiatry had certain limits and weaknesses, exhibiting signs of destabilization. I will claim, however, that the destabilization of domestic psychiatry was not caused by the rise of the asylum and professional psychiatry per se: its decline was mediated by those societal forces that promoted asylum-based psychiatry, rather than by the institution of psychiatry itself.

Two further considerations have led me to investigate madness at home in early nineteenth-century England. One is a general observation about the period; the other is the specific nature of the sources I have used for this book. The early nineteenth century was once considered the golden age of family in England, Western Europe, and North America.[5] Family was idolized as the essential basis of private affection and public virtue. In the last hundred years, numerous studies have debunked the myth of the Victorian "home sweet home," which hid ugly coercion and hypocrisy. Nonetheless, people's belief in the family was a concrete historical reality. Patterns of behavior of many men and women in the Victorian age were actually conditioned by the cultural emphasis laid on the family. I examine in detail the contours of domestic psychiatry in the context of the Victorian emphasis on the family. Suffice it to say here that one naturally expects that family members' attitudes toward mad members of their own family were strongly conditioned by their attitudes toward one another in general.

I have used materials that are particularly suitable for examining the family's response to its insane member. The major evidence used in this book is newspaper reports of the cases of commission of lunacy, which was a legal procedure to deprive persons of their civil rights because of their unsoundness of mind. The major thrust of the material is the family's perception of its member's inability to conduct his or her daily life, and the family's attempts to have the lunatic's inability demonstrated to the court.

One important and unique characteristic of these materials is that they were *not* concerned with confinement. Those in custodial institutions were a minority among the subjects of commission of lunacy during the period covered in this study. Some of them were under confinement of one sort or another, but that was not the point of the legal procedure. This feature of the source has enabled me to examine the family's attitude toward its insane member *outside* the context of institutionalization and confinement.

Incarcerating institutions have provided the major source for social historians of nineteenth-century psychiatry in England. This is a natural and obvious choice: a wealth of material is preserved in the archives of county asylums, mental hospitals, and some private madhouses, and it has been fruitfully employed by historians. Such exclusive reliance on institutional records, however, poses the danger of distorting the picture of the care and the control of the insane in a society as a whole.[6] Institutional records, after all, tell stories of those patients whose care and control at home was, at least temporarily, not available or given up. Their case histories do not often reveal much about what had been done at home before they came to the institution, and what would be done after they left it "uncured" or (partially) "relieved." What was done to those patients who remained at home has largely been left unexplored. The records of commissions of lunacy solve such evidentiary problems of institutional archives to a considerable extent. Many cases of commission of lunacy explicitly reveal the families' understanding, care, and control of lunatics in their own homes. With the help of such pieces of information, I have written a history of lunacy from the family's viewpoint. I should mention one caveat about the limits of my sources and my arguments. The subjects of commissions of lunacy came almost exclusively from the wealthy sector of English society during the period covered in this book. Working-class subjects were virtually absent in my data set.[7] Accordingly, my arguments throughout this book apply only to middle- and upper-class wealthy families.

I will not extensively summarize recent major works on nineteenth-century British psychiatry, for two reasons: first, because many are concerned with issues related to institutional confinement, which are not the major focus of this book; and second, because such overviews, particularly about institutional provisions for the poor, were recently given by Joseph Melling, Peter Bartlett, and David Wright.[8] Instead, I will provide a historiographical overview from a different angle, selecting issues that are highly relevant to this study.

D.H. Tuke's *Chapters in the History of the Insane in the British Isles* (1882) is perhaps the earliest work in English on the history of psychiatry based on a serious piece of historical scholarship.[9] Based on extensive research into primary sources, Tuke told the familiar story of the progress of humanitarianism centered on institutions for the insane. York Retreat and the 1815–16 Parliamentary Inquiry into extensive and shocking abuses at Bethlem Hospital and York Asylum (not to be confused with the Retreat in the same city) had pride of place in Tuke's narrative of the march of civilization in psychiatry, the culmination of which was John Conolly's successful implementation of the nonrestraint system at the Middlesex County Asylum at Hanwell in 1840. Tuke thus saw the history of psychiatry in the light of the nineteenth-century belief in progress: civilization and humanitarianism had been slowly but steadily overcoming superstition, ignorance, barbarity, and cruelty.

This high-Victorian narrative did not meet with full-frontal attacks until the 1960s, when it was challenged by Michel Foucault and by sympathizers of the antipsychiatry movement.[10] In scholarship inspired, but not dictated, by their penetrating and provocative attacks against asylumdom, Andrew Scull explored the history of the asylum and the asylum-based establishment of the psychiatric profession in nineteenth-century England. His *Museums of Madness* was published in 1979, setting a high standard of critical analysis based on close readings of historical materials.[11] It is mainly through critical response to Scull's seminal work that research in the history of nineteenth-century British psychiatry has been conducted in the last twenty-five years. Since the late 1980s, interpretations put forward by Scull and Foucault have been challenged by numerous historians, including Melling, Bartlett, Wright, Roy Porter, Len Smith, Jonathan Andrews, and Elaine Murphy, to name only a few. Despite their differences from Scull and Foucault and among themselves, these historians share one basic assumption with their targets of criticism: that the progress of humanitarianism and the benign intention of psychiatrists should not be the major analytical framework for understanding the history of nineteenth-century psychiatry in England. This negative statement loosely binds them together and justifies calling them "revisionist" historians of English psychiatry. This book is also a work of revisionist history in that sense.

In this broad revisionist historiography of the development of psychiatry from the early modern period to the nineteenth century, there are two interpretative models: one is the "public" model; the other is the "private" model. By categorizing major interpretations into the public and private models, I do not want to pigeonhole historians but rather to highlight one basic binary structure within which psychiatric facilities grew from the early modern period on. Admittedly, "the public" and "the private" are categories too broad or vague for use as analytical tools. Nonetheless, as Jose Harris's work on English society in the late nineteenth and early twentieth centuries has shown, these categories have great heuristic power, which enables historians to discover patterns in seemingly diverse events and to detect tensions in apparently simple phenomena.[12]

In the "public" model of the history of psychiatry, public authorities occupy center stage. Central and local governments' responses to troubles and threats of various kinds posed by lunatics are regarded as the driving force in the making of psychiatry and the care and custody of the insane. The most forceful advocate of this view is Michel Foucault. In his *Histoire de la folie* and many subsequent works, Foucault claimed that a prototype of modern psychiatric power was forged when public institutions were created for incarcerating lunatics with criminals and vagabonds. These institutions for "great confinement" were the French absolutist state's solution to the problems of the insane who were wandering and threatening public order. The subsequent unfolding of psychiatry was, according to Foucault, the development of different techniques to cope with the incarcerated insane within institutional walls.[13] Similarly, Andrew Scull's account of the making of English psychiatry is centered around the creation of a nationwide system of publicly funded county asylums, which emerging psychiatrists, or "mad-doctors," appropriated as the site to consolidate their professional status.[14] Recent critics of Scull, most notably Peter Bartlett and Len Smith, have shifted the focus away from the psychiatrist to local networks of power; still, they share with Scull a focus on public authorities or those elites who set the scene for the care and custody of the insane, although their detailed analysis of the roles of central government, local authorities, and voluntary initiatives has opened a new and promising vista for further research.[15] Foucault, Scull, and other historians have assumed that the initiatives taken by public authorities and members of the elite were the ultimate force behind the creation of psychiatric institutions, the setting of basic parameters for their use, and the shaping of the discipline of psychiatry. For Foucault and Scull, the influence of the state and the central government was paramount, whereas Bartlett, Smith, Melling, and Murphy have emphasized the role of local governments and locally based elites. Prominent in Foucault and Scull, but less so in Bartlett and others, are attempts to identify larger societal changes that prompted public authorities to adapt their machinery of social control or welfare provision. Foucault identified the social change that predisposed the creation of *hôpitaux générales* as the early modern problem of vagrancy. For Scull, it was the advent of capitalist society and "commercialization of existence."

The "private" approach, on the other hand, emphasizes the importance of the family's private need to cope with the problem of the lunacy of a family member. The works of Michael MacDonald best represent this direction of investigation for early modern England. In his examination of Richard Napier's practice on two thousand patients with various psychological problems, MacDonald has clarified that Napier's psychiatry took the form of personal encounters initiated by the clients. Napier's clients (the patients and their families) disclosed their personal and domestic problems, and the clergyman tried to console the patients, soothe their personal agony, and, if possible, cure them.[16] Roy Porter concurs with MacDonald in his emphasis on private initiative, despite the former's criticisms of the latter's chronology, which painted the eighteenth century as a dark "Middle Ages" in psychiatry. In particular, Porter has underlined the emergence of profit-making institutions for the insane as one of the keys to understanding the development of English psychiatry. These institutions were private enterprises designed to meet the increasing demand from well-off families troubled by insane family members. In response to the rising demand for high-quality care, market-conscious entrepreneurs invented a gentle psychiatric regime in a genteel environment. One of the components of the new psychiatry identified by Porter was personal maneuvering techniques—some subtle, others histrionic—to manage and control insane patients, which was, Porter suggests, the prototype of "moral treatment."[17] In the approaches taken by MacDonald and Porter, the basic parameter of psychiatric practice was practitioners' responses to the demands of their clients. MacDonald has claimed that the early modern worldview, deeply embedded in religion and magic, conditioned both the complaints of patients and their treatment by practitioners. Porter has emphasized that both the demand for and the supply of new psychiatry were products of the advent of the commercial society, forged in the affluence of London and the urban renaissance of English cities. In both historians' accounts, public authorities of any kind play conspicuously small roles in setting the scene for psychiatric clinical encounters.

"The public" and "the private" quite often coexisted in a single psychiatric facility, and historians have recently paid close attention to the intersection of the two. Sometimes, public authorities demanded psychiatric facilities, which private enterprise supplied; a handful of privately run and profit-making madhouses in London had grown into gigantic institutions by the end of the eighteenth century through accepting public patients sent by parish authorities. On the other hand, many public asylums for "pauper lunatics" in the nineteenth century also housed fee-paying patients. Voluntary subscriptions were combined with county rates to build and sustain asylums, many of which housed patients from diverse social classes.[18] In Len Smith's apt phrase, the "mixed economy of the care of the insane" was an eminent feature of English psychiatric provision in the eighteenth and nineteenth centuries. Just as psychiatric institutions operated in the mixed economy, psychiatrists often held posts in public institutions and at the same time had extensive private practices.[19] Jonathan Andrews and Andrew Scull have highlighted in fascinating detail the tensioned coexistence of these two aspects in the career of a prominent eighteenth-century mad-doctor, John Monro, who combined his appointment at a charity hospital with an extensive private practice for wealthy patients.[20]

Moreover, attempts have been made to integrate the public and the private and/or the supply and the demand for psychiatric facilities by examining the interaction of the asylum and the family.[21] Many historians have applied the "push-and-pull" model to the process of confinement in psychiatric institutions; families pushed out their troublesome members, whom the asylum pulled within its walls. Having the two variables in mind, Mark Finnane and John Walton have explored asylum committals in Ireland and Lancashire, respectively.[22] Building on their work, David Wright has proposed an "analytical framework for understanding the interface between the family and the formal medical institution" in an important paper published in 1997.[23] His monograph on the Earlswood Asylum has shown that such framework can be usefully applied to archives of individual institutions.[24]

Such historiographical innovations are not limited to the study of British psychiatry. Around the same time in the 1980s and 1990s, French, German, and American historians of psychiatry started to research the relationship between the asylum and the family, the supply side and the demand side of psychiatric care. American and European historians have, however, pursued lines of research somewhat different from those of British-based (or British-educated) historians. While historians of British asylum psychiatry, most notably Smith, Bartlett, and Melling, are keener to grasp the administrative structures and their socioeconomic background, historians of French, German, and American psychiatry are more interested in investigating the psychiatric culture of the interactions within and outside the asylum, or between psychiatric practice and domestic concerns. In other words, British historians tend to emphasize the "hard" organization of asylum psychiatry, while European and American historians put, relatively speaking, more stress on the "soft" content of the asylum. In Fernand Braudel's phrases, the former investigate the legal-administrative structure while the latter examine sociocultural events.

French, German, and North American historians of psychiatry thus have given much more attention to doctor-patient-family relationships and their incorporation into psychiatric concepts. Developing Robert Castel's view of French asylum committal as the postrevolutionary replacement of *lettres des cachet,* Yannick Ripa has argued that the way in which domestic problems were settled was influenced by the presence of public asylums in the day-to-day landscape of late nineteenth-century French society. Ripa maintains that the "voluntary" committal of lunatics gave the family another means to resolve family discord by mobilizing public authorities' intervention, and that asylums served the purpose of suppressing juvenile and female domestic rebellion as well as silencing political and social protest.[25] In her article on a late nineteenth-century Parisian asylum, Patricia Prestwich has explored a question similar to Ripa's but has reached a subtler conclusion.[26] Prestwich has shown that families' demand for institutional psychiatric service created a new role for the asylum and its doctors: the asylum and alienists were increasingly seen as a convenient and temporary access-point for settling or relieving domestic problems.[27] Likewise, Ruth Harris has perceptively shown that late nineteenth-century psychiatrists sanctioned women to redress injuries done to them by their husbands and lovers, and, at the same time, imposed on them an inferior "feminine" role. In the American context, Nancy Tomes has given a benign picture of what she has called "the collaboration between doctor and family," but she concurs in emphasizing the integration of the asylum and the family into a new psychiatric culture in the nineteenth century.[28] Similarly, Elizabeth Lunbeck has shown that in the early twentieth-century Boston Psychopathic Hospital, asylum doctors transformed themselves into hospital psychiatrists who were specialists in everyday psychological life, with expertise in dealing with patients' domestic problems.[29]

European and American historians' insights into the cultural interaction between psychiatry and its clients might well be incorporated into nineteenth-century British psychiatry. British historians' concentration on the administration of lunacy has generated one lacuna in their historiography: their failure to incorporate the experience of the doctor, the family, and the patient and to analyze their multilayered interactions. They are strong and solid on the societal structure in which confinement of lunatics took place, but often neglect to explore in depth how both laypeople and doctors understood, conceptualized, and felt about madness. Legal and administrative history of lunacy often fails to address the cultural history of madness, to examine the "meaning" of madness. This does not mean that the cultural history of the meaning of madness has been absent in the British historiography of psychiatry. Indeed, it has been a subject of extensive and lively scholarship. Sander Gilman, Elaine Showalter, Helen Small, and many others have studied medical, literary, and visual materials on madness with considerable dexterity.[30] Many of their analyses are, however, somewhat separated from the actual context in which the meaning of madness was created in a dynamic way. The meaning of the illness was not just adopted from the cultural showcase in which ready-made representations were displayed, as Gilman and others occasionally assume. It was forged from the specific life and circumstances of an individual patient, as Arthur Kleinman has perceptively suggested in his patient-centered hermeneutics of chronic illness. Kleinman has called for the anthropological study of transference of the vital significance from the patient's life to the illness experience. The patient, argues Kleinman, "[fashions] serviceable explanations of the various aspects of illness and treatment."[31] As Nancy Tomes has demonstrated in her close study of the diaries and papers kept by a female patient in Pennsylvania Hospital before her committal to the asylum, patients' life histories and their experience of mental illness before their institutionalization intersected with doctors' treatment strategies.[32]

These works by British, European, and American historians in the last generation have collectively suggested that psychiatry in the past was shaped by a multitude of complex bilateral interactions among three agents: the private needs of families, the public concerns of policy makers and administrators, and the professional strategies of psychiatric practitioners. Public psychiatric policy with medical apparatus penetrated the domestic realm, sometimes reinforcing patriarchal power over wives and children, sometimes transforming the power structure within the family. On the other hand, the psychiatric apparatus was under constant improvisation by clients, to whom administrators and doctors had to respond by inventing—sometimes unwillingly—new roles for themselves. Still another dimension of interaction is that between public authorities and doctors, which could be cooperative but occasionally became acrimonious and tense.

My account adopts this comprehensive framework of tension and symbiosis among the three species of agencies, namely, the doctor, the family, and the forces outside the doctor-family relationship. Employing this framework, I examine domestic care and control of lunatics as complex interactions among them. Chapter 1 serves as a general introduction to the records of commissions of lunacy and elucidates major problems illuminated through the examination of such sources. Chapters 2 and 3 examine psychiatrists' involvement in families' decision making about matters related to the lunacy of family members. Chapter 2 looks into the clinical aspects of the relationship between the doctor and the family, and establishes that doctors were intellectually dependent on the information provided by the families despite the fervent aspiration to scientific autonomy expressed in the printed pages of medical treatises. Chapter 3 turns to the ideological aspects of psychiatric practice and investigates the patterns of psychiatrists' conceptualization of their role vis-à-vis families' concerns about the protection of their property. Chapter 4 moves away from dealing with medical practitioners to illuminate the family's own understanding of and ways of coping with the family member's lunacy. Here, I emphasize the power and potential of "domestic psychiatry." Chapter 5, on the other hand, reveals the limits, weaknesses, and problems of the domestic control of lunatics, placing such practice within the context of the ways in which the public and the private spheres intersected in the early nineteenth century. Chapter 6 widens the scope of inquiry and examines the ambiguous relationships between the family and public authorities of various sorts over the question of managing lunatics within the household.

ONE

Commissions of Lunacy

Background, Sources, and Content

IN FEBRUARY 1823, THE READING public of England was shocked by the disclosure of yet another scandal in high places.[1] The major dramatis personae of the scandal were the third Earl of Portsmouth, his second wife, Mary Anne, and her lover, William Rowland Alder. Lord Portsmouth was born in 1767 and married Grace Norton in 1799. Grace died in 1813, and less than four months after her death, Lord Portsmouth married Mary Anne Hanson. Mary Anne was the eldest daughter of John Hanson, who was an attorney and Portsmouth's principal trustee.[2] Alder was a lawyer who had been acquainted with the Hanson family.

Shocking stories of the depravity and perverted sexuality of the three were revealed one after another. Unlike many contemporary aristocrats whose sexual misdemeanors outraged the public, Lord Portsmouth was not sexually profligate. Actually, he was almost certainly impotent.[3] He became, however, the center of the depraved excess of the ménage à trois, which, coming very close to the imagined world of the Marquis de Sade, overshadowed most other scandals disclosed during the period. Lord Portsmouth was morbidly fond of brutality, blood, and death. He severely whipped his horses and servants without cause or provocation; he gave harsh correction to children of St. Giles's School, to which he acted as a governor.[4] He took a great liking to bleeding and purging his servants, and he wandered about and asked to be bled by women he met, obviously to derive erotic pleasure.[5] He frequented a slaughterhouse and knocked animals down with an ax that was specially made for that purpose. He was fascinated by funerals, following mourning coaches in his phaeton while laughing and shaking his whip at the coachmen. These perversities of His Noble Lordship were more than matched by the depravities of Lady Portsmouth and her lover. They constantly abused Lord Portsmouth, both physically and mentally. They carried their adulterous affair on openly. Most shockingly, they invited the impotent lord to the bed on which they were making love.

An avalanche of evidence was given by an army of witnesses, whose testimonies demonstrated the adultery, on the basis of which the marriage was to be dissolved. The trial was, however, not for a "criminal conversation," which often accompanied a divorce case and provided material for pornographic publications. Demonstrating the adultery was not its legal aim.[6] The real goal of the trial was to demonstrate that Lord Portsmouth was insane and to dissolve the marriage for that reason. By showing that His Lordship was incapable of managing his own affairs at the time of his marriage with his present wife, those who started the trial wanted to nullify the marriage retroactively. All the depraved acts of the lord were recounted in order to show that he was and had been a lunatic, or, according to the legal parlance of the time, "of unsound mind."[7] Evidence of the bare-faced adultery was presented in court in order to demonstrate that Lord Portsmouth's mind had been so deranged that he knowingly let his wife and her lover carry on an adulterous affair. Using the threesome on the bed as the key evidence, a counsel claimed that "[the] adultery existed under circumstances which no man could fail to have seen but a madman."[8]

This type of legal procedure was called a "commission of lunacy" or "commission *de lunatico inquirendo.*" This procedure is now relatively unknown: historians of nineteenth-century English psychiatry and lunacy are much more familiar with the confusingly named "Commission *in* Lunacy" or "Lunacy Commissioners," a governmental body created in 1845 by the "Act for the Regulation of the Care and Treatment of Lunatics" (8 and 9 Vict.c.100) to inspect county pauper asylums, hospitals for the insane (except Bethlem Hospital, which was exempted from the Lunacy Commission's inspection until 1853), and licensed houses for the reception of the insane in England and Wales.[9] Commission *of* lunacy was, however, hardly an obscure legal procedure in the earlier half of the nineteenth century. Commissions were held in public spaces such as taverns or coffeehouses and were very well attended by the public. They were also popular in the press: about two hundred such cases were reported in the London

Times between 1820 and 1860. About a dozen of them were the top news of their day: many columns, sometimes an entire page, were devoted to reporting on the proceedings. Such reports contained detailed descriptions of the deeds of the accused lunatic, which were (and are) shocking, comic, tragic, poignant, and disturbing and require us to rethink our assumptions about the nature of "mental disease" and its regulation. Above all, the reports were highly revealing about how lunatics were thought of, treated, neglected, or abused by the members of their families or households, and how people responded to lunatics taken care of by their own families. On the basis of these hitherto neglected sources, this book casts new light on the history of nineteenth-century psychiatry and lunacy, seen from the viewpoint of the family.

BACKGROUND: REFORM IN LUNACY AND TRANSFORMATION OF THE FAMILY

The case of Lord Portsmouth is "interesting" in its own right. It did make news in its own day, and might well provide material for retrospective tabloid journalism.[10] The significance of Portsmouth's case lies, however, not in its scandalous details, but in its juxtaposition of two sets of historical events, which have been studied separately in the present history of psychiatry. Instead of being just an interesting vignette in this book, the episode of 1823 serves as an opening through which to investigate the intertwining of two major historical developments in the early nineteenth century: reform in lunacy and the transformation of domesticity.

The first line of development I would like to relate to Lord Portsmouth's case is what has been loosely called "reform in lunacy" in the early nineteenth century. In 1815–16, eight years before the Portsmouth case, an event took place that was to become a landmark in the history of psychiatric provision for the insane in England. It was the disclosure, by a House of Commons Select Committee, of abuse in asylums. The horrendous findings of the committee, the jolt they gave to the nation, and the subsequent battle over the issues of who should be responsible for taking care of mad people—all have been told many times and are aptly analyzed by Andrew Scull.[11] Unlike its predecessor in 1807, the Select Committee of 1815–16 had enormous ammunition to support its call for reform in lunacy. Godfrey Higgins, a Yorkshire magistrate and the first witness to be examined by the committee, repeated what he had found in his private investigation of the York Asylum in 1813: "maltreatment of the patients extending to rape and murder; forging of records to hide deaths among the inmates; and extraordinary widespread use of chains and other forms of mechanical restraint; massive embezzlement of funds; and conditions of utter filth and neglect."[12] The climax of Higgins's testimony came when he narrated his discovery of hidden cells in which thirteen women had been kept at night. Defying the staff and forcing his way into these cells, Higgins found a dungeon of filth, walls of which "were daubed with excrement." He vomited, unable to stand the odor. After Higgins, the committee disclosed another shocking abuse. Edward Wakefield and others reinforced to Parliament and the public what they had found in Bethlem in 1814, particularly the terrible situation of James Norris, who had been chained in a horrible apparatus for at least nine years, night and day. Numerous similar investigations were undertaken and their results were reported to the committee. Naturally, only a few institutions satisfied the reformers. Nine out of ten investigations found that the situation of those who were confined in asylums, especially those who were poor and supported by their parish or by charity, were highly unsatisfactory. Through such findings, the Select Committee of 1815–16 set a pattern for the reformers in lunacy for the following couple of generations. The formula for reform was established: find a glaring abuse in an asylum, publicize the result of an investigation, shock the public, humiliate those who were involved in managing the institution, and win the reform. Numerous subsequent efforts of reform in lunacy followed this pattern.

The Parliamentary Select Committee of 1815–16 had thus one important aspect in common with the commission of lunacy against Lord Portsmouth in 1823: disclosure of the abuse of a lunatic. Although the professed aim of the commission was to demonstrate the insanity of the lord, the petitioners also laid great stress on the abuse of the patient by Lady Portsmouth and her lover. The testimonies of the witnesses moved back and forth between two tactics, the demonstration of the insanity of the subject and the disclosure of acts of cruelty toward His Lordship. One Richard Jones, a gardener to Lord Portsmouth, testified as follows:

> I [Jones] heard that he was knocked down, and I ran out; his Lordship had just got up; Mr. Alder was standing by him; his Lordship ran behind me for protection; he was crying very much; he showed me his hand and desired to wipe it; it was filled with gravel . . . his Lordship then went and sat under a tree in front of the house; he cried very much. Lady Portsmouth nor Miss Laura [Hanson], nor Mr. Alder came to sit by him; but Mr. Alder came to

> him, and shaking his fist in Lord Portsmouth's face, said "you must prepare to fight a duel with me to-morrow morning." Mr Alder then walked up the steps, and went arm-in-arm with Lady Portsmouth into the hall; his Lordship remained under the tree for nearly two hours.[13]

Likewise, many witnesses catalogued physical violence, verbal insults, and mental cruelties directed against Lord Portsmouth, as well as giving evidence of conspicuous displays of inappropriate intimacy between Lady Portsmouth and Alder.[14] Technically speaking, such evidence of cruelty and abuse was not relevant to the purpose of the legal procedure, which was the demonstration of the insanity of the subject. Evidence of abuse was used to delegitimize Lady Portsmouth and her allies as trustworthy persons to be responsible for the care of the weak-minded lord. In effect, the petitioners of the commission asked for a "reform" of the present unsatisfactory regime for the care and management of the lunatic, which meant, in this context, the dissolution of the marriage. The parallel with the strategies of the Parliamentary Committee of 1815–16 is obvious: disclose abuses committed secretly behind walls and publicly discredit the regime that was responsible for the care of the lunatic.[15] The two scandals were presented in the same language, which conflated the private and the public, despite great differences in their legal or legislative aims.

It is important to note, however, that the parallel stops there. A fundamental difference existed between the two sites in which the lunatics in question were taken care of. Both York Asylum and the Bethlem Hospital were "public" institutions in the sense that they were accountable to their governors, who paid subscriptions, whereas the membership of Lord Portsmouth's family was strictly private. Lunacy in the latter case obviously needs a historiographical framework different from one suitable for the former case, despite considerable overlap between the two.

The development of domestic ideology is thus the second set of historical events in which I would like to contextualize the case of Lord Portsmouth. The most convenient single event to examine the domestic ideology is the agitation caused by the Queen Caroline affair, which galvanized the entire nation in 1820, just three years before the Portsmouth case.[16] Just as the 1815–16 Parliamentary Select Committee was the culmination of other inquiries into the abuses at incarcerating institutions from the late eighteenth century on, the Queen Caroline affair was the climax of a long trend. From the late eighteenth century on, the private misdemeanors of the famous and the powerful were increasingly used for the purpose of radical critiques of the corrupted establishment, helped by the wider circulation of newspapers, magazines, and cheap prints.[17] The Grub Street exploitation of trials of adultery cases ("criminal conversation" or "crim.con" literature) for political and pornographic publications became all the more intensified when the fervor stirred by the revolutions in America and France turned many radical publishers to energetic reporting of the sexual misbehavior of aristocrats and members of the royal family.[18] The Queen Caroline affair in 1820–21, which fed unprecedented interest in the sexual misdemeanors of the royal couple, was the climax of public outrage against George IV—both against the unmanly means by which he damaged the feminine honor of the "wounded queen" and against his own notorious libertinage. It was an Indian summer for English radicalism.[19]

The extraordinary popular agitations in support of Queen Caroline had a background wider than the profound unpopularity of George IV and the momentum in the English radical movement, as Thomas Laqueur, Leonore Davidoff, and Catherine Hall have asserted. The affair was discussed in terms of domestic ideology, a doctrine then gaining momentum in the middle class: domestic virtue is the condition of participation in public activity. According to Davidoff and Hall, it was "one of the first *public* moments" in which one view of domestic and intimate conduct was "decisively rejected in favour of another."[20] The Queen Caroline affair thus both signaled and confirmed the new middle-class ethos that forged an important link between the private sphere of the family and the public sphere of politics and economic activity: happy marriage and domestic virtue were necessary conditions for political and economic roles in the public sphere. This conflation of the domestic and the public connected the Queen Caroline affair and the Portsmouth case. They were both exposés of marriages without love, and they both used the failure of a family in the private sphere to disqualify that family from assuming a public role. The ideological rhetoric, if not legal logic, behind such criticisms went like this: the present Portsmouth family should be publicly disqualified as a proper psychiatric regime because of its failure to meet the standard of domestic virtue. This rhetoric signaled an attitude related to lunacy and the family that turned out to be crucial: lunatics kept in the private family were proper objects of public concern if the family did not meet the standard of domestic virtue. The Portsmouth case is important not just because it made a legal precedent and because it provided yet more material for political radicals' denunciation of the old guard's corruption. It was certainly the first report of a commission of lunacy case in the *Times*, and arguably the first news that made the abuse of a lunatic in a private family widely known to the public. It thus established a pattern of public scrutiny of the private, familial sphere in which a lunatic was kept.

The case of Lord Portsmouth thus straddled two important historical changes in the early nineteenth century, which have been studied separately by historians in different specialist fields. The Portsmouth case echoed the reform in lunacy, which has been studied by Andrew Scull and many other historians of psychiatry in nineteenth-century England. It also resonated with the formation of new domestic ideals, closely studied by Catherine Hall, Leonore Davidoff, and many other historians of family and gender in the late eighteenth and early nineteenth centuries.[21] My intention in this book is to bridge the two fields: I examine the problems of lunacy in the domestic setting and from the viewpoint of the family in the upper ranks of English society.

SOURCES AND THEIR BACKGROUND

Commission of Lunacy: General Observations

In many ways, the records of the court of commission of lunacy provide uniquely rich material. Although this book does not aim to study the legal procedure per se, a brief overview of the history of the commission of lunacy is in order.[22]

During the period covered in this study, roughly 1820 to 1860, commission of lunacy was a legal procedure allowing a person (called the "petitioner") to ask the Lord Chancellor to examine whether the person in question was a lunatic or an idiot. If the examination established the lunacy or idiocy of the subject, the subject was deprived of his or her civil rights, in consequence of which committees were appointed to take care of the subject's property.[23] The examination or "inquisition" was a complex and large-scale process. The Lord Chancellor appointed one or several lawyers, called commissioners, to investigate and settle the issue. The commissioners arranged a hearing of evidence before a jury. To prove the insanity of the alleged lunatic, the petitioner produced witnesses testifying to the subject's lunacy. These were often family friends, neighbors, or servants of the household, whose experience with the alleged lunatic was reported in detail. Opposition to the commission could be put forward by a family member, a relative, or any other party. The opposition, too, brought forward witnesses, testifying to the subject's sanity. If no opposition had been put up and the alleged lunatic did not consent to be declared insane, he or she could act as the opposing party. The alleged lunatics were personally examined by the commissioner in front of the jury. After all witnesses had testified, the lunatic had been examined, and counsels for and against the commission had entered pleas, the commissioner summarized the case. Then the jury returned a verdict, specifying the date from which the subject had been *non compos mentis.* The date was very important, because a commission was often used to retroactively annul a contract that had been made years before. The nullification of the second marriage of Lord Portsmouth was the object of one such commission.

Commission *de lunatico inquirendo* had a long history. The procedure went back at least to the fourteenth century, when it developed from the notion of the Crown as *parens patriae* (guardian of the kingdom): the Crown had a royal prerogative for the care and custody of the persons and estates of those who were deemed *non compos mentis.* Instead of directly exercising its authority, the Crown delegated the power to the Lord Chancellor.[24] In 1540, the functions of the Crown as *parens patriae* was transferred to the newly established Court of Wards. The Court effectively protected the property of lunatics and idiots, preventing those who managed lunatics' and idiots' estates from taking advantage of the situation. Although the Court tried to expand its protection to humbler men and women, commission of lunacy remained a legal procedure serving the needs of the wealthy.[25] During the Civil War and the Interregnum, the Court of Wards came under attack as an institution that symbolized the unjust power of the Crown over its subjects. The Court ceased to operate during the Long Parliament and was formally abolished in 1660, when the function of protecting the estates of lunatics and idiots passed to the Court of Chancery.

The Court of Chancery in the early eighteenth century was notoriously corrupt, although its rules and procedures were basically fair on paper. As Michael MacDonald has shown in his analysis of a scandal in 1725, Masters of Chancery embezzled considerable amounts of money entrusted to them by suitors of the Chancery, including the guardians of lunatics. Earl of Macclesfield, the Lord Chancellor for 1718–25, was impeached for making illegal profit from the property of the estates of many widows, orphans, and lunatics, as well as for selling masterships.[26] Moreover, the abuse of the legal machinery of the commission *de lunatico inquirendo* was not limited to this case or to lawyers in high places, but extended to wider sections of the society. There was at least one case of abuse in which an impoverished baronet in Lancashire was accused of gaining a dubious commission of lunacy against his father-in-law for the purpose of making illegal profit.[27]

Judging from what Daniel Defoe and others wrote about illegal confinements in early private madhouses, it is not unlikely that there were further cases of abuses of the commission of lunacy in the eighteenth century.[28] In this respect, MacDonald is right in sounding a note of caution against the optimistic picture of eighteenth-century lunacy painted by Roy Porter.

From the beginning of the nineteenth century, there was a series of important legislative attempts at reforming the practice of commissions of lunacy. I shall examine these reforms in detail in chapter 6. Suffice it to say here that they shared the common goal of expanding the range of protection offered by reducing the costs and delays for the execution of the legal procedure. Such reforms culminated in 1853 in the form of an "Act for the Regulation of Proceedings under Commissions of Lunacy" (16 and 17 Vict.c.70).[29] Under this Act, the Lord Chancellor appointed two full-time Masters in Lunacy, who, for the handsome salary of £2,000 each, performed the duties that had been discharged by commissioners appointed for each commission.[30] Two important Amendments were made to this Act, in 1862 and 1882. The Amendment in 1862 further extended the availability of the commission of lunacy by allowing the cases to be tried in one of the superior courts of common law at Westminster.[31] It also empowered the Lord Chancellor to allow people even of modest means to obtain a commission without the lengthy, complex, and costly process of inquisition: when the property of the alleged lunatic did not exceed £1,000, or £50 per annum, the person could obtain a summary commission at the Lord Chancellor's discretion.[32] Because of this Amendment, people possessing only a small amount of property could expect to obtain a commission at a substantially reduced cost. The Amendment in 1882 (45 and 46 Vict.c.82) raised the ceiling value of property that qualified a person for this exemption from inquisition to £2,000, or £100 per annum.[33]

The Lunacy Act of 1890 (59 Vict.c.5) amalgamated and consolidated numerous Acts and Amendments related to lunacy that had passed in the previous half-century.[34] Its impact was great in many issues related to lunacy, and a drastic change was brought about in commission of lunacy. Although the office of Masters in Lunacy was retained and the procedure for a commission of lunacy remained in operation, the Act established major ways by which people could bypass a commission of lunacy.[35] Before the 1890 Act, commission of lunacy and certificate of lunacy were completely separate matters. The former was necessary to deprive a person of his or her civil rights, while the latter was a requisite to confine him or her:

one thus needed to petition for a commission in order to put a person's property under protection, even if he or she had already been confined under a certificate of lunacy.[36] The Lunacy Act of 1890 explicitly indicated that the same protection of the property of a lunatic as that afforded by a commission of lunacy could be obtained under an order of a judge, without going through the legal procedure.[37] Clause 1 of section 116 of the Act specified six categories of persons whose property could be protected and who could be deprived of their rights. The first category is those who went through the legal procedure of a commission and the accompanying inquisition; the other five categories are those who could be exempted from the process.[38] Among these, the most important is category C, which reads: "every person lawfully detained as a lunatic [under a certificate of lunacy] though not found [a lunatic] by inquisition." This meant that protection of a lunatic's property could be secured if he or she was confined under a due order and if a judge granted an exemption from a commission of lunacy. Section 116 thus made commission of lunacy redundant for many cases, as a contemporary author predicted.[39] After the Lunacy Act in 1890, followed by further Amendments in 1908 and 1922, commission of lunacy as a legal procedure fell into disuse.[40] By 1927, the authors of a work titled *Management and Administration of Estates in Lunacy* remarked that "[the] wide powers afforded by L[unacy]. A[ct]., 1890, s.116, as extended by L.A., 1908, s.1, and L.A., 1922, and the simple form of procedure thereunder, have rendered proceedings [of commission of lunacy] under inquisition exceedingly rare."[41] The 1890 Act thus effectively ended a legal procedure that had been used for more than five hundred years.

The legislation discussed in this section was related to the actual practice of commission of lunacy. Figure 1 represents the annual number of commissions of lunacy issued from 1627 to 1920. Figure 2 gives the data aggregated by decade.[42] Figures before 1660 are unlikely to represent the real number of commissions, for the Court of Chancery did not assume responsibility for commissions of lunacy until that year. From the late seventeenth century on, the records are fairly complete apart from some minor gaps.[43] The overall pattern of the rise and fall of commissions of lunacy is clear. In the late seventeenth century and throughout the eighteenth century, the number of commissions of lunacy fluctuated at a low level. During this period, the increase, if any, was very gradual. At the beginning of the nineteenth century, the number started to rise markedly. The growth in the first three decades of the century is particularly striking: in the last decade of the eighteenth century (1790–99), there were 131 commissions, whereas

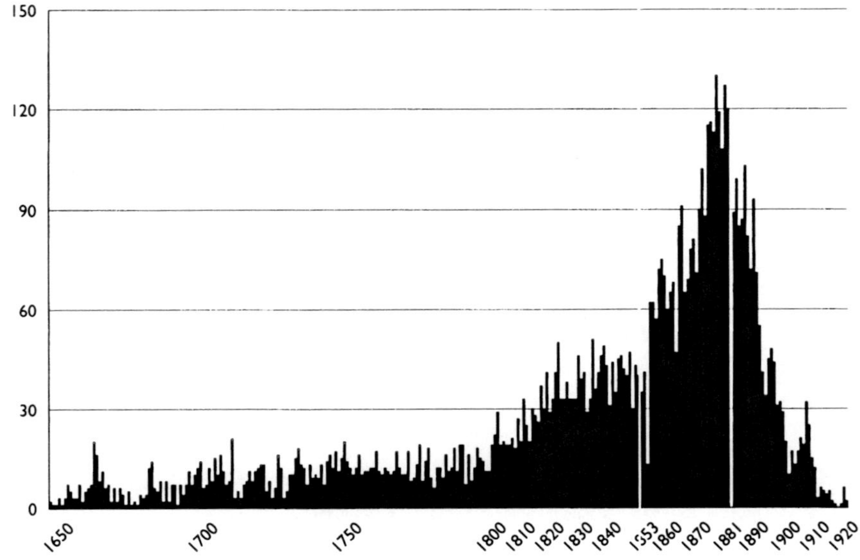

Figure 1. Numbers of Commissions of Lunacy, 1627–1920

the period 1820–29 witnessed 373 commissions, 2.8 times as many. These three decades of rapid increase were followed by two decades of stagnation between 1830 and 1850. From the 1850s, the numbers of commissions entered a second phase of increase at an even greater pace, which lasted until 1880. After the gap in 1881–82, the trend was abruptly reversed and a rapid decline set in. The minor surge around 1910 turned out to be temporary, and commissions of lunacy were reduced to near extinction after the First World War.

Some of the rises and falls in figures 1 and 2 were obviously related to legislative changes. The 1853 Act and its Amendment in 1862 increased the number of commissions by making a commission easier and cheaper to obtain. The Lunacy Act of 1890 prompted a precipitous decline, for it enabled people to seek a simpler form of the protection of the property of lunatics and to bypass a commission. After 1853, therefore, trends in the actual number of commissions followed legislative changes fairly closely. For the first half of the nineteenth century, however, no such obvious correlation can be discerned. Without the stimulus of new legislation, more people started to seek a commission around the turn of the century. I tackle this puzzle in chapter 6.

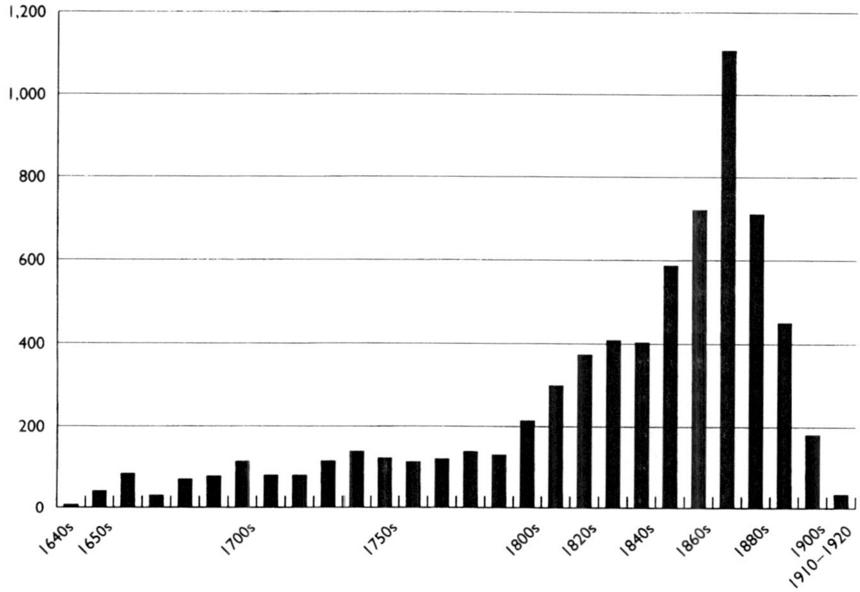

Figure 2. Numbers of Commissions of Lunacy Aggregated by Decade, 1640s–1910s

Two prominent features of the subjects of the commissions should be mentioned. First, they were predominantly male during the period covered in this book (see table 1). Of 3,301 commissions requested between 1620 and 1853, 2,206 (66.8 percent) were male. The ratio of male lunatics to females remained about 2:1 throughout the period 1660–1850, with no clearly visible change over time. This male predominance was mainly a result of the absence of married women. Among female subjects of the commission, 52.4 percent (n = 574) were spinsters or single women, and 35.2 percent (n = 386) were widows. Those who were identified as "wife" were only 2.8 percent (n = 31) of the total female subjects. (For the remainder, their marital status was not recorded.) Married women were vastly underrepresented because they did not possess *their own* property that would have needed protection by a commission of lunacy.[44] For the period covered in this book, women's civil as well as political rights were severely limited, mainly owing to the common law doctrine of "coverture": because the wife's legal personality was absorbed in her husband, all property of hers became the property of her husband. There was no need for a husband to request a costly legal procedure to deprive his wife of property rights, simply because she had no property rights to be deprived of. Only under exceptional cir-

TABLE 1

Male and Female Subjects of Commissions of Lunacy, 1620–1853

Years	*Male*	*Female*	*Total*	*Male Percentage*
1620–1629	1	—	1	—
1630–1639	1	—	1	—
1640–1649	5	—	5	—
1650–1659	33	9	42	78.6
1660–1669	66	19	85	77.6
1670–1679	23	8	31	74.2
1680–1689	47	24	71	66.2
1690–1699	50	29	79	63.3
1700–1709	82	33	115	71.3
1710–1719	54	27	81	66.7
1720–1729	58	23	81	71.6
1730–1739	76	40	116	65.5
1740–1749	88	51	139	63.3
1750–1759	79	44	123	64.2
1760–1769	66	48	114	57.9
1770–1779	87	34	121	71.9
1780–1789	89	50	139	64.0
1790–1799	95	36	131	72.5
1800–1809	157	57	214	73.4
1810–1819	205	94	299	68.6
1820–1829	255	118	373	68.4
1830–1839	261	147	408	64.0
1840–1849	251	152	403	62.3
1850–1853	77	52	129	59.7
Total	2,206	1,095	3,301	66.8

cumstances did a wife became the subject of a commission. Men numerically predominated as subjects of commissions of lunacy principally because married women were virtually excluded from the population at risk.

Second, the social status and occupations of the subjects of the commissions display a strong bias toward the social elite (see table 2). Only a very rough picture can be presented, because the sources I have consulted give

TABLE 2
Status and Occupations of Male Subjects of Commissions of Lunacy, 1627–1853

Status or Occupation	*Number*
Esquires/gentlemen	1,077
Tradesman/artisans	272
Farmers/yeomen	147
Noblemen/titleholders	104
Professionals	74
Others	99
Not stated	433
Total	2,206

only brief, vague information about the occupations of the male subjects of commissions.[45] The two most numerous entries were "esquire" and "gentleman": together they constitute 48.8 percent (n = 1,077) of the male subjects of commissions. Although both "esquire" and "gentleman" were highly ambiguous social statuses in the eighteenth and nineteenth centuries, it is certain that subjects from these groups were persons of relatively high social standing. These two categories dwarfed "artisans and tradesmen" (12.3 percent, n = 272), and "farmers and yeomen" (6.7 percent, n = 147). Although small in number, "noblemen and other titleholders" (4.7 percent, n = 104) are remarkably overrepresented, considering that they constituted only a tiny fraction of the total population. Equally conspicuous is the absence of manual laborers, who constituted the bulk of the population. These figures on the occupations and social statuses of the subjects of commissions suggest that the legal procedure was largely, if not exclusively, a measure sought by the elite sector of English society between 1627 and 1853.

Reports in the Times, *1823–1861*

Commissions of lunacy before 1853 always took place before a jury and large audience. They were, at least from the mid-1820s, often attended by shorthand reporters for national newspapers, whose accounts of the examinations appeared in the paper. Between 1820 and 1860, there are about 200 reports of the cases of commission of lunacy in the *Times*. These newspaper reports, which have so far been utilized only partially by historians of psychiatry and lunacy, form the core material for my argument throughout this book.[46] I have to rely on newspaper reports, which have many obvious shortcomings as sources for historical research, because the original documents of the commission of lunacy during the period covered in this study were destroyed, unavailable, or scattered.[47] I have used only the abstracts and indexes to the commissions from the mid-seventeenth century to 1853 that are now left in the Public Record Office in Kew.[48] Some copies of legal papers concerning commissions of lunacy are scattered both in the Public Records Office and in local archives, and painstaking research will no doubt bring more materials to light.[49]

In total, 196 commissions of lunacy were reported in the *Times* from 1823 to 1861, the years, respectively, of Lord Portsmouth's case and W. F. Windham's case. The majority of those reports (n = 177) were published between 1825 and 1845, during which period 263 commissions took place in London and Middlesex, the location of most of the reported commissions (see table 3). The *Times* thus covered about two-thirds of the cases heard in the metropolitan area during the period 1825–45. One can be reasonably confident that the material examined represented a substantial portion of all commissions in the metropolitan region during the period in question.

Why were commissions of lunacy reported in the *Times* during these two decades? Its beginning is easier to explain than its end. When the *Times* started to cover this type of legal procedure, there were two successive cases that certainly made good material for journalistic and commercial purposes. The first case was the commission against Lord Portsmouth in 1823. As is evident from my brief account at the beginning of this chapter, the case was difficult for the press to ignore. The second case appearing in the *Times* had similar appeal, with tremendous power to attract public attention.[50] It contained a vivid story of adultery between a clergyman's wife and a "rupture doctor" (a medical practitioner specializing in the treatment of hernias), spiced with tales of the husband having sex with prostitutes. Those two sensational cases perhaps served to establish regular coverage of legal proceedings in this category. These were, however, exceptions to the rule. The overwhelming majority of cases did not have this pornographic character. The journalistic appeal of the rest of the cases seems to have lain in people's interest in incidents of lunacy and their desire to know the situations the lunatics were put in. This editorial decision was in harmony with the general conviction that the problem of lunacy should be a public concern, not something left to the discretion of those who were directly involved in the care and management of the insane.

TABLE 3

Numbers of Reports on Commissions of Lunacy in the London *Times*, 1823–1861

Year	*Male Subjects*	*Female Subjects*	*Total*
1823	1	—	1
1824		—	
1825	2	—	2
1826	1	2	3
1827	3	1	4
1828	3	—	3
1829	3	1	4
1830	4	3	7
1831	3	2	5
1832	3	2	5
1833	3	2	5
1834	8	5	13
1835	6	3	9
1836	9	2	11
1837	8	4	12
1838	12	6	18
1839	8	5	13
1840	6	3	9
1841	10	3	13
1842	9	4	13
1843	6	5	11
1844	6	2	8
1845	8	1	9
1846	—	—	—
1847	—	—	—
1848	—	—	—
1849	—	—	—
1850	4	1	5
1851	2		2
1852	—	3	3
1853	2	—	2
1858	3	1	4
1859	—	1	1
1860	—	—	—
1861	1	—	1
Total	134	62	196

The abrupt termination of the *Times*'s reporting of commission of lunacy cases is harder to explain. As table 3 shows, the *Times* suddenly stopped regular coverage in 1845, and reports resumed sporadically in the late 1840s through the 1850s. This is only partly explicable. A legal reform in 1853 allowed the Masters in Lunacy to settle a commission without a jury or in a closed court, unless in their judgment the case was complicated and a jury was necessary. A principal effect of this reform was to make many routine cases inaccessible to reporters. Accordingly, all cases reported in the newspaper after 1853 were hotly contested and argued before a jury, each taking more than two days to complete.[51] But the problem with relying on this line of explanation is that the *Times* stopped regular coverage *before* the 1853 Act. Why was this the case? Did the editors become concerned about issues of privacy and the feelings of the families? Perhaps, but there is no independent evidence for this claim. It is true that there was some disquiet about the practice of publicizing in the newspaper the strange acts committed by the insane and bizarre delusions held by them. The pain the family felt in bringing the case in front of the public was regularly referred to. On one occasion, a reporter for the *Times* was blamed in court for practicing tabloid journalism. During the commission against Rev. Paul Saumarez in 1834, a sheriff's officer at the court told the reporter, "you must not report this in the papers," and declared that "if he [the sheriff's officer] had known for what purpose I [the reporter for the *Times*] attended the inquiry, he would have closed the door against me."[52] However, on the following day, the commissioner explicitly endorsed the propriety of the press reporting on its proceedings: "Mr Commissioner Whitmarsh directed the attention of the jury to a letter which appeared in the *Times* yesterday, complaining that a sheriff's officer had threatened to close the door to a reporter who attended an inquiry of this description. . . . He [the commissioner] begged to state that inquiries of that kind should be thrown open to the public. He believed that that was the feeling entertained by the under-sheriff, and he felt confident that [the] gentleman would not sanction such a threat as had been made by the officer."[53] Thus, even in this single instance of criticism raised against the practice of reporting, the *Times* won a clear victory. Henry Brougham expressed a similar distaste for journalistic practice during the case of Edward Frank in 1825. Brougham pleaded to the jury to sympathize with the alleged lunatic, who was being subjected to a "severe scrutiny . . . [of] . . . his whole life," with the result exhibited in open court and in the newspapers.[54] In this case, however, Brougham acted as a counsel against the commission, and his statement may be seen less as a genuine expression of his opinion than as a legal tactic to cast the petitioner (who was the son of the subject) in an unfavorable light. Protests against the practice of reporting cases were thus rare and insubstantial, nor did they meet with a favorable response. The *Times*'s abrupt stopping of its coverage of lunacy cases was certainly not the result of mounting criticism against the practice.[55] Nor did the newspaper stop publishing cases in which "interesting" lunatics played some part, either in commissions of lunacy or in other types of trials.[56] The reason for the termination of the regular reporting of commission of lunacy cases around 1845 remains a mystery.

LUNATICS ON STAGE

The content of the reports naturally varied, and Tolstoy's oft-quoted remark—all happy families resemble one another, but each unhappy family is unhappy in its own way—is particularly apposite when applied to the two hundred families who were troubled with the insanity of family members and asked for legal intervention to help them resolve their troubles. In order to give a sense of the general picture emerging from my sources, I shall briefly delineate some characteristics of the cases.

At the outset, note well that they were published in the newspaper. A commission of lunacy could become a piece of news, in which the public was interested. Some evidence suggests that the newspaper reports themselves were keenly read. In at least three cases, reports of a commission were separately published after appearing in the newspaper.[57] One diarist recorded his opinions about two cases of commission of lunacy, one in 1829 and the other in 1832.[58] Sometimes the reports prompted those who had read them to participate in the examination or to volunteer as witnesses. Readers sent letters to the editor of the *Times,* asking for corrections or giving supplementary information.[59] When a commission against Daniel Gundry was reported, one Jerome Goodrich, an old acquaintance of the subject, came to the court to give evidence, "having come to town two or three days ago, he had that morning seen in *The Times* newspaper a report of the first day's proceedings under the commission against Mr. G."[60] These casual participants must have been thrilled to be part of an important event.

The popularity of commission of lunacy cases can be gauged also from the fact that the actual legal proceedings were very well attended by the public. Although my major sources are from London, interest in commissions of lunacy was not restricted to the metropolis but extended from Windsor to Wales. In 1839, the *Times* reported that the commission of lunacy against

Miss Eleanor Lloyd excited much interest in Cloughjordan.[61] The core part of the attraction varied from one case to another. Some cases allured people by salacious stories. In the commission against Rev. Edward Frank, the Gray's Inn Coffee House was much crowded, for the case excited great interest, no doubt owing to the pornographic details people expected from the case.[62] As the details of the sexual misconduct of the clergyman, his wife, and her lover further unfolded, excitement mounted. On the fifth day of the trial, the passages were so full of people that lawyers and witnesses could get into the room only with extreme difficulty.[63] Other cases gathered crowds for the thrill of watching a fierce legal feud. The commission against Hon. Jervis Jervis excited a great deal of interest, "not only from the circumstances connected with it, but on account of the rank of the party, and the resolute opposition which, it is understood, will be made to the commission."[64] Commissions of lunacy against persons who were already famous naturally attracted great attention.[65] The commission against Richard Weeks "excited considerable interest, owing to the publicity that has been already given to the death of Mr Weeks' aunt, who bequeathed him £120,000."[66] At least one commission had been advertised through precirculated reports, whetting people's appetite for the curiosities to be revealed. The commission of Thomas Dutton Rothwell, "a gentleman of high respectability and attainment," was stated to have excited the greatest interest because of "several reports having been [for] some time in circulation as to the extraordinary nature of the delusions under which the unfortunate gentleman laboured."[67]

Owing to such publicity and the popularity of commissions of lunacy, the commissions provided an ideal platform for broadcasting one's opinion. For example, in the commission against William Stevens in 1840, enthusiasts for nonrestraint denounced in court the use of straitjackets. Two visiting justices of Hanwell Lunatic Asylum used a cross-examination as an occasion for advocating the nonrestraint system, which was at that time being implemented at the asylum. The tactic must have worked, because several of the jurors then present sent a petition to the Lord Chancellor to discontinue the harsh treatment of this patient.[68] Next year, another ad hoc attack on physical restraint was made, again during cross-examination of a witness.[69] These incidents of questioning about the use of excessive restraints also pointed to the disclosure of abuse and neglect practiced behind closed doors. The pattern set by the 1815–16 Parliamentary Select Committee is only too evident.

The major attraction of the commissions lay, however, in watching the lunatics themselves. The personal examination of the subject of the commission was almost always the most important part of the proceedings. Accordingly, the court often went to considerable lengths in an attempt to secure such an interview with the lunatic.[70] In one case, when Mrs. Sarah Eliason, a deranged old widow, refused to come out of a carriage, the commissioners and the jury went out of the building to speak to her in the carriage.[71] In another case, they proceeded to the subject's residence, "[as] it was impossible that the unfortunate woman could be removed from her residence without great danger."[72] Such examinations of the lunatic sometimes turned out to be a reconfirming and routine ritual to meet the criteria of law. More often, however, the appearance of the lunatics and the examination of them were occasions for intense drama. The style of newspaper reports often became emotional and lyrical with the entrance of the subject on the scene. This was the moment when a legal procedure was suddenly infused with a sense of human drama and poignancy. One lunatic was described as a "melancholy picture of despondency"; another "a great mind in ruins—occasionally sensible of its original dignity"; still another "excited much feeling of commiseration from all present."[73] Pathos prevailed in the report about the commission of lunacy against Feargus O'Connor, a former member of Parliament and a leading Chartist, who recited a verse that had once been popular among his followers (quoted in full in the *Times*): he "betrayed much of that bold address which distinguished his oratorical displays in former days." Dame Esther Filmer's long delusional rambling about the absence of her viscera and her request to be buried alive was quoted in full, and perhaps almost verbatim:

> I have a very extraordinary request to make, it will appear a very extraordinary one to you, gentlemen, no doubt, but it must be granted, it must indeed; I am convinced I shall never die; and I must not be kept above ground any longer; I hope you will consent to my being buried alive. I am not human, I am a million times worse that the Devil himself. . . . All I earnest[ly] solicit is that I may be interred, I am a mere shell; it is so, indeed, and you know it is so. . . . I have no heart, no bowels, nothing but lights; that is my only request, it is absolutely necessary, it must be done. When will you let me know? Do not delay it beyond Monday. It is absolutely necessary, and when that is done Sir Edmund Filmer will settle everything but I must be buried, it must be done.

As the *Times* reported, this soliciting "excited the greatest sympathy in all present, several were deeply affected."[74]

A strong sense of drama thus infused the procedures of commissions of lunacy, the lunatic being the major character. Naturally, the performances of the lunatics varied. In one case, which was arguably exceptional but nevertheless telling, the subject of the commission did play an actor making his debut: John Barns, a wealthy gentleman, "sent out some hundreds of invitations to his tenants in the neighbourhood of Mile-End, Stepney, &c. to attend the inquiry." This accounted for the large audience assembled at the trial.[75] The subjects of the commissions could take center stage, and the audience clearly enjoyed their performance. William Eusden could not find any legal assistance to oppose the commission, and he cross-examined the witnesses testifying to his insanity, much to the amusement of the court.[76] Some could not respond to questions appropriately. George E. Liebenhood did not utter a word, appearing "completely lost." His sister Lucy Christian Liebenhood was absorbed in her own merry interior world, humming a tune all the way up the room to her seat, moving as if she were dancing, talking rapidly but incoherently, and placing her legs up on a chair.[77] In a few cases, the subjects of commissions appeared to admit their inability to manage their own affairs. Admiral Sir Ross Donnelly was called to the court and examined, only to admit that one of his sons should be in charge of his affairs: "that my son, the barrister, who is very good and kind indeed should manage my property."[78] Likewise, when making a brief summary report about Mr. Charles Cater, an inmate of Northumberland-house Private Asylum at Stoke Newington, the *Times* stated that "[one] unusual feature in the case was, that the unfortunate gentleman expressed himself perfectly happy, and exhibited great anxiety to get back to Northumberland-house."[79] Caroline Ann Tweedale gave up her civil rights in a less dignified way: she talked rapidly and incoherently about her numerous titles ("Duchess of Austria, Countess of Uxbridge, and Lady Byron"), but when asked if she was capable of managing her own affairs, she admitted that she was incapable.[80]

The sense of tragicomedy was heightened when the lunatics opposed the commission but only confirmed their madness in their insistence on their sanity. Reporters quoted with relish the strange words and deeds of the major characters. Joshua Richard Wilkinson bared his arm and told the jury that "though he had only the wrist of an infant, he had the fist of an elephant."[81] Mrs. Sarah Bird, a seventy-six-year-old widow, understood the nature of the inquiry pretty well, but betrayed her insanity in her attempt to demonstrate her sanity:

> I know the object of this inquiry—I am quite able to take care of myself and my property. I am not advanced in life. Some blackguards have been talking about me, and I should like to catch them. This year is 1839, and the month is August. [Actually, it was May 1843.] I won't tell you (the Commissioner) nor the jury how much money I have got, and I shall not say where it is. I worked hard for it, and (striking the table vehemently) no one has any business to ask me such questions. As for the Lord Chancellor, only let him come and see me cook a dinner. Good God! what a fool he must be to allow himself to be imposed upon.[82]

Likewise, Miss Elizabeth Fisher, a niece of one Silvester who inherited a huge property of £20,000, was quoted to have remarked to the commissioner: "I see you are a tyrant by your eyes; but I will not be tyrannized over by you, you blackguard, although you have black whiskers."[83]

The commissioners were far from cool observers or guides of the legal proceedings, but often took an active part in the drama of lunacy on the public stage. Very often, they showed their own dramatic capabilities by skillfully playing a role in order to elicit manifest delusion from the subject of the commission. Commissioner Phillimore drew out the delusion by a single stroke from Isabel Sprout, who was stated to labor under the delusion that "she was Empress of the whole world, except the East Indies, which was too hot."

MRS. SPROUT—	Stay down there, Sir.
PHILLIMORE—	I will. Pray, whom am I addressing?
MRS. SPROUT—	The empress of all the world, except the East Indies.

Admittedly, commissioners wanted to elicit clear evidence of delusion as a part of the legal proceedings. There is, nevertheless, an unmistakable relish for comedy or psychiatric freak show in their behavior.

These cases represented the alleged lunatics in a more or less expected light. Their grandiose ideas, bizarre delusions, and irrelevant remarks were familiar hallmarks of madness. In a sense, they came to the court to act a preordained role, scripted by those who petitioned for the commission. On the other hand, quite a few lunatics did not conform to the assigned role and disrupted the preconceived smooth scenario. Actually, unpredictability of performance of the major character was an integral part of the attraction of the drama of the commission of lunacy. Continuing the age-old tradition of the wise fool or sanity in Bedlam, some lunatics impressed the audience with their clever remarks. Despite her manifest delusions, Mary Jones, a maiden lady forty-two years of age, "surprised all the court" by her astuteness and shrewdness.[84] Richard Dunn, a lunatic who was arrested because he had sent offensive letters to several upper-class women, demanded that a witness repeat John Locke's definition of madness.[85] Some lunatics used the occasion of the commission to reveal the truth of their ill-treatment. Miss Louisa Ridge, a woman haunted by the image of a man whom she had met only once, "complained of ill-treatment at Monro's madhouse" and expressed her wish to go back to her family. Although her delusions completely undermined her insistence that she was sane, the report in the newspaper suggests that people found some truth in her remarks.[86] Likewise, Andrew Mitchell Campbell's criticism of Whitmore House, where he had been confined—"[it] is very old, and, from its construction, calculated to deprive people of their reason and make them mad"—was taken seriously. His complaint received special mention in the *Times,* and the jury took special steps to advise the petitioner of the commission to remove him to another residence. More ambiguously, John Tatham addressed the jury:

> He was, he assured the jury, the victim of the most dreadful conspiracy and persecution. He had exuded away in his body, but he did not talk like a madman. No, no. He would assure the gentlemen before him, that he was perfectly in his senses, and he would open the most dreadful things. He had been taken to a house in Hackney, and a strait-waistcoat was put upon him for nothing. He was totally ruined, and had destroyed his family, and it was all owing to Dr. Monro and those people. He had been sent to Hackney in June, 1826, and had been detained there for 3 years and a half. His size had been altered, for he had been 5 feet 7 inches before the conspiracy, and who could say that he was that height now?[87]

Mixing truth, half-truth, and utter delusion, his incoherent speech went on, until at last "with difficulty and by force he was taken out of the room."[88] The audience and readers were ready to be surprised by the unexpected rationality of the lunatics' remarks or to find kernels of truth in their apparently incoherent ramblings. They were aware that the lines between utter madness, sanity in madness, and sanity were proverbially difficult to draw. Lunatics appearing in commissions of lunacy cases thus varied, as did people's expectations of them.

To judge by the tone of the reports in newspapers, unpredictability was an important part of a commission's attraction as a drama. The scenario was quite fluid, and some lunatics were able to put the outcome of the commission at serious risk. Dame Sarah Lydia Seymour, who put forward an opposition to the commission against herself, delivered a performance that impressed everybody.[89] She almost defeated the commission by her "extremely prepossessing appearance," rational manner of speech, convincing explanations of almost all her acts that had been put forward as evidence of her lunacy, and candid admission that "I have been excited a great deal at different times, and I know I have talked a great deal of nonsense." Her criticism of the treatment she had received at Norman House Lunatic Asylum, Fulham, was also perfectly rational. When asked by the commissioner whether she had "any complaint to make against any person," she was composed enough to first thank the commissioner for the chance he gave her, and then delivered a cool assessment: "The nurse is violent sometimes. She does not appear to understand my character and disposition. I think, by this time, I should have been much better if I had received mild treatment. I am very nervous, and was much frightened at first by the screams of the other inmates of the house where I am. I was not accustomed to it, but now I hope to get stronger and better in a week or two." These impressively rational remarks were completely at odds with testimony to her insanity. The jury therefore could not reach a conclusion, and the commissioners had to adjourn the court to obtain further evidence.[90] On the next occasion, however, her manner was completely different: "In place of the mild and sympathetic cast of countenance which distinguished her before, there was a vacancy in her look and wildness in her manner."[91] On seeing her in this state, the jury at last returned a verdict of insanity, adding that she had had a lucid interval on the day when she appeared in the court for the first time.

Lady Seymour was not an isolated exception in putting the outcome of the commission at risk through her performance. The commission against Mrs. Mary Hartley was almost defeated when the jury visited her in her own residence to find her perfectly rational, composed, and able to provide satisfactory explanation for every strange behavior cited as evidence of her insanity:

BARLOW— She [Hartley] had any claim to the English crown?

HARTLEY— Certainly not. What claim could I, as simple Mrs. Hartley, have to the crown?

BARLOW— But did you ever state so to any person by work or by writing?

HARTLEY— No, I did not. I have seen the statements made in the papers of the evidence given before the commission, and they are all false and erroneous.

BARLOW— Did you not mention to Mr. Bransby Cooper that you had a box of very peculiar construction by which you could communicate with the foreign ministry?

HARTLEY— (laughing)—Oh, yes, I told him so, but it was only my nonsense. You can't call that insanity. It was only [a] joke.

This performance must have alarmed the petitioner of the commission and those medical witnesses who had testified to her insanity. No doubt sensing the danger the commission was put in by this impeccable performance, the next day the medical witnesses used all their might and expertise to show that the rational answers she had given did not exclude the possibility of her unsoundness. Sutherland, a physician to St. Luke's Hospital for the Insane, quoted similar precedents, in which apparently rational subjects of commissions of lunacy were judged insane. Another doctor tried to explain the apparent rationality as a product of "tutoring": "It is well known that insane persons in some cases, if pre-informed of the points on which they are considered to be insane, will fence with and parry the questions put to them with much ingenuity."[92] Perhaps thanks to the weight of these medical testimonies, the jury returned a verdict of unsound mind. Through their persistence, medical experts managed to snatch victory from the jaws of defeat.

These cases of near defeat should not mislead us into believing that the voices of alleged lunatics arguing for their sanity were, in the end, always overwhelmed. Actually, there were three alleged lunatics who *did* defeat the commission. Miss Barbara White was one. When the commission was first held on 17 March 1841, she asked to adjourn the court "in order to provide herself with professional assistance." Two weeks later, with one Mr. Bateman attending on her behalf, she was able to defeat the commission, mainly by her own rational explanation of her condition, showing that "[the] nefarious excuse that she was insane was utterly unfounded." In addition, she was released from her present confinement at home, in response to her accusation of two "masculine women" committing various cruelties to her and her anxious plea "to be released from the *surveillance* of her keepers."[93] Likewise, the commission against Stephen Woodcock was defeated by the shrewd remarks the subject made during his examination.[94]

The most dramatic case of this kind was the commission of lunacy of Thomas Telford Campbell, the secluded and mildly eccentric son of the poet Thomas Campbell. Thomas Telford then resided at a private madhouse at High Beach in Essex owned by one Dr. Allen, who had been in the habit of taking "low-spirited or desponding" patients without certificate of lunacy, a practice of a dubious nature.[95] Although the commission was formally unopposed and no counsel appeared on behalf of the alleged lunatic, the jury was impressed by "the greatest urbanity, coolness, and composure" of Campbell's performance. No sign of insanity was found in the manner in which Campbell cross-examined the witnesses testifying to his insanity, answered the questions put to him, and addressed the jury about the harm caused by his residence in an asylum. After long consultation, the foreman finally announced that "although he and another juror objected to give a verdict at variance with the medical testimony, yet that 14 jurors out of 16 were of opinion that Mr. Campbell was of sound mind."[96] Single-handedly, Campbell had fought against medical testimony and had defeated the commission. Both the audience of the commission and the readers of the report must have been thrilled at the unfolding of an unpredictable drama.

The enormous popularity of the commission of lunacy as a performance on a legal stage and a journalistic narrative was thus a part of the public's keen interest in matters related to lunacy. A parallel can be drawn with the notorious entertainment, popular in the seventeenth and eighteenth centuries, of visiting the Bethlem Hospital or "Bedlam." Inmates of Bedlam provided entertainment to visitors and inspiration to playwrights and painters until visiting was restricted in 1770 to those who obtained a ticket signed by a governor.[97] Attending a commission of lunacy continued this tradition of watching mad persons. The end of unrestricted visits to Bedlam thus did not mean the establishment of the modern sensibility that shrinks from the freak show of insanity. More than a half-century after the restriction of visits to Bedlam, people watched subjects of commissions of lunacy and the press reported their antics with few qualms. More important, the public's interest in commissions of lunacy was multifaceted. Relish for comedy coexisted with the sober pathos of watching a tragic malady, and fascination with freakish delusions coexisted with earnest outrage against restraint. It is simplistic and naive to condemn the practice of displaying the subjects of commissions of lunacy as cruel voyeurism. Most important, commissions of lunacy played an ambivalent role in both empowering and disempowering lunatics. Those commissions certainly disempowered lunatics: depriving lunatics of their civil rights was the point of the legal process. On the other hand, the legal mechanism prepared a stage on which lunatics could act, make speeches, and explain themselves.

Put in a larger context, the popularity of commissions of lunacy as a dramatic or journalistic entertainment was a part of the complex historical changes in matters related to lunacy. In England from the late eighteenth century on, an increasing number of mentally disturbed people were shut up in institutions, and, at the same time, public interest in watching, observing, knowing, listening to, and reading about them grew. As the insane were increasingly hidden behind walls, they became more visible within what Michel Foucault called discursive space. As Roy Porter and Alan Ingram have pointed out, the beginning of the publication of autobiographical accounts by mental patients (or those who were alleged so) coincided chronologically with the rise of psychiatry and its institutions.[98] From around the middle decades of the eighteenth century, writings by those who went through psychiatric confinement started to emerge, until it became a kind of minor but well-established genre in the late Victorian period.[99] In all probability, psychiatry and its institutions thus created a discursive space in which patients spoke aloud of their delusions, agonies, and sufferings and expressed praise for and criticism of mad-doctors. Psychiatrists, in turn, avidly collected writings and speeches of mad people, and published them in psychiatric treatises and medical journals. The medical interest in the first-hand experience of mad people was matched by the contemporary literary fascination with the representation of what was happening in the morbid mind.[100] Readers of *The Pickwick Papers* need only to be reminded how the eponymous gentleman was absorbed in reading "a madman's manuscript."[101] Psychiatric discourse in the nineteenth century thus both empowered and disempowered patients: empowered by giving them the space to speak out, disempowered by confining them. The same paradox is clearly visible in cases of commission of lunacy. Michel Foucault's famous statement on Western power/knowledge of sexuality aptly applies to the role of commissions of lunacy and other apparatus to manage and regulate lunacy: they formulated, rather than prohibited, the subjectivity of madness.[102] The chance to have a first-hand experience of the formulated subjectivity of real-life mad people might well be the major attraction of the cases of commission of lunacy.

TWO

The Structure of Psychiatric Practice

IN AUGUST 1827, ALEXANDER MORISON, who had recently started to practice psychiatry in London, received two sets of letters, informing him of the mental disease of Mary and Helen M——. Each set contained two letters, one from the sister of Mary and Helen, the other from Dr. Davidson, who had visited the sisters at the licensed house of Dr. Stewart, where they had been kept.[1] The contrast between the sister's narrative and that provided by the doctor is striking. The sister gave seven pages of detailed accounts of Mary and Helen's personal circumstances, in which she presented her often acute observations of her sisters' personalities from childhood onward. The doctor, in contrast, provided brief supplementary information about the recent development of the disease and largely restricted himself to describing the bodily states of the patients. The doctor's information was of lesser substance, and apparently of lesser significance, than that provided by the layperson.

The sister had an ax to grind. She told Morison that she did not approve of the treatment Mary was then receiving at the private asylum and that the family disagreed over the costly treatment of the patients. She criticized her mother, Dr. Stewart, and Mary's servant for overindulging Mary: "indulging her in whatever she has a desire for is not necessary." The patient should not be spoiled into becoming a nervous valetudinarian and a drain of the family's financial resources, but rather should be braced by firmness: "Dr Stewart has not been aware of what firmness would do with Mary." The informant's long and intimate acquaintance with Mary as a family member enabled her to supply numerous arguments against indulging the patient and for treating her with firmness. In her youth, Mary "looked angry and menacing with those she thought she could frighten, but with any person who was firm she instantly became calm." Mary got rather better when the most indulgent servant was temporarily away from home, and she did not suffer at all when the doctor did not attend.[2] On the basis of her own assessment of the case, the sister asked Morison to take the rather drastic step of moving Mary to a public asylum:

> Against a public asylum there may be many medical reasons of which we can be no judges, and far would [we] be from wishing to offer any opinion to Dr. Morison. We only wish to make him acquainted not only with the progress of her malady, but also with the state of her family, and the treatment which she has received. We know that Mary is Dr. Morison's patient, and that what is best for her must be his object, but his directions for her must be guided by circumstances, and that he should know how his orders will be obeyed is very necessary to inable him to judge what orders to give.[3]

This is a polite but forceful statement. The author showed respect for Morison's expert status but did not hesitate to recommend to him the type of treatment strategy she herself believed in. Perhaps her long and frustrating relationship with Dr. Stewart had taught her how to cope with status-conscious medical practitioners.

Morison's reply to this letter is most interesting. The alienist described the narrative given by the sister as an "excellent and feeling description." He then proceeded to tailor the treatment he recommended to Dr. Davidson rather precisely according to the demands of the sister. Morison endorsed the sister's opinion, writing that Mary needed to be pulled out of her present indolence: "considerable improvement might be effected by a change of system, for at present she seems to be entirely given up to follow her own will and to dwell without ceasing on her delusion," although there was no hope of complete recovery. She needed to have a well-disciplined life and to be subjected to "a regular mild system of restraint," in which she "ought to be made to rise at a certain hour to take her meals and exercise or amusement at stated times." Morison assumed a studied ambiguity on the question of placing Mary in a public asylum or a private one, perhaps discreetly avoiding getting involved in a family row by refusing to take sides too clearly. Apparently suggesting a compromise, he stated that a system of mild restraint could be pursued in either type of asylum. Morison gave unmistakable encouragement to the sister, however, by stating that public asylums possessed "one decided advantage" in that they insisted on a strict adherence to rules.[4] It seems that here he was not paying lip service to the sister, but was genuinely convinced, to a considerable extent, by her account. The core part of the doctor's clinical decision making was thus heavily influenced by what the layperson told him. What had dictated his prognosis and treatment was not so much his own and Dr. Davidson's medical examination and observation as the sister's account of Mary's personality and the family's circumstances. Although Morison took Mary's pulse and examined her tongue when he visited her, he did not find anything particularly informative, commenting that there were no symptoms indicating decided corporeal disease.[5] The decision was a result of negotiation between the client and the medical practitioner, not dictated by professional authority drawn from scientific expertise.

In valuing the sister's information and in incorporating her opinions into his own, Morison was not doing something exceptional for medical practitioners at the time. Indeed, what Morison did was a typical example of the "traditional" pattern of medical practice and clinical encounter, and his reliance on the layperson's narrative had been a familiar and basic component of medicine for centuries. Historians of medicine have maintained that before the advent of reliable physical examinations of the patient's body (symbolized by stethoscopy), diagnosis of disease and other types of clinical decision making were heavily dependent on laypersons' narratives of sickness, for doctors did not enjoy any clear advantage over laypersons in terms of the information the two parties possessed about the disease.[6] In one of her studies of eighteenth-century English medicine, Mary Fissell has remarked that the early modern doctor-patient relationship was characterized by a balance of power in which the doctor and the client were put on a "near-equal hermeneutic footing."[7] In the episode of Morison's clinical encounter, the client-informant was more than equal. She enjoyed superior status in terms of interpretative authority, largely because the informant disclosed many pieces of crucial information that were completely out of reach of medical observation—Mary's childhood personality being the most obvious example. The cogent assessment of the patient's character, which was known only to close and long-term acquaintances, naturally carried more weight than the medical knowledge gained through a cursory examination of the surface of the body. The lay narrative enjoyed clear priority over medical observation, at least partly because of the former's inherent relevance in terms of treating chronic disorders of the mind.

The episode I have just narrated reveals a largely neglected side of psychiatry in the nineteenth century: its *practice.* Like medicine in general, psychiatry had theoretical and practical aspects that did not always conform to one another and sometimes differed considerably. The divergence of science and practice in medicine has long been noted by historians, particularly since Erwin Ackerknecht's advocacy of the "behaviorist approach" in the history of medicine.[8] In a classic paper published in 1967, Ackerknecht maintained that one should distinguish historically between "what a doctor did" and "what a doctor thought," and that medical historians had lavished attention on the latter at the expense of the former or had been insufficiently critical in identifying the two sides of medicine, which interacted with each other but were nevertheless two distinct categories. Ackerknecht's observation of the duality and distinction of medical science and medical practice applies forcefully to psychiatry in the nineteenth century. Indeed, perhaps in no other branch of medicine was the contrast greater, for psychiatric practice, especially for the rich, was shrouded under a thick cover of secrecy because of the stigma of madness. (It is symbolic that the family name of Mary M—— was made illegible by thick lines by Morison's descendants who deposited the documents at the Royal College of Physicians in the late nineteenth century.) Although psychiatric science was publicized in medical treatises, journals, and textbooks, psychiatric practice for the wealthy was done under strictly private circumstances. To study psychiatric practice is thus to investigate psychiatry in the private sphere.

This duality of the public and private spheres of psychiatry characterized doctors' involvement in commissions of lunacy. As I described in the previous chapter, commissions of lunacy were public examinations and declarations of the insanity of their subjects, played out on a public stage. Doctors were regularly called to testify before the jury about the state of the mind of the subject of the commission.[9] Many of these medical witnesses were specialists in psychiatry or mad-doctoring, but nonspecialists—both general practitioners and elite consultants—were included as well. Those doctors who appeared in court at a commission of lunacy perfectly recognized the significance of the occasion: they had to perform in front of a large audience, and their testimony would be quoted in the newspaper. Those who owned private madhouses may have regarded the occasion as an opportunity for advertisement. As a novice mad-doctor, Alexander Morison practiced how to testify in a commission of lunacy in the presence of other more experienced specialists in the trade.[10] In the commission of lunacy against Rosa Bagster, John Haslam cut an extremely fine figure, mixing humor and pathos, and impressing the audience with his urbanity.[11]

On the other hand, involvement in a commission of lunacy also meant intensely private and discreet business with the petitioners for the commission, who were usually family members or relatives of the subject of the commission. Before the public drama started, the doctors were often consulted by the families about what should be done. Such a phase of the medical involvement was intensely private and usually hidden from both the public's eye and the historian's reach. There existed, however, one case of commission of lunacy that throws extraordinary light on the ways in which psychiatrists conducted their business with patients' families. The case is a commission of lunacy against Edward Davies in 1829. During the procedure for the commission of lunacy against Davies, searching inquiries were made into the practice of George Man Burrows, then one of the most successful psychiatric practitioners in London. Because of another legal case of a similar nature, which also involved Burrows and had taken place earlier in the same year, enormous attention was drawn to the dealings between mad-doctors and their clients during and after the Davies case.[12] Arguably, the Davies case was the hitherto unrecognized first wave of panic against wrongful confinement. With the help of documents on this case, I shall throw light on doctors' relationships with patients' families and on the practice of psychiatry in the private sphere. In so doing, I will argue that the alienists' diagnosis and other medical decisions were heavily influenced by the information they received from patients' families. The cases of "wrongful confinement" in which Burrows was involved were not so much exceptional conduct of an unscrupulous practitioner or a moral hazard generated by defective laws, as an indication of the structure of psychiatric practice.[13] My emphasis is thus less on the lack of moral uprightness or legal correctness of psychiatrists than on their behavioral patterns. Moreover, because Burrows excelled in both the intellectual and scientific aspect of psychiatry as well as the practical and business aspect of psychiatric practice, one has an occasion to examine both his theoretical approach to the science of psychiatry and his practical habits in dealing with the clients of his business. In other words, Burrows enables a historian to compare, on detailed evidence, what he told his professional brethren with how he behaved to the patrons of his trade.

In what follows I first examine Burrows's theory and practice, focusing particularly on the contradiction between what Burrows preached and what he actually did, a contradiction that largely echoed that between medical science and medical practice. I then proceed to show that the two cases of wrongful confinement in which Burrows was involved were outcomes of this contradiction. I will conclude the chapter by assessing some impacts the Burrows case had, suggesting that English alienists at this time became clearly aware of the indispensable but troublesome role of the family in their business.

SCIENCE AND PRACTICE OF G.M. BURROWS

Advocating Somatic Psychiatry

George Man Burrows was first noticed by doctors as the organizer of general practitioners and the hero of the Apothecaries' Act (1815).[14] In 1816, he "retired from the arduous duties of general practice, and confined himself to the treatment of insanity."[15] While developing a flourishing psychiatric practice based on his own licensed houses in the metropolis, he was keen to improve the scientific status of psychiatry, preaching a rather extreme form of somatic psychiatry in a journal he edited. He finally established his *scientific* fame with his *Commentaries upon Insanity* (1828), a magnum opus of more than seven hundred pages, the most comprehensive and up-to-date work on psychiatry in the English language at that time.[16] He is known to historians of psychiatry as one of the most prominent proponents of the somatic medicalization of lunacy in the early nineteenth century, particularly as the first English doctor who reported Bayle's work on general paralysis of insanity.[17] His overall aim was to establish psychiatry as a branch of medicine by adapting the former to the standards of the latter, or, to use his own words, "to adhere to those principles of pathology which ought to be our guide when viewing all the other diseases of the human body."[18] This advocacy of somatic psychiatry had a political and ideological dimension: he claimed that opinions of medically qualified persons must be given priority not only in the management of asylums but also in the regulations that governed lunacy. Accordingly, he criticized the government's intervention in matters of lunacy as the "interposition of Parliament in medical affairs."[19] He also attacked what he regarded as the peril of excessive reliance on moral therapy, for it had been derived from the most detrimental "scholastic dogma" and "German mystifications" of metaphysics of the mind, which would obstruct scientific inquiry into the nature of insanity based on the consideration of the body.[20] He dared to criticize the York Retreat, which had become a model of moral treatment and the epitome of reform in the treatment of lunacy, for its limited use of medicinal means.[21] In short, he cut a figure familiar to historians of psychiatry: the professionalizing and somaticizing alienist who wanted to bring the trade of mad-doctoring in line with the science of medicine.

Several factors conspired to make him a militant supporter of the medicalization of the care of the insane. First, his particularly keen concern to secure a medical monopoly on psychiatry must be related to his experience in the passage of the Apothecaries' Act (1815), whose major goal was to bar unqualified practitioners from medicine.[22] When Burrows attacked James Lucett, an entrepreneurial madhouse owner and an inventor of a new treatment that was patronized by some members of the royal family, Burrows's language of condemnation was centered on Lucett's lack of medical scientific education and the way he advertised the new treatment. He used the same rhetoric when, in another context, he condemned "empirical" and unlearned nostrum-mongers, the target Burrows had tried to exclude by means of the Apothecaries' Act.[23] Second, he had good reason to feel that he and his colleagues were under threat and to react sharply to this situation, because he started to practice psychiatry just as the 1815–16 Select Committee was raising fundamental doubts about the propriety of trusting lunatics to medical men and was promoting the model of practice established at the York Retreat, which was started by a tea merchant on deeply antimedical principles.[24] To the hero of the Apothecaries' Act, the direction of reform in lunacy set by the Parliamentary Select Committee in the same year must have appeared profoundly mistaken.

His hostility to "psychologists" caused Burrows to underrate every part of psychiatry related to the psychological study of the deranged mind per se. He deemed the present "inquiry into the state of a patient" or analysis of the mental affection pernicious, for it would put "the [metaphysical] science of reasoning or logic" at center stage and lead the medical practitioner astray from the more important part of his study: "Where is the utility of studying the characters of the mental delusion? Ought we not to prefer examining the various signs which indicate functional or structural lesion, and endeavour to find out whether the attendant delirium is idiopathic, symptomatic, or sympathetic?"[25] In all probability, his self-confidence as a down-to-earth general practitioner kept him from incorporating philosophy of the mind into his thinking. Philosophy of the mind was an academic and gentlemanly discipline, to which the self-made leader of general practitioners responded with mixed feelings. There was a tone of surprise and irony when he found that John Mayo and Thomas Forster, both Oxonian MDs, attacked the use of metaphysical philosophy in psychiatry.[26]

Because the study of the mad mind was of little value, it should not, Burrows argued, be a guide in the classification of madness. He preferred classification by bodily etiology to that by mental symptomatology.[27] He insisted that even when there was an obvious moral cause, doctors should try to find an underlying and hidden bodily cause. Burrows therefore criticized Philippe Pinel and his French followers for placing too much emphasis on moral causes, suspecting they had overlooked what they would have found *had they followed his advice:* "Extensive as I conceive the influence of moral causes in the production of insanity, I cannot assign it so wide a scope as many foreign writers. I entertain very strong doubts of the fidelity of the catalogue of moral causes which they enumerate with so much affectations of minute accuracy."[28] He was aware that brain dissection had done little to find bodily causes. Moreover, brain localization, if successful, would have helped phrenologists, of whom he was highly critical. These concerns turned him toward other parts of the body for the seat of mental disease. He thus picked up from J. E. D. Esquirol's writings a suggestion of the thoracic and abdominal viscera as the possible site of the sympathetic seat of insanity. He went on to publish a call for collaborative study and invited contributions in the *London Medical Repository,* the journal he was then editing, to test the hypothesis of a visceral localization of insanity.[29] Reports of autopsy findings trickled in to the journal, all of which appeared, not surprisingly, to confirm his hypothesis.[30]

When he talked about diagnosis, he grudgingly admitted that "an intimate knowledge of the moral faculties of man" would help doctors to arrive at a more correct diagnosis of insanity. The knowledge was, however, merely commonsense knowledge of human nature, "a knowledge which is acquired by association with the world only."[31] The pathognomic tools that Burrows emphasized as helpful were all concerned with the patient's body rather than his or her mind, that is, physiognomy, position, sensations, muscular powers, fasting, and odor.[32] He had remarkable confidence in his olfactory power and boasted that he could "smell out" mania: "I consider [the maniacal odor] a pathognomic symptom so unerring, that if I detected it in any person, I should not hesitate to pronounce him insane, even though I have no other proof of it."[33] Within a year after he published this claim, this passage turned out to be a hostage to fortune.

The Power of Lay Narrative in the Case Histories of Burrows

Burrows's research program for somatic psychiatry was confidently expressed to his professional brethren and looked extremely fine in the pages of medical textbooks and journals. Burrows faced, however, enormous difficulty in carrying it out in private practice, where he had to negotiate with clients, who were usually his patients' relatives. Take, for example, autopsy, a cornerstone of somatic psychiatry at that time.[34] Burrows's *Commentaries* are filled with resentment at his failures to get permission to dissect interesting cases. Burrows had been obviously itching to open up and look into the cadaver in a case of puerperal mania, but his hope was frustrated by the family's refusal to allow an autopsy. On that occasion, he wrote: "[There] can be little doubt that the encephalon would have exhibited in this case evidence of cerebral congestion." In other cases, when he did succeed in getting permission, it turned out to be too late, "for decomposition was very rapid."[35] Because systematic pathological anatomy could be carried out relatively easily at public hospitals, Burrows wrote enviously of medical officers of public asylums and of French asylum doctors for their opportunities to dissect "hundreds of bodies of insane persons." Indeed, he unsuccessfully applied for the post of physician to Bethlem Hospital in 1816, although access to the cadavers of lunatics must have been far from the sole reason for his application.[36]

The numerous case records he included in his publications show that he often had to make concessions to his clients. The relatives of patients intervened in medical issues such as regimen, treatment, and the site of treatment.[37] When a melancholic cavalry officer consulted him, Burrows "earnestly recommended that he should be completely separated from all intercourse with [his wife] and his connexions," advice that was flatly disregarded by the officer's wife.[38] Burrows resented the delay in obtaining a cure, which he was convinced would have followed, when a husband repeatedly opposed the introduction of seton near the occiput of his new wife, who had become insane.[39] Burrows also insisted that patients' families tended to overlook the approaching symptoms of insanity or to turn a blind eye to them. Indeed, their "pride, suspicion, deception, avarice, and caprice, are all opposed to the free agency of the physician in the treatment of insanity."[40]

Burrows was clearly frustrated by laypersons' failure to appreciate and act in accordance with scientific expertise and advice. He was strongly aware of the discrepancy between his ideal and the reality, and aspired to adjust the latter to the former. It seems, however, that he was blind to, or at least did not explicitly recognize, his reliance on the information provided by the family for medical decision making. As for his reliance on his clients' information, Burrows did not show any clear sign of his being aware of his own behavioral pattern. Clients' narratives made their way into almost all the case histories in Burrows's publications, without any particular comment from him. This shows that despite his medical scientific professionalism, his case histories retained the core characteristics of eighteenth-century "old" case histories.[41]

To be more precise, each one of Burrows's case histories had two distinct parts, the first dominated by lay narratives, the second by his own observations. Burrows's entrance on the scene announces the beginning of the second part, in which medical observations reign over objectified patients.[42] The case history of Mrs.——, "a young lady of 22 years of age," may serve as the best example of the conjunction of the two heterogeneous genres of narrative, one lay and the other medical. The subject of the case history was a "remarkably fine young woman." The earlier part of the case history was concerned with a melodramatic chronicling of the character, fortunes, and misfortunes of a beautiful and virtuous maidservant who married her master, who was almost certainly the narrator. She went into service as the housekeeper to a widower, who "conceived a passion for her person, [and] made proposals of a nature not to be accepted by a virtuous woman."[43] Although she found the suitor otherwise agreeable, the virtuous maid could not accept the offer of becoming his mistress. She then left the house for London, where the beautiful woman was soon courted by another suitor. On learning of the development in London—perhaps the woman informed him—her former master came to London, and this time made a proposal of marriage to her, to which she happily consented. A happy ending did not immediately bless this psychiatric Pamela, however. Soon after she accepted the offer of marriage, her period came prematurely. She could not disclose "a circumstance of so much delicacy" as an excuse for delaying the consummation of marriage, and "the fear of losing a match so advantageous violently agitated her feelings." In such a situation, the newly married couple traveled by a coach to the place where the marriage was to be consummated. Here the narrative became the most private and erotically intimate: "[During] the journey her passions were highly excited and subsequent intercourse was attended with much pain."[44] After having slept for about an hour, she suddenly awoke in a violent alarm, and then maniacal symptoms followed. Medical assistance was sought to no avail, and in the meantime, she was sent to Burrows's madhouse.

The doctor's entrance on the scene drastically changed the style and the subject of the narrative. Replacing the story of personal anxiety in a novel-like situation, the medical gaze dominates the second part of the case history in a style resembling Hippocratic writings on fever, which recorded the clinical first-hand observation of bodily symptoms in precise and curt phrases: "Her countenance was sullen and pallid; the eyes heavy, turgid, and cast downwards; the tongue foul; bowels inert; the pulse rather full and slow; the surface of the skin, and especially the extremities, below natural heat. She answered few questions, and those only in monosyllables; and she was very averse from moving."[45] In subsequent entries, Burrows regularly recorded her symptoms in the same manner, until she was eventually discharged cured.

This case history is thus a combination of two very different narratives. The first part is a story about a Richardsonian heroine, most certainly narrated either by herself or by her husband. (How else could the doctor know about her passions in the coach?) The second is a clinical description based on medical observation. The structure of this case can be read in two ways. On the one hand, it could suggest the Foucauldian triumph of medical gaze over objectified patient after the patient was institutionalized.[46] On the other hand, it could be read as evidence of the client's grip on the doctor's understanding of the patient's disease, at least up to the threshold of institutionalization, suggesting continuity with an eighteenth-century pattern of practice.

It is important to note that Burrows himself explicitly valued the lay narrative of madness as a means to assess the disease's etiology. Comparing practice at the public psychiatric hospital and private practice for the well-off, Burrows found one definite advantage of the latter over the former, and that is the narrative provided by friends of the patient. Examining the role of religion as a cause of madness, he wrote: "Medical writers, who have derived their chief experience from public practice, are most apt to err in this particular. The previous history of lunatics admitted into public asylum is rarely known; therefore the moral cause of malady is frequently inferred from the tenour of their mental aberrations; than which nothing can be more deceptious. . . . In private practice the opportunities of obtaining this essential information [of the patient's previous history] are superior; and upon a point of such serious importance, I have not omitted to avail myself of them."[47] Obviously, the source of the private patient's previous history could not be other than the patient's family. As a practitioner who based his income and knowledge on a licensed house for private patients, it was natural for Burrows to acknowledge his debt to the information provided by his clients. No doubt he valued obtaining information about the hereditary predisposition, the psychological characteristics, the events leading to the development of the disease, and many other aspects of the etiology and pathology of the disease. In the search for the cause of the disease, the patient's mental aberrations and symptoms, of which *the doctor could have first-hand observation,* should not be relied on. Instead, one should rely on the narrative of the previous history, which was inaccessible to the doctor by himself but was provided by the patient's family. The intimate observations by the family of the patient's psyche supplemented the clinical picture drawn by Burrows, who concentrated on the patient's bodily symptoms and underrated the clinical value of his or her mental or psychological manifestations. Despite his desire for a scientific and professional psychiatry, therefore, Burrows's practice retained the core of a client-centered clinical encounter, that is, the doctor's dependence on the client's narrative of illness. Indeed, because he neglected to observe the psychological state of the patient, his reliance on the client's narrative of the patient's mental state became even greater. The vacuum resulting from his obsession with the patient's bodily state was filled by the layperson's story. One should note two crucial things here. The first is that the dependence on the family's account was heavy *before* the patient's institutionalization: the doctor could confine a patient only on the basis of the family's account. The second is that Burrows does not seem to have been particularly worried about this pattern in his practice. Danger thus lurked in the structure of the psychiatric practice of this proud doctor fervently aspiring to scientific and somatic psychiatry.

THE FALL OF AN EMINENT PSYCHIATRIST

The Case of Freeman Anderdon

In 1829, just when he might have been basking in the success of his major work, Burrows was involved in two successive cases of wrongful confinement. Both cases were centered around the issue of the status of relatives' narratives in the diagnosis and certification of lunacy. The first case, that of Freeman Anderdon, seems straightforward: no doubt was raised about the sanity of Anderdon, against whom Burrows had issued an *equivalent* of a certificate of lunacy without seeing him and had attempted to confine him only on the basis of the family's account.[48]

Freeman Anderdon was a son of a well-known, wealthy merchant, and his brothers were coproprietors of the bank where Anderdon had his account. Anderdon was fond of a retired and frugal life: he did not see his family and he led an "ungentlemanly" existence, living by himself in a poor area of the city, mixing with people from the working classes, and enjoying wearing peculiar clothes such as a waterman's coat and a straw hat.[49] He had, however, never been suspected of insanity by his neighbours.[50] In short, he was an eccentric gentleman with strange habits that certainly did not amount to madness. He possessed a considerable fortune and he invested part of it in paintings, whose value was estimated in total at £15,000–20,000. Although the investment had been fairly successful, one of his brothers was afraid that Anderdon might squander the money, which the brother expected to inherit at Anderdon's death. The brother, therefore, refused to cash the check Anderdon brought to the bank to purchase another picture. Anderdon protested and threatened legal action.[51]

A few days later, on 2 November 1829, two men, John Shelly and Thomas Hazord, came out of the blue to Anderdon's house and told him that they were to confine him there as an insane person. Although they behaved with civility (or what madhouse attendants considered civility), they carried cords, manacles, screws, and other items of their trade in their bag.[52] Anderdon's cries for help brought his neighbors to the scene, and they demanded that the two men explain their actions, at which one of the men produced a paper that bore the words "By direction of Mr. Oliver and James Anderdon, I hereby authorise the bearers to take charge of Mr. Freeman Anderdon, he being insane, and confine him in his own house. [Signed] G. M. Burrows, M.D."[53] On the following day, Burrows appeared at a police hall, where he admitted that he had not seen Freeman at all and had signed the document only on the representation of the brothers. Daily papers reported the case, which immediately caused a storm of outraged protest. One James Wells, who had been certified as a lunatic, wrote to the *Times,* asking "what is . . . the difference between a 'Lettre de cachet' and a 'Certificate of Lunacy?'" He vehemently criticized Burrows as "a man styling himself M.D., a self-interested mad-doctor and physician," committing a "deed of monstrous cruelty, of hellish inhumanity."[54] Subsequently, Anderdon sued Burrows for assault. The case was beyond argument. At the trial, held in April of the next year, even the lawyer who acted on Burrows's behalf meekly ended his defense by asking for mercy: "He admitted that the verdict must be against the defendant; but unless he was painfully mistaken, the smallest possible damages would be given." On the contrary, Burrows, having lost the case, faced punitive damages of £500.[55]

Unyielding and hard-nosed, Burrows tried to defend his deeds, resorting to a string of legalistic quibbles. The *London Medical Gazette* pronounced itself unimpressed and advised that "he ought to know that it is better to suffer a false step to be overlooked in the general respectability of his character, rather than thus to provoke criticism by attempting to justify it."[56] Burrows should have followed this advice, for by not doing so he played into the public fear that many alienists were regularly performing two types of ethically and legally dubious actions.

First, they were in the habit of issuing an equivalent of a certificate of lunacy, which was practically effective but defined nowhere in the lunacy law. Burrows justified his deed as follows:

> It frequently happens, in removing a lunatic from one place to another, that he is very violent, or endeavours, by making artful appeals to those near him, to attract their attention, and raise a feeling to rescue him. In such a case, the populace are almost always sure to side with the lunatic, and sometimes liberate him. The production of the regular certificate generally proves a passport, stops further interruption. When the case requires no certificate, if the attendants, whether relations or keepers, are interrogated, and have no document to shew that they have an insane person in charge, they would not only be interrupted, but commonly be defeated. In those cases of removal where a certificate is not understood to be necessary, I, in common with other medical gentlemen, upon a principle of precaution, have been in the habit of sending by the keeper a note, addressed to some one in the house where the lunatic is, specifying that the bearer is the person confided in to take the care of, or to remove him.[57]

This is a pseudo certificate of lunacy, so to speak. Although there was no law against creating such a document, the aim of doing so was clearly to dupe the people around the alleged lunatic to facilitate his or her confinement. The unmistakable tone of boasting in which Burrows laid out his and his fellow alienists' precautions and ingenuity must have irritated contemporary readers.

Second, Burrows acknowledged that he had not conducted a personal examination or a medical interview before he judged that Anderdon was insane and sent his attendants equipped with manacles and cords to confine him.[58] Here, Burrows's self-defense betrays that his and other alienists' clinical encounters were structured in the ways I have just described. Burrows admitted, to be sure, that "medical examination of a suspected or alleged lunatic should always precede . . . his being placed under restraint." But he believed that he was blameless for acting on the evidence adduced by the Anderdon brothers, for he knew they were gentlemen of the highest character and had been for some years personally acquainted with them.[59] From such trustworthy family members, Burrows was saying, one could naturally expect only honesty and integrity, totally neglecting the fact that he had not heard the other side of the story from the "patient." Burrows ventured further still, contending that family narratives were indispensable: "Others conceive that an opinion on the sanity or insanity of a person's mind ought not to be found and decided upon any representation at all. Yet, from the history of a case we can often draw the clearest inference, while a personal examination without it will elicit nothing."[60]

This was exactly, I argue, what Burrows had been doing in his psychiatric practice. His belief in the value of what he called "the history of a case" remained firm. In a pamphlet published the next year, Burrows still insisted that his actions had been proper and maintained that "there is no malady to which humanity is liable, where the judgment and moral treatment of it must be guided so much by representation or description as insanity." To make his point, he relied partly on a familiar and stale argument: making decisions about remedies, control, and restraint only on the "representation" of third parties was often necessary, he contended, because an alienist was sometimes consulted by a country practitioner by post, or because procrastination could end up in suicide or homicide in an urgent case.[61]

More significantly, he argued that the presence of the patient was harmful to composing a correct picture of the situation, writing that "the real state of his case can rarely be properly described to the physician by his friends or attendants *in his presence* [my emphasis]." By this, Burrows probably meant to allude to the problems that might be caused by the patient who noisily contested what the family told the doctor, suspicious that the family was engaged in a malicious conspiracy. When in 1828 Burrows visited one L. Phillip to examine his mental state for a commission of lunacy, the patient was excited, showed utmost violence, and declared that the family beat him and wished to rob him. Phillip abused his wife and threatened to strike the son who accompanied Burrows.[62] All these violent and wild scenes caused by a protesting patient could and must be avoided. The ideal psychiatric clinical encounter as Burrows conceived it should consist in the relationship of a doctor and the prospective patient's family or relatives. The family members rationally and calmly represented the state of the patient, and the doctor attentively listened to the narrative and made diagnosis and judgment. Since clamorous patients disturbed the communication between this ideal pair, it was often essential that they be excluded from the scene. In other words, Burrows was saying that an ideal psychiatric clinical encounter was one *without the patient.* Trying to defend himself, Burrows thus betrayed an unpleasant reality of his everyday practice.

Despite Burrows's emphasis on the diagnostic value of the scientific examination of the bodily symptoms of a patient—such as maniacal odor—as expressed in his published medical works, in his *practice* he centered his diagnostic decision making on the relatives' lay narrative of the patient's tormented and disturbed psyche. Nevertheless, there is no reason to believe that Burrows was insincere when he preached a somatic research program and when he boasted of his ability to smell out maniacs. Perhaps the person who was the most deceived by what he wrote in his *Commentaries* and his many journal articles was Burrows himself. In all probability, his self-deception was severer than that of his fellow alienists because of his genuine belief in the value of somatic diagnosis, his keen aspiration to develop scientific psychiatry, and his sense of competition with English lay reformers of lunacy.[63]

The Case of Edward Davies

The Anderdon case was just the beginning of the mad-doctor's troubles. While Burrows was being criticized over the Anderdon case, he was simultaneously drawn into another case of alleged lunacy, that of Edward Davies.[64] Davies's father was a pub-keeper, his mother a cook. From such lowly beginnings, he quickly climbed the social ladder and had become a successful tea broker, earning £2,000 a year, with property estimated at between £10,000 and £12,000. At the time of the commission, he was age twenty-seven, single, and living with his mother, now Mrs. Bywater, who controlled Davies "like a hard mother over a child."[65] Most important, she did not allow him command of his purse and frequently ordered him to give money to members of the Bywater family. Davies attempted to be independent, but his mother did not give way. The conflict between them grew intense in 1828–29.[66] Having been a shy, eccentric, and nervous valetudinarian, Davies was obviously highly agitated by his confrontations with his mother, who made up her mind in June 1929 to try *every* means to prevent his assertions of independence.[67] Burrows and William Lawrence, then serving as a surgeon to Bethlem, were asked to attend Davies in early July, and they concluded that he was insane. Anticipating his mother's plan, Davies had asked his attorney, Francis Hobler, to intervene.[68] Subsequently, in early August, Davies ran away from his own house and took lodgings at the Furnival's Inn Coffee House, where he refused to see his mother and the doctors.

On 4 August, Burrows sent two men to Furnival's Inn. A string of events identical to that in the Anderdon case occurred: the two men showed the innkeeper a note that read, "[the] bearers are two of my attendants, authorised by the family of Mr. Edward Davies, who is insane, and also by me, to take charge of him, and convey him to his house, signed by G. M. Burrows, M.D."[69] Using this pseudo certificate as their authority, the two men brought Davies to his own house. The next day, on 5 August, Thomas Brundell of the London Dispensary visited Davies, declared that he saw indisputable signs of insanity, and signed a legal certificate of lunacy. William Lawrence signed the other certificate, thus completing the legal requirement of two independent medical certificates. On 19 August, Davies was brought to the Retreat at Clapham, a licensed house owned by Burrows. Davies's mother petitioned for a commission of lunacy to prove Davies's lack of civil competency on the basis of insanity. For reasons that remain unclear, the commission against Davies did not start until 14 December, by which time Burrows's conduct in the Anderdon case had already tarnished his credentials.

The inquiry for the commission of lunacy lasted a full two weeks. The *Times* reported the proceedings and examination and cross-examination of witnesses in detail every day, regularly devoting several entire columns to the testimony. On 17 December, it devoted almost an entire page. The case became the biggest news of the day in late December 1829. Although Hobler's minor celebrity may have contributed to the public's attention to the case, the exceptionally heavy coverage more likely resulted from the involvement of Henry Brougham, a Whig politician, an eminent lawyer, one of the founders of University College London, and a leading Benthamite legal reformer, with whom the *Times* was then on very close terms.[70] Brougham cut an impressive figure, leading the team of four lawyers against the commission, trying to show that Davies was *compos mentis* and could manage his own affairs.[71] Ever since he had made his name through his opposition to slavery and to suppressive measures enacted during the Napoleonic War, Brougham was known to show talent, zeal, and unmatched eloquence in cases that touched on some principle of individual or political liberty.[72] The Davies case proved to be an ideal occasion for him: toward the end of the commission, Brougham delivered a speech that lasted five hours, pleading for the principle of individual liberty and warning against the danger of mad-doctors' wish "to monopolize all the soundness of intellect as well as the cure of all the unsound intellects."[73] Moreover, Brougham had an ideal opponent. The counsel for the commission was led by Sir Charles Wetherell, the favorite of Lord Eldon and an ultra-Tory politician who opposed every legal and political reform.[74] On the very first day of the inquiry, Wetherell and Brougham exchanged jabs, the former making a sarcastic comment about the University College, London, the latter immediately answering it.

The Anderdon case, which had come to light just a month before, cast a dark shadow over Burrows, and Brougham made effective and shrewd use of it to damage the alienist's credibility. When Brougham cross-examined Burrows, he asked, "[Did] you ever give any order of any kind for detaining a person as insane, without seeing him?" Wetherell anticipated the obvious peril for Burrows and objected that this line of questioning was not related to the present case. The commissioners, however, allowed Brougham to go on, after assuring Burrows that he was not bound to answer the question:

BROUGHAM—	Now I repeat the question, Dr. Burrows, and you may answer it or not, as you like. Did you ever give any order of any kind for detaining a person as insane, without seeing him?
BURROWS—	I must decline to answer questions as to matters not connected with [the present case].
BROUGHAM—	Very well: you decline to answer it.[75]

In his summing up, Brougham took advantage of this triumph, reminding the jury of "the alarm we feel . . . when we hear refusal to answer to such a question."[76]

The Anderdon case not only served to lessen Burrows's credibility, but also revealed to Brougham's team a fundamental vulnerability of the medical witnesses: their dependence on the family's representations about the state of an alleged patient. The cross-examination of the medical witnesses who testified to Davies's lunacy shows that the lawyers had a clear grasp of this built-in structural problem of psychiatric practice, recently revealed by the Anderdon case and in Burrows's subsequent attempt at self-justification. Burrows himself admitted that an alienist's diagnosis of madness depended at least as much on representation as on personal examination. The most effective way to undermine the claim of medical witnesses was, therefore, to show that their testimony was based on second-hand information acquired from a biased source rather than on their own observations. In other words, Brougham's team tried to construct the Davies case on the model of the Anderdon case. The following cross-examination of Dr. Algernon Frampton by Brodrick exemplified this strategy:

BRODRICK— Did you prescribe for him at Crouch-hill?

FRAMPTON— I gave him a prescription.

BRODRICK— You gave him physic for his mind, I suppose—pray did you examine his bodily health?

FRAMPTON— I did not.

BRODRICK— What! do you prescribe for your patient without examining into his state of bodily health?

FRAMPTON— Dr. Cobb prescribed for him, and by my sanction put my name to his prescription.

BRODRICK— Do you put your name to a mad certificate at the request of a friend, without examining the party who it is to deprive of liberty?

FRAMPTON— That's quite another matter.[77]

The doctors did not seem to have been particularly worried about their omission of any bodily examination. Indeed, Dr. Cobb was proud of his ingenious use of physical examination as a camouflage for doing something else: "I took hold of his hand, pretending to feel his pulse, but in reality to examine a slight eruption on his hand." Thanks to the veneer of a physical examination, the doctor perceived a slight cut on his hand, which suggested Davies's attempt at suicide.[78]

With all his agitation, confused behavior, and eccentricities, Davies did not show any palpable delusion, then the sine qua non of the legal definition of *non compos mentis* in the criminal context.[79] This maneuver involved some legal sleight of hand, since delusion was not necessary in the context of the commission of lunacy at that time, as I shall show in chapter 6. The hard core of the doctors' argument was that Davies's antipathy to his mother was *delusional:* Mrs. Bywater was a nice mother, full of maternal love, and Davies's antagonism to her had no ground and was irrational. Brougham's team, on the other hand, tried to show that Davies had good reason to react angrily, implying that the mother was a wicked old hag. In so doing, they tried to prove that the doctors grounded their argument for *delusional* antipathy on the information they had obtained from other people.

Adolphus's cross-examination of Sir George Tuthill, then physician to Bethlem, marked the point of triumph of the defense lawyers:

ADOLPHUS—	Was there any point in his narrative of matters of fact on which you could judge of the truth or untruth of what he told you, from any other source than the information which you derived from the persons in the house, or [the Clapham] Retreat, or from his mother?
TUTHILL—	It is not from any communication from his mother that I judge him insane.
ADOLPHUS—	That is not an answer to my question, Sir George, and you know it as well as I do. I will repeat the question to you again. [He repeated the question.]
TUTHILL—	No, there was not.
ADOLPHUS—	*No, there was not*—and that answer I have got at last.[80]

Adolphus here conclusively showed that Tuthill could not produce a single example of Davies's "delusion" the falsity of which Tuthill could confirm from first-hand observation. The lawyer demonstrated that Tuthill believed that Davies's ideas were delusional because Tuthill had been told so by other people. In other words, the ultimate basis of Tuthill's diagnosis was other people's representation of Davies, not his own observation.

Following this exchange, the two medical witnesses who appeared the next day gave up the argument for the existence of delusions, and instead produced extremely feeble testimony. Sir Edward Roberts, senior physician to St. Bartholomew's, admitted that there was no solid fact that proved that Davies was suffering from delusion: "Whether his complaints were true or not, I say that his relation of the facts was that of a madman. I formed my opinion from the circumstances generally, . . . not from any one separately." Burrows attempted to show that lack of evidence of delusion did not necessarily imply the sanity of the subject in question, arguing that many insane persons could conceal delusion.[81] In taking this approach, however, the medical witnesses implicitly admitted that they could not provide any solid first-hand evidence of Davies's delusion. Although it is extremely difficult to assess which part of the defense lawyers' argument was the most effective, there is no doubt that the contest over the basis of doctors' diagnoses played an important part in the process of their advocacy. At a relatively early phase of the examination, the outcome of the commission became increasingly clear. On 27 December, the jury finally interrupted the examination, stating they had already learned enough to return a verdict.[82] As expected, they voted unanimously against the commission, announcing that Davies could manage his own affairs and should be set free.

The two cases devastated Burrows. His name was now irretrievably associated with wrongful confinement. Lucett took a belated revenge, advancing still another case in which Burrows kept a man without certificate.[83] In his *Lunacy and Liberty* (1832), William Griggs, an ex-patient of Kensington House, wrote that the wrongful confinement of Davies in Burrows's madhouse was the most horrible one he had ever seen.[84] J. J. Stockdale and Thomas Little, obscure underground publishers of pornography and pamphlets of political radicalism, issued a lurid *Mad-Houses!* (1831), writing that they were inspired by the recent "occurrences between Burroughs *[sic]* and the Messieurs Anderson *[sic]*."[85] More damaging, *Quarterly Review,* an influential high-quality journal, joined the chorus bashing the mad-doctor, when an anonymous author of its article coined a term *the Burrowsed,* meaning those wrongly confined.[86] When Burrows protested that he had become a target of a conspiracy of lawyers and the press, the *Times* assumed an openly contemptuous attitude, writing, "Let Dr. Burrows not think that any 'conspiracy' is hatching against him. Without any disparagement to his talents, experience, or reputation, we would say that he is scarcely of sufficient importance to be the subject of a conspiracy like that which he describes."[87] Thundering criticism of his behavior thus echoed in both the mainstream and the radical press.

Burrows also found himself subjected to direct protests and threats. After the Anderdon case and during the Davies case, about 250 protesters visited his Clapham Retreat, "most of whom came with a notion that [Davies] was not insane, and therefore looking with a jealous eye, and a disposition ready to cavil at all they saw here." During the inquiry, Burrows received numerous anonymous threatening letters. On the day after the verdict, he received an additional forty letters, one of which read, "Dr. Burrows is cautioned to take care of himself. His consummate villainy will be expiated by blood only."[88] The mixed use of social protest and threat of violence suggests a style of protest against wrongful confinement in the 1830s with more affinity with underground radicalism than with the tactics of the Alleged Lunatics' Friend Society, a pressure group organized by upper- and upper-middle-class ex-patients and respectable radicals such as Thomas Wakley in the 1840s.[89]

Burrows's prosperous practice seems to have completely collapsed.[90] One of his sons could not finish his university education, another had to give up his study for the bar at Lincoln's Inn.[91] In 1831, Burrows wrote a desperate letter seeking the Lord Chancellor's patronage for his third son, whose career as a novice attorney was in danger for lack of resources. Most ironically, the Lord Chancellor then was Brougham himself. In the letter, Burrows told Brougham that although his friends had helped to restore his reputation and fortunes, "ruins [are] impending on myself," reminding the Lord Chancellor of his "hopeless condition." This epitome of professional success and pride had to beg for mercy at the feet of a man who had ruined him.

His scientific output ceased completely. Burrows, then fifty-nine years old, bitterly recognized that his medical-scientific efforts and eminence did nothing to help him in a time of hardship: "Perhaps I had the vanity to think it would be remembered, that I had shewn a zeal in the study and practice of this branch of the healing art, that entitled me to be distinguished from those who had continued to tread the routine course of bygone years, and that this would have insured me more liberal treatment. . . . I will yield to no British physician for industry and personal exertions, and, I may add, pecuniary sacrifices in the pursuit of that knowledge which was essential to improvement."[92] Disillusioned, Burrows drew a bitter lesson that there was in the English psychiatric world no established system to evaluate scientific achievements of medical men; that all the enthusiastic reviews of his *Commentaries* had not changed an iota of his status as a mad-doctor in the market place, a social position that Brougham had compared to that of a shopkeeper during the Davies case.[93]

It should be noted, however, that Burrows was not acting only from greed or monetary concern. Brougham's accusation was only partially true. Burrows's overriding concern was the pursuit of scientific psychiatry, modeled after Parisian hospital medicine. His aspiration to scientific psychiatry demanded that what he observed in the patient should be the major, if not sole, basis for medical decision making. But that aspiration was virtually impossible to realize in practice. Given the relative urgency of the decisions he had to make, and the contrast between the small amount of time during which he familiarized himself with the patient with the long period during which the family knew the patient, it was extremely impractical to discard the information provided by the family and to depend on medical observation only. Burrows perhaps overlooked his problematic dependence on the family's narrative and trumpeted an alluring but impractical dependence on physical signs. He aspired to an impossible version of medical professionalism, and made his actual practice subservient to his clients' expedience in a most unprofessional manner.

The two successive cases in which Burrows was involved were not the first major cases of wrongful confinement in England, nor the first expression of the public's concern over the threat psychiatrists posed to "liberty." Nevertheless, Burrows's legal travails held a particularly important place in several respects. First, the publicity given to the cases, especially that of Davies, was unprecedented. It resulted not just in a handful of articles, exposé pamphlets, or novellas. For a full two weeks, the case was the top news in the *Times,* then the most important daily national paper in England.[94] Burrows was one of the best-known, if not one of the most prestigious, medical and psychiatric practitioners in the metropolis. His fame among his fellow general practitioners and alienists perhaps matched the fame of his adversary Henry Brougham among the general public. Although Burrows might not be the first psychiatric practitioner whose career and reputation were destroyed by his involvement in a case of illegal confinement, certainly his fall was the most spectacular.

More important, this disaster, which hit the most respected and successful practitioner of the profession, constituted an important lesson to early and mid-nineteenth-century alienists. Many practitioners must have learned that epistemological duality was an unavoidable, built-in part of their business, which they neglected at their peril. The optimistic advocacy of the ideal of scientific diagnosis, independent of information passed from clients, looked fine in the pages of psychiatric treatises, but it was next to impossible to practice according to this ideal. One could not, in short, smell out insanity. Such careless boasting about clinical acumen could backfire on the bragging psychiatrist. However unsatisfactory it might be from the viewpoint of building an ideal of scientific, somatic, and autonomous psychiatry, one had to listen carefully to and rely on what the client had to say. At the same time, the doctor had to ask himself whether the representation was trustworthy. Alienists had to recognize their own dependent status in terms of the epistemological basis of their diagnosis, and, simultaneously, bear in mind that they relied uncritically on the family at their own grave peril. Burrows's ruin revealed that the business of psychiatry was a catch-22, inset within the unsolvable dilemma of science and practice. The challenges facing a psychiatric practitioner were serious indeed.[95]

In the next chapter, I touch on some of the consequences of the new awareness of the difficulty in psychiatric diagnosis in the 1830s and 1840s.

I would like to conclude this chapter, however, by examining J. C. Bucknill's advocacy of a compromising style of diagnostic procedure in *The Manual of Psychological Medicine,* which Bucknill coedited with Daniel Hack Tuke in 1858. Bucknill and Tuke's *Manual* was the work that succeeded, after thirty years, Burrows's *Commentary* as the most comprehensive and authoritative standard manual for psychiatric practice in its day. One can reasonably assume that a comparison of the two books reflects the changes in the attitude of the profession in the thirty years in question.[96] The contrast between the two works in terms of diagnostic guidelines is striking indeed. Recognition of the structural difficulty of diagnosis and the call for a very cautious approach, rather than overoptimism about the possibilities of physical diagnosis, are evident in Bucknill and Tuke's *Manual.* The change of attitude in the thirty years deserves closer analysis.

Unlike Burrows, whose optimism and confidence were evident in his work, in the *Manual* Bucknill told psychiatrists that they should assume utmost caution. No other diseases were, Bucknill warned, so various, ambiguous, and full of "infinite variety of light and shade" as insanity.[97] No other disease "taxes so much the ingenuity and patience of the physician." Diagnosis of mental diseases was particularly difficult, according to Bucknill, because one could learn very little from observation of physical and somatic signs: "The diagnosis of almost all other diseases depends principally upon weighing the evidence afforded by physical signs and symptoms, upon evidence addressed to the senses; but in mental disease, it is, for the most part, dependent upon evidence which is cognizable by the intellect alone, and upon data which the senses furnish to us only at second hand."[98] Here is a forthright acknowledgment that it was impossible to conduct psychiatric diagnosis in exactly the same manner as diagnosis of somatic disease. The ambition to make psychiatric diagnosis "scientific" by making it depend solely or mainly on tangible sense data—the aspiration embraced so fervently by Burrows—should be given up.

Accordingly, Bucknill and Tuke recommended that psychiatrists regard their business as strictly and explicitly consisting of two parts: listening to the family's explanation of events *and* personally examining the patient. When a psychiatrist was called to see a suspected patient, he should not, advised Bucknill, proceed directly to personal examination, but listen carefully to the narrative of the family or "the near relations of the patient." By so doing, the doctor could expect to gain vital information about hereditary tendency toward the disease, previous attacks, and changes of habit and disposition. Particularly the last of these was vital in helping the practitioner reach a diagnosis, because that offered him a yardstick against which the present behaviors of the patient could be measured and judged. Only after completing inquiries into those matters with the patient's family should psychiatrists start a personal examination. The interview with the family now became a separate category of psychiatric information-collecting: the *Manual* gave a detailed and extensive guide to that part of the process, running to six pages.[99] Bucknill and Tuke threw in many caveats, warning the doctor against taking the family's testimony at face value. Families' accounts tended to be unreliable or misleading, and sometimes families even tried to deceive psychiatrists. Similar difficulties were, however, also acknowledged with the personal examination. No infallible or unequivocal signs of insanity could be obtained through examination of the patient's dress, bodily condition, gesture, or physiognomy.[100] Physical signs were no trump card by themselves.

Bucknill and Tuke's basic message is clear: psychiatrists had to live with the dual structure of their practice, in which neither the family's representation nor the personal examination provided a solid or infallible test of insanity. The alienist should give up the impractical if attractive mirage of the personal examination as a single key to the process. He should also avoid overreliance on the family, lest he should be misled by an interested party or duped by an unscrupulous or scheming one. This advice from Bucknill and Tuke may sound like a compromise, but its compromising attitude is a sign of psychiatrists' maturity or their explicit recognition of the complexity of their business, which Burrows failed to acknowledge, to his own peril.

It is important to note that these emerging guidelines for psychiatric diagnosis proceeded along the direction of incorporating information given by laypersons, not excluding it. As the century progressed, the business of madhouse-keeping matured into the profession of psychiatry. The psychiatrists' professional organization was established, journals were started, and some clinical courses, if perfunctory, were established. Bucknill's formulation of diagnostic procedure was itself an important part of the professionalization of psychiatry and a means of raising the standard, perhaps following a similar trend in medicine in general.[101] The title of the work itself—*Manual of Psychological Medicine*—speaks of the authors' aspiration. Most important, at the time when Bucknill and Tuke published their *Manual,* the ultimate clinical and institutional basis of the psychiatric profession was solidly established in the form of the county asylum. This process toward professionalization and establishment of psychiatry was *not* accompanied by the establishment of narrowly scientific aspirations or research programs but by the consolidation of the role of the family. Unlike the model proposed by many historians of medicine in the late eighteenth and early nineteenth centuries, the rise of psychiatry did not disfranchise the lay narrative, at least in the context of diagnosis of madness.[102] The lay interpretation of madness turned out to be resilient. Indeed, the family received an explicitly sanctioned place at the core of psychiatric practice. My findings thus corroborate a recent revision proposed by David Wright in the context of the certificate of lunacy. Wright has criticized the view that sees the nineteenth century as a period of linear growth of the power of the psychiatric specialist, and he has pointed out that "ironically, over the course of the nineteenth century, power over certification devolved away from the so-called experts in the asylums to non-resident medical practitioners and the lay public."[103] The psychiatric profession in England learned this lesson—that one should incorporate the lay narrative into one's practical guidelines—through the painful experience of witnessing the fall of its most eminent theorist and practitioner.

THREE

The Problems of Liberty and Property

THE PREVIOUS CHAPTER APPROACHED A familiar question of psychiatrists' misdemeanors from a new perspective. Instead of attributing incidents of wrongful confinement to the lack of professional conscience or legal regulation, I attempted to uncover the epistemological structure underlying psychiatric practice. The practitioner's trust of family members and the high status accorded to information they provided were key factors in the cases of Anderdon and Davies. Alienists had two kinds of information that helped them to judge whether the person in question was insane or not: what they observed in the patient and what they heard from the patient's family. They in effect prioritized the latter because the former was deemed of less assistance in forming a medical judgment. Another reason for the alienists' dependence on the information provided by the patient's family was that they made their living through providing psychiatric service in the medical marketplace. The status of the family as the alienist's client must have affected psychiatric decision making. The family was in a situation that demanded sympathy and assistance from alienists; they were ready to pay the alienists a fee for the help they would receive. Most important, it was not the patient but the family who held the purse strings. As Brougham and many others had forcibly argued, it was in the economic interest of an alienist to listen to the plea of the family and decide that the person in question should be judged insane. When the practitioner himself owned a licensed house, believing what the family told him would lead to direct financial gain for him. The epistemological choice between two kinds of information was made with practical gain in mind.

There existed yet another important dimension in the psychiatrist's relationship with the family, which is the question of the protection of property. This aspect has not received due attention from historians of psychiatry, many of whom have framed cases such as Anderdon and Davies under the rubric of "wrongful *confinement*." Of course it is perfectly right to regard these cases as examples of wrongful confinement, for both men were indeed confined or about to be confined—Davies in the Clapham Retreat, and Anderdon in his own house. However, in both cases, the curbing of personal liberty was not the ultimate concern of those who sought the services of the psychiatrist. The threats Anderdon and Davies posed were not directed against other people or against their own persons. If one closely examines these cases, the real bone of contention was control of their property rather than personal liberty. It should be remembered that the brothers of Freeman Anderdon were unhappy at Freeman's purchase of paintings, which appeared to them to be wasteful of money they would inherit after his death. This led to the family dispute, and the brothers took the drastic measure. In the Davies case, the dispute developed between Davies and his mother, when he asserted his financial independence of his mother and her family and the mother tried to block the attempt, which led to her seeking a commission of lunacy. The legal procedures had, technically speaking, nothing to do with confinement, but rather were concerned with the alleged lunatics' civil rights over their property. It was only by Brougham and his team that the commission of lunacy against Davies was transformed into a question of liberty. This was a shrewd strategic move, for the magnitude of the public's anxiety or even panic about Davies's psychiatric confinement grew out of the well-established English belief in liberty, which Brougham skillfully exploited in 1829. However, one should not be misled by Brougham's rhetoric and the fervor of the public outcry. A domestic dispute over the disposal of property was at the root of the case of Davies, as well as that of Anderdon. In other words, when the psychiatrists' dubious conduct in private disputes over property was brought to the notice of the public, it was reconstructed as a threat to liberty.

Family disputes of this sort may be almost universally observed. But in England in the nineteenth century, the legal as well as social situation fostered "family feuds" over property.[1] From the mid-seventeenth century on, despite the rule of primogeniture, aristocratic estates were increasingly held together by the legal mechanism of "entailment," a device that restrained the incumbent's power to sell land. Under this legal practice, family members other than the first son were drawn more extensively into the outer circles of the benefit from the estates. The legal properties of middle-class families were complicated, too. Sons, brothers, and in-laws were drawn into the family business to become business partners, and under such a situation control over one's own property was not a concern just of the individual who owned it, but very frequently that of the family and relatives as well. During the period under review, both law and custom failed to give the owner of property complete discretion over its disposal, for a degree of personal property could be retained within families by various forms of private trust.[2] The question of how to dispose of a person's property was a rich source of family disagreements. It is thus not surprising that the charge of lunacy was often raised when family members were not happy at the way in which an individual managed his or her own property. Numerous cases of attempts to secure a commission of lunacy, to be examined in chapters 4 and 5, fall into this pattern. The English family in the early nineteenth century quite often actively interfered in the management of property owned by one of its members, to prevent him or her from squandering it. The tacit assumption underlying such cases was that management of property should be not left to the discretion of the individual who owned it, but was a joint concern of the family members and relatives who drew benefit from the property.

When a psychiatrist was invited by a well-off family to judge the sanity of one of its members, he faced a complex situation, dealing with the ambiguity of the question of the disposal of the family's property. The question was not just one of personal liberty or freedom from confinement, but often also that of the right to manage one's property, which "belonged" also to the family. The family asserted that a person was damaging his or her own personal property through lunacy and should be prevented from doing so by putting the individual under a commission of lunacy. More often than not, the individual repudiated the charge of insanity and denounced the family as acting on greed. Disregard of the damage done to one's own estates or business was often stated as a sign of madness in the context of commissions of lunacy. *The capacity of managing one's own affairs and property* was the phrase routinely used in that kind of legal procedure. Tactics suitable to such concerns could be employed by psychiatrists involved in a commission of lunacy case or, broadly speaking, in the question of the lunacy of a person with substantial property. Even the definition of madness could be adapted to the aim of the protection of property. At one time, John Haslam even testified that doing damage to one's property was ample evidence of "delusion," though such an opinion represented a stark departure from the usual definition of the term. At a commission in 1835, the foreman of the jury asked Haslam, who gave his testimony as a medical witness: "Can you define why miserly habits are a criterion of judging of a man's mental condition, as to his soundness or unsoundness of mind?" With his typical panache, Haslam's answer went right to the point of the commission: "If those miserly habits trench on the health or on the *property* of the individual, then I can conceive that his actions are delusions."[3]

Broadly speaking, psychiatrists thus had two different duties. The first was protecting society from the possible harms done by an insane person—homicidal maniacs should be confined, and those who attempted to assassinate the king while laboring under delusion should be exonerated but put into custody at Bethlem. The other duty, which psychiatrists performed for the patient's family, was to protect the property of individuals from being wasted, mismanaged, and squandered away by their misbehavior. While the former was a psychiatric service to the public, the latter function was performed for the family's private and discreet, if not secret, interest.

The vital question was: *whom* should a psychiatrist serve? Here, the question of the double agency of the alleged lunatic and the family at the psychiatric bedside became especially pressing and ambivalent, for both parties had a stake in the ownership and management of the property. The *Times*'s comment on the Davies case is blunt but succinct: that mad-doctors "are generally called in by wealthy relatives, who desire to protect the property of the patient, which may ultimately be theirs."[4] However, things were not always as simple as the *Times* depicted: psychiatrists did not always conspire with the family against the alleged lunatic. There was considerable room for the expression of different opinions among psychiatrists. This chapter analyzes how radically psychiatrists differed over the question of the role of alienists in the protection of property in the early 1830s.

In the immediate aftermath of the Davies case, there were calls to rethink the psychiatrist's relationship with the patient and the family, especially in the context of commissions of lunacy. I shall examine three forms of reaction, which were all, in one way or another, responses to the crisis in psychiatry brought about by the fall of the most eminent practitioner in the field. They were: an unpublished paper read at the Royal College of Physicians (RCP) in 1830–31; *The Indications of Insanity* (1830) by John

Conolly, then a professor of medicine at University College London; and the writings of Charles Dunne, a radical entrepreneur and lecturer who had received a medical education in Paris. They proposed different programs to recast psychiatric practice, inspired by different ideologies and concerns. The anonymous paper at RCP reinforced the conservative and gentlemanly role of the guardian of family property; Conolly expressed staunch liberalism and stauncher legalism; Dunne embraced out-and-out scientism and medical authority. These three proposals were all made in the immediate wake of the fall of Burrows in 1829 and were directly related to the question of commissions of lunacy. I shall also examine J. C. Prichard's concept of "moral insanity" in this context. First formulated in a publication in 1833, Prichard's newly formulated diagnostic category provided an escape route from the catch-22 in which psychiatrists found themselves, by endorsing the old family-dependent diagnostic pattern and, at the same time, insisting that the diagnosis was a scientific one.

THE IMPACT OF THE TWO CASES

One of the impacts of the scandal in 1829–30 in which Burrows was implicated was that it made medical practitioners keenly aware of the existence of the legal procedure of a commission of lunacy, in which court the Davies case was examined. In spite of its ancient origin, the commission of lunacy had been a relatively obscure legal procedure and had not loomed large in contemporary psychiatric treatises until the huge publicity or notoriety given to the case of Lord Portsmouth in 1823. Once the Portsmouth case had popularized, if not created, the new notion of "unsoundness of mind," this legal procedure started to attract the attention of the authors of psychiatric works.[5] Prompted by the Portsmouth case and its problematic notion of "unsoundness of mind," John Haslam published a treatise in which he wrote critically about the introduction of the new concept, which was "a morbid state of intellect, which is neither idiotcy nor lunacy."[6] In 1825, another scandalous case—that of Rev. Edward Frank—was heard, which was similar to the Portsmouth case in many respects: neither of the two alleged lunatics exhibited any clear-cut delusion, and both might just as easily have been called sexual perverts, as I have briefly touched on in chapter 1. With these famous cases as background, the case of Edward Davies was brought to public attention in 1829–30. This time, the upshot was not just one wealthy eccentric person being pronounced a lunatic. Instead, the career and reputation of an eminent medical practitioner was devastated and the entire trade of psychiatric practice or mad-doctoring was disparaged. All of a sudden, English doctors made a series of quick and fervent responses to the problems inherent in their role in the question of lunacy in general and in commissions of lunacy in particular.

The reaction of the medical world to Burrows himself was mixed and varied. Some expressed hearty sympathy with Burrows, ample testimony of the respect he had hitherto enjoyed among medical practitioners. About twenty members of the Surrey Medical Society published a letter of support in major medical journals, expressing their dismay at the unjust misrepresentation and traducement of Burrows by the public newspapers, and "their sympathy and the assurance of their most cordial and undiminished regard for you."[7] Reviewing their colleague's effort at self-defense, the *London Medical and Physical Journal* stated that the book had shown that "Dr. Burrows has not stepped in one degree from the high station he has always maintained" both morally and professionally.[8] Medical and professional pride was certainly wounded by the outcome of the Davies case, and some called for revenge against the legal profession. An eminent West End doctor boycotted another commission *de lunatico inquirendo* held in 1830, in protest against "the unjustifiable manner in which the lawyers treated [medical witnesses] in the case of Mr. Davies."[9]

On the other hand, some sectors of the medical press assumed a critical attitude toward Burrows. In the *Lancet,* Thomas Wakley made a brutally sarcastic comment on Burrows's boast about his sensitivity to the maniacal odor as a pathognomic symptom, comparing Burrows to the witch-finder Matthew Hopkins, who had boasted of his skill in smelling out witches.[10] Although the *London Medical Gazette* expressed sorrow for the unjust aspersions cast on Burrows, it put the blame on mad-doctors and the "exclusive monopolizers of insanity," who signed certificates of lunacy too easily.[11] The *Medical Examiner* was more explicit in its support for Brougham's "admirable speech" and likewise attacked the monopoly of the lunacy trade by alienists.[12] These remarks suggest intraprofessional animosity toward mad-doctors in early nineteenth-century London.

The impact of the two cases went far beyond such clamors against biased public hostility, protests against the tyranny of lawyers, and criticisms of the monopoly of the lunacy trade by specialist practitioners. There were several attempts to reformulate codes and guidelines of the part of forensic psychiatry that was related not just to questions of personal liberty and the certification of lunacy but also to issues of civil competency as these bore upon commissions of lunacy.[13] The central question discussed in these works was the structure of psychiatric practice, especially what a doctor should do when confronted with an alleged patient and his or her family members. Such attempts could be placed in the partly overlapping maps of the intraprofessional strife in the medical world and of the political strife and agitation at Westminster and beyond.

PHYSICIAN AS A GUARDIAN OF PROPERTY: DIAGNOSTIC MANUAL FOR COMMISSIONS OF LUNACY

The Royal College of Physicians, from whose ranks many of the men who testified at the Davies case were drawn, made a quick response to the crisis that ensued. In an unpublished paper written perhaps around 1830–31, deposited at the college's library around the same time, and titled "An Attempt to Simplify and Explain the Diagnostics of Insanity, with More Immediate Reference to Commissions of Lunacy," an anonymous author explained what a physician should do to persuade the jury for the commission *de lunatico inquirendo.*[14] The paper starts with a very brief summary of associationist philosophy concerning the state of the healthy mind, and then it proceeds to show the role of a physician in a medical examination for a commission of lunacy. The organization of the work, in which the author proceeded from the normal to the pathological, was the typical structure in textbooks of forensic psychiatry at that time.[15]

The most conspicuous element of the paper was its advocacy of the role of a physician as a guardian of family property. The ultimate goal of the treatise was to show how to demonstrate the insanity of an alleged lunatic at the court of a commission of lunacy, when no clear-cut manifestation of delusion was easily available. The emphasis was squarely on how to discover hard-to-find insanity, rather than how to differentiate the fine grades in sanity, eccentricity, and madness. The aim of such psychiatric detective work was of course to protect the family from ruin. Indeed, the author emphasized, a doctor must consider whether the alleged lunatic was in a financially and legally secure and protected state: when the property had already been securely protected, "such a state of things should remain undisturbed" and there was no need to establish his or her lunacy. When the security was in doubt, however, the commission should be immediately issued to "relieve him . . . from the possible intrigues and machinations of interested individuals."[16] The doctor spoke with some bitterness of a case in which his failure to establish the insanity of a young lady caused the dissipation of her property and hence hardship for her offspring.[17] Obviously, this was a remarkable bending of psychiatric decision making to the practical needs of the financial situation of the family. The expediency of the clients, not objective criteria of medical diagnosis, was the top priority for this anonymous Fellow of the Royal College of Physicians (FRCP). So as to avoid the family's ruin, he recommended that a doctor should have recourse to every means at his disposal.[18]

Nor was this strong concern with family property exceptional among the FRCPs. Indeed, Sir Henry Halford, the president of the college for twenty-four years (1820–44) and the doyen of elite consultant practitioners in London, had expressed a similar concern for the protection of family property in a paper read at the college in June 1829. Halford told the audience how he had saved a family from ruin and a solicitor from trouble.[19] A gentleman of fortune, in a state of senile insanity, stated that he would make his solicitor his heir, leaving little to his two natural children. Faced with this will, which meant disaster for the gentleman's children, Halford remembered a passage from *Hamlet,* hitting on the idea to "see whether our patient could re-word the matter, as a test, on Shakespeare's authority, of his soundness of mind." The old man could not reword the will, on the basis of which Halford helped to nullify it successfully.[20] Works of great poets of antiquity, Halford added, also had insights that would be of help in such cases. This is typical Halford: humanistic, learned, witty, wise, and exhibiting a total disregard for the earnest pursuit of scientific rigor. It is quite unlikely, however, that this piece of learned witticism was appealing to general practitioners, who increasingly embraced serious professionalism based on science.[21] Nor is it likely that Brougham and other lawyers would have found evidence of this sort satisfactory.[22] His approach embodied the gentlemanly aspirations of the RCP at that time, providing exquisite service to upper-class clients.

The anonymous author of the 1831 treatise sought to provide more practical advice, the essence of which was that a doctor should closely cooperate with the family to gain firm evidence of insanity. The doctor needed to ask the family questions about the alleged lunatic's habits and social life, and must examine letters of the alleged lunatic obtained with the help of the family, if possible. Echoing the lesson of the Anderdon case, the author emphasized the necessity of personal examination, in order to skillfully detect the irritabilities of the alleged patient and to trigger hidden delusions that would without question persuade the jury of the insanity of the person being examined. In his search for concealed signs of madness, the doctor needed the family's help, in the form of detailed information about the patient's character: "I have dwelt the longer on this part of my subject as it is that on which medical men meet with most difficulties when consulted on commission of lunacy; . . . those most conversant with insanity must often be deceived, unless the particular point on which the derangement hangs be fairly *communicated* to them."[23] When asked to examine an alleged lunatic, the doctor was engaged in, so to speak, a combat with the patient, who might try all sorts of tricks to conceal his or her delusion and to deceive the doctor and the jury.[24] To win the game, the doctor needed to observe the patient closely, but he should do this by skillfully using delusion-detectors provided by the family. The treatise urged that a doctor should observe the patient through the framework prepared by the family.

The anonymous treatise, thus, told FRCPs to strengthen communication and ties with the family in order to collect more information from them. This was, essentially, a reinforcement of the style of clinical encounter that alienists had been practicing and that Brougham and his team had criticized. Although this advice did not satisfy the lawyers, it certainly pleased families of patients with property, the most important clients of the Collegiate doctors. The anonymous manual about how to proceed in commissions of lunacy in 1830–31 advocated a family-centered model of psychiatric practice.

WHIG ADVOCACY OF LIBERALISM AND LEGALISM: JOHN CONOLLY'S 'INDICATIONS OF INSANITY'

Enquiry Concerning the Indications of Insanity was John Conolly's first major work on a psychiatric subject. Because Conolly was the most prominent and revered figure in English psychiatry in the nineteenth century, the work has received close attention from psychiatric historians. However, his major biographers, including Hunter and Macalpine as well as Scull, have overlooked the fact that Conolly's *Indications* was a direct response to the crisis of psychiatry in 1829.[25] Conolly's explanation of his direct concern was rather straightforward and seemingly difficult to miss. At the end of the introductory chapter of the work, whose manifest aim was "to render the recognition of insanity less difficult," Conolly wrote: "It is my desire to avoid direct allusion to recent circumstances, which, belonging to the *system* followed with respect to cases of supposed lunacy, rather than to the individuals concerned, have reflected very undeserved odium on a gentleman. . . . I allude to Dr. Burrows."[26] It was not just modern biographers who failed to see the point of the book: as Conolly himself complained, the reviewer of the book for the *Lancet* also missed the point.[27] In retrospect, this was mainly Conolly's fault. This book was not well written. The lengthy, repetitive, and clumsy summary of the Common Sense philosophy, which occupied the first nine chapters (70 percent of the book) certainly bored and misled contemporary reviewers and modern historians alike. Admitting that defect of the book, Conolly himself asked his readers to skip all the rest and read only the tenth chapter, "Application of the Inquiry to the Duties of Medical Men, When Consulted Concerning the State of a Patient's Mind."[28] If we focus on this single chapter, setting aside the first 360 pages, which the author himself declared redundant, one encounters a book with the same structure that the anonymous RCP paper followed: a brief summary of the philosophy of the normal mind, followed by advice about how to declare somebody insane. Conolly's own clumsiness in the first part has masked the fact that the crucial portion of the work belongs to the genre of forensic psychiatry for the purpose of commission of lunacy.

Conolly's *Indications,* however, offered advice diametrically opposed to the suggestions made by the anonymous FRCP's treatise. While the anonymous FRCP complained of the inefficient protection the law gave to the security of family property, Conolly's aim was to show the opposite: that "insane persons are not sufficiently protected by the existing regulations and practice" and "every eccentric man is actually in danger of being treated as a madman."[29] For Conolly (in 1830 at least), freedom of the individual was sacrosanct; individual freedom should be given priority over anything else, including the protection of family property:

> It is repugnant to every idea of that rational freedom which all ought to enjoy, that a man should not do as he chooses with his time, or his property, so long as he does not inflict direct injury on others. . . . An old bachelor may indulge in a thousand extravagances, and imprudences, and absurd freaks, . . . and may end in the destruction of his own health or property; but I do not see how any restraint can be put upon such a man, without endangering the safety of every one who allows himself at any time to depart from formal rules of living.[30]

The role of the doctor was, therefore, to serve as the guardian of individual freedom over one's property: "let the practitioner never forget, that he may be the patient's last and only hope."[31]

Why did Conolly embrace such an extreme form of liberalism? There were clearly two factors. First, his personal belief in liberal ideology played a major role. From the beginning of his career, he had been moving in Whig and liberal circles.[32] Also at the metaphysical level, Conolly was loyal to the liberal tradition of the denial of innate reason started by John Locke.[33] Conolly argued that the rationality of a person would fluctuate, since personality depended on acquired habits and various circumstances, rather than immutable innate reason. Hence, "insanity is often but a mere aggravation of a little weakness, or a prolongation of transient varieties and moods of mind, which all men now and then experience."[34] Resistance to easy certification of lunacy and commission of lunacy was thus a safeguard of everybody's personal liberty and freedom over the disposal of one's own property.

The second factor was Conolly's relationship to Brougham at that time. Conolly had gotten the professorship of University College London, a huge jump for a provincial general practitioner, mainly through Brougham's influence and patronage.[35] Conolly was thus worried about the medical profession's antagonism to Brougham. Just before the draft of *Indications* went to the press, Conolly learned that a medical man had boycotted a procedure of commission of lunacy in protest against Brougham. Conolly was clearly embarrassed at this and told his medical fellows to listen to Brougham.[36] Conolly's *Indications* was, therefore, published at the very moment when his legal patron was under attack from his fellow medics. It was, in a sense, a medical defense of a lawyer who had destroyed the reputation of an eminent medical practitioner.

Accordingly, Conolly's suggestions incorporated and developed ideas that Brougham's team had argued in the Davies case. Personal examination was absolutely necessary, without exception: "If a practitioner undertakes to give advice in any case, he should, with whatever inconvenience to himself, never fail to see the patient for whom he prescribes. If he cannot do this, he ought to refuse taking any share whatever in the case."[37] Conolly went on to argue, unlike the anonymous FRCP, that the aim of personal examination was not to find signs of insanity. He therefore repudiated all the tricks with which alienists "discovered" the hidden or concealed delusion of a lunatic.[38] Signing a certificate of lunacy or declaring somebody to be insane was not for the purpose of exhibiting clinical acumen or practical shrewdness. Treatment and regimen must be guided by *medical* concerns in which medical expertise and inventiveness was valued, but declaring someone to be insane was, Conolly argued, a quite distinct *medico-legal* concern. Conolly warned against the danger of extending the former to the latter: "On the first [medical] question hangs the medical treatment and superintendence; on the second [medico-legal], restraint, confinement, deprivation of authority, and control over property. Medical care and superintendence may be necessary in every case; but the mistake has been to conclude, that restraint and the other circumstances are also necessary, which they certainly are not."[39] In short, Conolly was preaching here *not* to insist on one's medical expertise when signing a certificate of lunacy or declaring somebody of unsound mind. One did not need to develop or exhibit special skill for that purpose. From the viewpoint of promoting psychiatric professionalism, this was a very strange strategy, to say the least. This makes sense only when one remembers that Conolly's career was promoted by the patronage of a lawyer who was fiercely opposed to mad-doctors.

To achieve the end of the protection of liberty and freedom, Conolly proposed a mode of clinical encounter that was strikingly idiosyncratic. Because the personal examination must serve as the only guide in the diagnosis and certification of lunacy, Conolly maintained that the doctor should discard all information from the family as harmful and biased. Conolly warned that a medical practitioner "cannot avoid deriving first impressions from the representations of those who apply to him."[40] When he was asked by a family of rank and fortune to declare some members of the family to be insane, the temptation of "wealth and patronage" was also great.[41] Yet he insisted that the doctor must free himself from the influence of the family and exercise independent diagnosis in a one-on-one relationship with the patient. Conolly's distrust of the family was extraordinary in its extent. Medical practitioners were warned to guard against tricks done by the family to irritate the alleged lunatic and to present the alleged patient in a frantic state. Conolly told the story he experienced of a scheming wife.[42] Wishing to be rid of her weak-minded husband, she vehemently abused him in front of Conolly until the husband was exasperated and bounced out of the room, slamming the door violently. Achieving this victory, the wife exclaimed, "you see what a state he is in; he does this twenty times a day; there is no living with him." Fortunately, Conolly happened to have had an interview with the husband without the wife. The one-on-one encounter convinced him of the sanity of the husband. When the wife reentered the scene, Conolly found that she verbally provoked her husband and disturbed the proceedings between Conolly and the alleged patient. This example was a precise mirror-image of Burrows's remark that the ideal psychiatric clinical encounter took place between the family and the doctor, with the patient excluded.

In promoting this stance, Conolly was well aware that he was preaching something that was deeply unpopular with both medical practitioners and clients, something whose only merit was its legality: "That kind of conduct may give great offence [to the family of the patient], may be very prejudicial to our immediate interests, but the opposite conduct would be a crime."[43] From our vantage point, we can readily understand why Conolly's prescription to remedy what he saw as a major problem for contemporary psychiatric practice was almost entirely neglected.[44] Its denial of the role of expertise in the practice of psychiatric diagnosis certainly did not appeal to those who believed in the value of scientific expertise; few practitioners were willing to sacrifice economic gain and favor with clients just to flatter lawyers; and its stated disregard and suspicion of the motives and desires of patients' relatives undoubtedly offended clients. Most important, there was serious doubt about the practicability of the idea of psychiatric practice without the family. Conolly's *Indications* must have pleased, therefore, nobody except those who either were determined libertarians or had to conform to the preference of lawyers.

RADICAL CRITIQUE OF THE SOCIAL STATUS QUO: CHARLES DUNNE IN THE BRAND CASE

As is sufficiently clear from the account I have given, neither the anonymous FRCP nor Conolly sought a program of medicalization or professionalization. Both recommended respect for values that cannot be called medical in a narrow sense—the former advocating judicious guardianship of family property, the latter putting the cause of liberalism and legalism before medical practice and expertise. The distinction becomes clearer when one examines out-and-out "medicalism" or the fierce advocacy of professional autonomy or monopoly that was manifested by Charles Dunne in his testimony in John Brand's case, another major commission *de lunatico inquirendo* held in late August 1830.[45]

John Brand, the subject of the commission of lunacy, had been educated at Winchester and Cambridge—from which the eminent mathematician Charles Babbage appeared as an acquaintance of his and as a witness testifying for his lunacy—and now possessed property of £4,000 per year. His case was rather hopeless, certainly by Victorian standards. He had a palpable hallucination about his deceased wife; he imagined that men around him had approached him for homosexual relationships. Such beliefs certainly qualified as delusions. Moreover, his lifestyle did not inspire confidence in his mental stability: he had squandered £1,500 in a chess match and £3,000 on seashells, although the latter may well have been a form of investment, just as Anderdon invested in paintings. Every day he drank two bottles of wine and smoked twenty cigars. He lived a promiscuous life with women he picked up in the streets or theaters, he spent thousands of pounds on one woman, promised marriage to another, and married yet another. What perhaps sealed his fate was a letter containing a death threat that he sent to Robert Peel. Brougham, whom Brand had asked to serve as his lawyer arguing against the commission, no doubt because of the lawyer's success in the Davies case, was on the north circuit and not available.

Charles Dunne involved himself in the Brand case in an extraordinary way. During the procedure, one Mr. Hughes, the medical attendant to Brand, testified as a medical witness that he thought of Brand as insane because he saw him frequently laughing during this inquiry. At this moment, Dunne, who happened to be among the audience, was "fired with indignation at the consummate folly of this witness" and requested permission to interrogate Hughes. This violent intervention was interrupted by the commissioners and drew reproach from one of them. Dunne, however, had Brand appoint him as a medical witness and in that capacity he became a tumultuous presence at the court throughout the rest of the examination.[46] He made abusive remarks about the counsel who first had interrupted Dunne's intervention, saying that the lawyer showed symptoms of insanity. He did not answer the questions put to him but talked on and on, entirely ignoring the frequent interruptions of the commissioners. When told that he must answer the question without any further explanation, he replied: "[He] was called upon by Mr. Brand to state all he knew of the matter in question. He would fearlessly do so to the best of his ability, disregarding the threats of any man."[47] Dunne's performance was very eccentric, to say the least, approaching *folie à deux* with his client Brand.

If we look at the turbulent career of Dunne up to that time, this wild performance becomes easier to understand. Beginning in 1807, Dunne had been a military surgeon for a few years until he was dismissed as insane. Dunne later argued that his dismissal was, in truth, due to his discovery of the systematic embezzlement at the hospital where he worked.[48] His first publication in 1808 suggests his firm belief in the role of medical science in surgical education, as well as his support for the radical social and educational reform inspired by the materialism of Baron d'Holbach.[49] After further medical study in Paris, he was authorized in 1816 to practice surgery in France, and read at the Institute of France a paper titled "De l'homme consideré dans l'état d'aliénation," which was published in 1819.[50] A former alleged lunatic, he had some claim to up-to-date expertise in psychiatry.

On returning to England, he set up Athenaion, an enterprise providing lectures in sciences and belles lettres. In 1824, he tried to submit a plan of surgical reform to the Parliament, a scheme that was dropped, according to Dunne, because of the malicious intervention of quacks.[51] He started litigation, but at the court one of the judges described Athenaion as "a ridiculous establishment altogether." At this remark, subscribers to the institution withdrew and it failed.[52] This experience seems to have confirmed his radicalism, and, taking the stance of a radical critic of what he claimed was an oppressive judicial system, Dunne published a pamphlet attacking the judiciary.[53] His bold defiance of the protocol of legal procedure and his abuse directed at a lawyer in the Brand case were, thus, a part of his criticism of the judicial system, no doubt intertwined with his sympathy for a fellow alleged lunatic. The political excitement and agitated atmosphere accompanying the question of Parliamentary Reform in 1830 may also have contributed to Dunne's heated performance in the Brand case.

Dunne expressed his opinions about how to restructure psychiatric practice and the legal procedures relating to lunacy in a separate publication in 1830, acknowledging that he was well acquainted with the Anderdon and Davies cases.[54] The work reveals that Dunne was not just an angry and excited eccentric, but was proposing a consistent, if impractical, model of psychiatric conduct. Generally speaking, Dunne's position was closer to Conolly's than to the anonymous FRCP's, but the difference between Conolly and Dunne was great. Dunne shared with Conolly the denial of the idea of innate reason, but his view was more Romantic: he believed that insanity was an essential part of human nature, stating that "every man has his deranged intervals" and "a uniformly cool and sedate reign of reason is rather an artificial . . . state of the order of the human mind."[55] He also shared Conolly's suspicion of the family of the alleged lunatic, and Conolly's ideal of independent diagnosis, which for Dunne, too, was to be based on a one-on-one clinical encounter: Dunne insisted that medical examination should take place "without the presence of any one of whom he [the patient] may stand in awe, or who is interested in his conduct."[56]

However, his angry resentment of the judicial system, coupled with his political radicalism, cast Dunne's strategy into a completely different form from that adopted by Conolly, whose major aim in *Indications* was to bring medical practice into conformity with the approach preferred by his Whig patron, Brougham. The core of Dunne's argument was that medical expertise should be the only guide in deciding cases of civil confinement. He wrote that at least one-half of the jury in lunacy cases should be medical men.[57] In court, Dunne did everything possible to turn questions into purely medical ones, and at every turn he found himself frustrated. At the beginning of his examination, for example, he begged the commissioner's permission "to lay before the jury, briefly, the moral and physical causes of madness," something he claimed it was necessary "for the jury to understand prior to their giving their verdict about a disease in which they were perhaps ignorant of its symptoms."[58] Later he repeatedly tried to read out extracts from his own work on insanity, and each time was stopped.[59] He argued the sanity of the alleged lunatic on the basis of the lack of bodily symptoms: "Witness formed his opinion of his insanity in a great deal from the look of the eye, and the tension of the temple. The pulse is generally quick, the tongue often furred. He had not perceived those symptoms in Mr. Brand. Smoking many cigars, especially if the stomach was foul, would make the tongue furred. He did not think that Mr. Brand belonged to any of the four genera, or twenty six species of insanity."[60]

As the final part of this remark shows, classification was the central question for Dunne. He challenged the medical witnesses, who testified to Brand's insanity, to specify the species and the cause of the madness from which Brand allegedly suffered: "In all cases of madness it is with the accusers to explain to the satisfaction of the court and jury the nature of the charge, by declaring to which of these different species of it, the supposed madman belongs; if they are unwilling to do so, such unwillingness argues their inability; and if they are unable to do so, the jury can never pronounce a conscientious verdict against the accused."[61] Dunne's strategy to identify classification with medico-legal decision making may be related to his first-hand experience of the situation in France, where the enterprise of psychiatry was centered around the management of large-scale asylums. There, French alienists could concentrate on the classification of those admitted to the institution. Then they could proceed to impose on the world outside the logic they had developed and firmly established inside the hospital walls.[62] Leading English alienists in the metropolis were facing at that moment quite a different task. Instead of the business of putting inmates into diagnostic and institutional pigeonholes, the precarious thresholds between sanity and insanity, liberty and confinement, and possession and dispossession of civil rights were the issues they faced. If they misjudged the threshold or were not careful enough, disaster awaited them. Dunne's preaching of medical monopoly of the act of deciding whether a person was insane or not was clearly an untenable strategy in the English context of psychiatric practice and within the context of commissions of lunacy at that time.

It is unlikely, therefore, that any significant number of English alienists welcomed Dunne's program. His obscure place in society and suspicious politics certainly did not make him a lot of medical friends. Likewise, Dunne obviously infuriated the judges. His argument does not seem to have impressed the jury, either. In the final analysis, one cannot decide whether he wanted to succeed in freeing Brand or he was just carrying out a political and personal protest against the legal establishment. Having said that, Dunne's strategy, had it been successful, could have cut the Gordian knot of the definition of madness with multiple layers in a radical way. It would have brought doctors a perfect independence from the yokes of the lawyers and the family, securing an autonomous realm of professional expertise.

The great diversity in these three proposals confirms that psychiatric practice was a complex field, with great room for disagreement among medical practitioners. There existed multiple actors: the patient, the family, the doctor, and the lawyer. A medical practitioner who was asked to perform his duty faced many choices, for example, whether to form an alliance with the family, or an alliance with the patient and lawyer, or to assert the absolute autonomous power of the doctor. Moreover, the examples analyzed in this chapter suggest that the medical practitioner's political or ideological leanings greatly influenced his conception of psychiatric practice. Without insisting on the generalization, we have more or less predictable attitudes from the Whig Conolly and the Radical Dunne. Although we do not know the identity of the anonymous author of the document at the Royal College, his single-minded valorization of the interests of the family fits well with the image of the college under Henry Halford as a group of conservative medical practitioners who tried to maintain their prestige through their service to upper-class clients.

J. C. PRICHARD'S MORAL INSANITY

There is firm evidence that the three proposals examined in this chapter aimed at reforming doctors' behavior in the context of commissions of lunacy, in response to the crisis of psychiatry in 1829. For J. C. Prichard's conceptualization of moral insanity, we do not have such direct evidence that demonstrates its link with that type of legal procedure. Nevertheless, some evidence clearly suggests that Prichard was concerned with the same situation that prompted the three proposals, cases of wealthy patients whose lunacy was suspected but was not established on the basis of clear-cut symptoms. I should like to argue that the new diagnostic category of "moral insanity" was suggested by James Cowles Prichard in the light of the crisis of 1829–30 and subsequent attempts at reformulating psychiatric practice, at least partly for the purpose of commissions of lunacy.

From the late eighteenth century on, the medical notion of madness started to expand, departing from a narrowly conceived model of madness as a disease of imagination or wrong image-making.[63] The higher faculty of judgment was increasingly regarded as central to the medical definition of madness. William Cullen's notion of madness as depraved association, Boissier de Sauvages's tripartite classification of madness, and Benjamin Rush's emphasis on the moral faculties all represented the search for a more inclusive definition of madness. Philippe Pinel's "*manie sans délire*" (mania without delirium), which would have been regarded as simply oxymoronic in the eighteenth century, was its most famous expression. Prichard's moral insanity was the English culmination of the psychiatric attention to moral rather than cognitive faculties.[64]

Prichard was one of the most important and respected figures in early Victorian psychiatry.[65] In addition to being the originator of the idea of "moral insanity," he served as one of the Metropolitan Commissioners of Lunacy, and his intellectual and social eminence was clear. Prichard put forward the notion first in the article "Insanity" in *Cyclopaedia of Practical Medicine* (1833) and later elaborated it in his *Treatise on Insanity* (1835). Although Prichard did not make direct mention of Burrows's 1829 cases, almost certainly he had them in mind. He himself testified in a commission of lunacy against the Earl of Kingston in July 1833. Moreover, in the testimony he treated his role as a medical witness in the legal procedure as intellectually serious work, citing five German authors about the fine grades of imbecility.[66] Prichard was also well aware of Conolly's efforts and his response to the problem presented by Burrows's cases. Prichard was one of very few medical writers who correctly recognized that Conolly's *Indications* was a work of forensic psychiatry. Although Prichard paid homage to Conolly (who was the editor of the book in which his original article was included), he made it sufficiently clear that he did not agree with Conolly: he admitted that "to Dr. Conolly's work I have not made so frequent references as might be expected."[67] As for the fine grade of eccentricity and insanity, he took the opposite position to Conolly's and declared that "some instances of this kind [of oddity and eccentricity] really constitute cases of madness."[68] The Tory Prichard must have noticed the unmistakably Whig nature of Conolly's proposal, which was pernicious both from his medical-professional and his socio-moral viewpoints.

On the printed page, moral insanity was presented as a scientific and medically autonomous diagnostic category. As Hannah Augstein has shown, Prichard was exceptionally well read in contemporary French and German medical literature—command of the latter language by English doctors being relatively rare at that time. In the context of practice, it is fairly certain that Prichard initially regarded "moral insanity" as a useful diagnostic category for psychiatric practice that had clear resonance for commissions of lunacy: judging the sanity or insanity of a wealthy patient and saving the family from the trouble caused by the damaging behavior of the troublesome family member.[69] He introduced the diagnostic category in a context similar to those we examined earlier: he wrote that there are a lot of "reputed persons of singular, wayward, and eccentric character" living at large—exactly the situation of Anderdon and Davies. When a head of family indulged himself in thoughtless and absurd extravagance and wild projects and speculations, Prichard continued, it was prudent for the rest of the family to ask for a commission of lunacy so as to avoid absolute financial ruin. The present laws were, however, inadequate, and if the man did not show delusions, the suit would likely be rejected. This situation, Prichard may well have hoped, would be corrected by the use of moral insanity as an accepted medico-legal diagnosis. Here Prichard was essentially aiming at the same thing as the anonymous paper presented to the RCP: the protection of family property. The only, if crucial, difference was that Prichard insisted that this aim should be achieved through *medical and scientific* means, not by the savoir-faire typically exhibited by Halford.

Moral insanity, therefore, reinforced the traditional pattern of medical practice with the key information held by the clients: the doctor was still dependent on the lay narrative of disease provided by the clients he served. At the same time, it allowed the doctor to pretend that he had made an autonomous and scientific diagnosis. Prichard combined, therefore, the anonymous FRCP's approach with Dunne's promotion of the paramount status of classification. In so doing, he consolidated the place of the patient's family in the psychiatric clinical encounter, which had been questioned and challenged by liberal-radical lawyers and doctors, in the autonomous medical-scientific classificatory scheme. Moreover, deviation from family values was promoted as the key pathognomic sign of moral insanity. Prichard argued that eccentricity of conduct and singular and absurd habits were not by themselves the definitive element of moral insanity, but when combined with the breach of domestic affections, they were justifiably called signs of moral insanity: "When, however, such phenomena are observed in connexion with a wayward and intractable temper, with a decay of social affections, an aversion to the nearest relatives and friends formerly beloved, . . . the case becomes tolerably well marked."[70] The family thus became the place where madness was not only discovered, but also measured and arbitrated.

The forging of the new diagnostic category thus served the purpose of helping the family to get out of trouble. If individuals behaved in eccentric, depraved, and troublesome ways that were detrimental to the interest and the well-being of their families, but still did not fit the narrow criteria of delusional madness, their families now could insist that they should be judged insane or put under the commission because they suffered from moral insanity. Moral insanity was subsequently invoked mainly in the context of debates about criminal responsibility, and fervent disputes followed about the possibility of volitional and emotional insanity without any vitiation of reason.[71] It should be emphasized, however, that the concept of moral insanity was originally conceived mainly in the context of a type of practice different from the criminal courtroom. It was conceived by Prichard, first and foremost, as a means to save the family from financial ruin and exposure to infamy. Commissions of lunacy, or, more broadly, questions of how to control the damage caused by wealthy "lunatics," must have been a major practical application of the diagnostic category Prichard had in mind. Moreover, the behavior of the subjects of several prominent cases of commissions of lunacy fit in very well with Prichard's characterization of moral insanity. Edward Frank was described as suffering from "the positive extinction of all moral feeling in one of the most delicate points of every married man."[72] One doctor appearing in the case of Edward Davies stated that Davies's strange and disjointed behavior deserved the diagnosis of insanity: "[suppose] a man [is] dancing about a room when he ought to be sitting on a chair, I would call it 'delusion of manner.'"[73] Another doctor in the Davies case stated that "[the] disturbance of the natural affections is a symptom of insanity," mentioning Davies's antipathy to his mother.[74] Had it been available to medical witnesses at those occasions, they would have certainly used the diagnosis of moral insanity.[75]

And it was not just Prichard who thought of moral insanity as a diagnostic category serving the interests of the family to control the behavior of its troublesome member through legal-psychiatric means. Those who grasped his notion immediately understood its merits and the context in which it could be used with great benefit. The example of John Addington Symonds, a medical practitioner at Bristol and later biographer of Prichard (and the father of the famous literary figure of the same name), throws valuable light on the concept of moral insanity in the context of psychiatric practice. After reading the article in the *Cyclopaedia,* Symonds sent Prichard an exceptionally candid letter about how he used the new diagnostic category. Symonds graphically depicted the calamity of the family of a person suffering from moral insanity, in a way that clearly betrays where his sympathy lay:

> [The patient of moral insanity is] to be despised and hated for singularities of manner and conduct; to scatter confusion and dismay over a once happy household by the development of unworthy passions, and intolerable irregularities of temper; to distract an affectionate and honourable wife by strange suspicions, and unfounded jealousies; to harass the timid child by irritability, violence, and tyranny, which no tender submission can appease, no fond attentions can mitigate; to plunge helpless dependants into ruin and beggary; and in all these several conditions to be considered a person fully responsible for his actions, and as capable of subduing evil tendencies as are other people:—these are but a few of the miseries incident to the victims of the malady in question, and however inferior they may appear in the picturesque to maniacal and melancholic visitations, they are productive of far more sorrow to the individual, and of far more lasting and wide-spread distress to those around him.[76]

Experience with one such case was described in Symonds's letter to Prichard. Symonds was consulted in the case of a gentleman of means. Before he had undertaken a personal examination, he was informed by the gentleman's family of his reckless expenditures, his publishing a book that contained abusive attacks on his family, and his writing vituperative letters to his son. Moreover, he was mismanaging his property: "[he] had latterly committed so great an injury to property in which he had only a life-interest, had involved himself so deeply in debt." To prevent such a calamity from deepening, something had to be done, to "enforce some restraint upon his action." The visit by Symonds, however, did not yield anything of help for the purpose of declaring the patient to be insane. Symonds had not been able to learn much about his bodily state. At the interview, the gentleman exhibited enmity to a member of his family then present, and made a lot of allegations about the family, which Symonds knew to be "groundless." (Of course, as Brougham would have been quick to point out, Symonds knew them to be *groundless* solely on the basis of the representation made by his family.) Symonds could not find any solid evidence of delusion: "I endeavoured, by a variety of expedients, to discover any latent hallucination, but failed in my attempts." The medical interview did not add anything new to what he had already learned from the family as evidence of the lunacy of the gentleman. Nevertheless, Symonds concluded: "After due deliberation I came to the conclusion, that, although I had been unable to trace any positive intellectual error, there was such a morbid condition of the feelings, habits, and motives, as to constitute a case of what has been correctly designated by Dr. Prichard as moral insanity. I therefore did not hesitate to sign the usual certificate."[77] Moral insanity acted here as an ingenious device to turn a clinical failure into a diagnostic narrow victory, by putting a medical scientific gloss over a means for helping the family. In short, its role was to lend scientific status to the expediency of the propertied family.

Symonds was not exceptional. His use of moral insanity very much resembled the conceived use of commissions of lunacy suggested by A. L. Wigan, now mainly known as one of the first advocates of the double-brain theory. In his work, Wigan maintained that the commission would be better issued "long before the case arrives at the point which justifies perpetual restraint," like *lettres de cachet:*

> The "Lettres de cachet" in their origin (before they were abused for political purposes), were only granted on a petition of the man's family, setting forth that he was a wantonly extravagant spendthrift, and was dissipating the property of his wife or children in foolish and blameable self-indulgence—that is, that he did not exercise self-control; and this, for all social purposes, justified personal restraint, just as much as if he had absolutely lost it. . . . If such a law could be executed in this country, how many families might be saved from disgrace and ruin, and how many men prevented from disgusting the world with the exhibition of their shameless vices and filthy depravity?[78]

These accounts show that Prichard and other English psychiatrists in the 1830s and 1840s perceived that the family was not served well by the present laws of lunacy, particularly those concerning the lunacy cases of the wealthy. Psychiatrists could not help them, because of the lack of a clearly defined diagnostic category useful for that purpose. In all probability, they understood the diagnostic category of moral insanity as a means to help families by depriving not-so-evidently-mad but still troublesome family members of their civil rights.

In this chapter I have examined the responses by doctors to the crisis in psychiatry in 1830 that was prompted by the fall of G. M. Burrows, and I have attempted to put the idea of moral insanity in the context of the needs of the family and the constraints of commissions of lunacy. One can draw three important insights from the analysis of these pieces of evidence.

The first point is the timing of the scandal. Historians of psychiatry have so far identified 1858–59 as the first of the two major lunacy panics over wrongful confinement in the nineteenth century, the other being in 1876–77. Most recently, this chronology has been suggested by Helen Small.[79] My findings push back the date of the "first" panic to the years 1829–30. It is true that the cases of wrongful confinement in 1829 did not apparently inspire major sensational novels, as the cases in the 1850s did. But the sheer size of the stir the cases in 1829 caused in the early 1830s and their impact on the medical world should nonetheless command our attention. The word *panic* does not, however, well describe the varied and quick responses made by doctors, or the different practical concerns and ideological sympathies that were exhibited in the early 1830s. Many doctors were very anxious to change their behavior and strategy in response to the crisis caused by the events in 1829, lest they should be involved in a scandal. They tried to restructure their bedside practice in ways that were consistent with their ideological convictions and practical priorities. *Responses to crisis,* not *panic,* captures better the situation of the doctors I have described.

Second, emphasis should be placed on the importance of the family's financial concerns. The protection of the property of the lunatic *and* the family was the major concern around which the new paradigms of doctors' behavior at the psychiatric bedside were centered. This observation adds, I argue, an important new dimension in our understanding of the relationship between the family and the psychiatric profession. So far, much attention has been paid to the emotional aspects of the family with a patient suffering from mental disorder. In her analysis of Kirkbride's practice at the Philadelphia Hospital, Nancy Tomes has perceptively shown how the asylum superintendent incorporated the concerns of the families of incarcerated patients into his practice in the asylum.[80] To assuage the guilt felt by the family, Tomes argues, Kirkbride forged a model that emphasized gentle persuasion. Tomes has stressed the doctor's response to the *emotional* trouble experienced by the family; my examples suggest that, in a different context of psychiatric practice, the *economic* concerns of the family were paramount. Families of lunatics, or alleged lunatics, sought help from doctors to facilitate their control over the lunatics' property. Doctors felt the need to respond to their clients' needs: they developed ingenious methods to reveal obscure delusions; they picked up interesting tests of sanity from literary authors; and they put a scientific gloss on a type of behavior that was, in essence, nothing but inconvenient eccentricity that threatened the family's property. All these efforts were made less to address the emotional needs of the family than to serve their financial concerns. Tomes is certainly right in pointing out that the emotions arising from domestic trouble were one of the important parameters that formed Victorian psychiatry: the next chapter will examine the emotional side of the story. My argument in this chapter does not negate, but rather supplements, the claim made by Tomes and others. Doctors had to address both the emotional and the economic needs of the family and to construct their psychiatric practice accordingly. As I have shown, the language used by Prichard, Symonds, and Wigan illustrates that both emotional and economic aspects were taken into account by psychiatrists judging the mental state of a patient. In the context of a commission of lunacy, the economic needs of the family were clearly of greater importance.

Third, stress should be laid on the diversity of the medical conceptualizations of psychiatric practice and the resonance of different concepts with larger trends in political thought. Because questions of the status of property rights and the liberty of the individual were an integral part of psychiatrists' testimony in commission of lunacy cases and their certification of lunacy, one might naturally expect that doctors' priorities were influenced by their political or ideological allegiances. To portray all doctors as alike, either as aspiring to professional autonomy or as nodding sycophantically to clients, is a gross oversimplification. The three reactions to the crisis of psychiatry in the early 1830s, especially those put forth by Conolly and Dunne, show that different psychiatrists conceptualized ideal psychiatric practice more or less in the frameworks of their individual political tenets.

Theory and practice were, however, completely different matters. Chapter 2 suggested that what doctors wrote in their medical treatises is a very unreliable measure of what they actually did in their daily practice. In published materials such as Conolly's or Dunne's, they talked about what ought to be, rather than about the realities of their practice. One should not mistake what was written in polemical and political pamphlets, as well as in medical textbooks, for the reality of their practice. Nor should we take the ideals expressed there at face value and let them lead us to assume that alienists of liberal-radical political creeds were more likely to put priority on personal liberty and less likely to expand the boundaries of insanity. One should remember that Dunne had no practice to lose in his radical advocacy of the patient's liberty, and Conolly *had to* act as a medical spokesman for his patron, Brougham. One cannot draw conclusions, from these materials, about the importance of the liberal-radical political creed to the *actual,* rather than conceptual, structure of psychiatric practice at that time.

Indeed, some fragmentary pieces of evidence suggest that one's political affiliation or sympathy did not greatly affect one's pattern of *actual practice,* in contrast to one's pattern of *belief in the ideal.* At least two doctors of impeccable liberal-radical credentials were involved in cases of wrongful confinement in the first half of the nineteenth century. One of them is James Parkinson. As an early member of the London Correspondence Society and a discoverer of the disease that bears his name, he was the epitome of the combination of scientific eminence and political radicalism. He is the last doctor one might expect to be involved in the sordid business of easy certification and toadyish subservience to his clients. Nevertheless, in 1810, he was involved in a case of wrongful confinement when he was asked to sign a certificate of lunacy for one Mrs. Daintree. When he first examined Mrs. Daintree, he found the patient rather rational, and declined to sign the certificate until he had gained more information. Then he went to the street where she lived and sought information from her neighbors, and talked as well with her son. Both the neighbors and the son confirmed that she was mad. Then Parkinson went back to examine and interview the patient again. This time, he was convinced of her lunacy and signed a certificate attesting to this conclusion, only to be later accused of being involved in a wrongful confinement.[81]

The other example is Conolly himself. Ironically, the youthful champion of personal liberty and the individual's rights over his or her property was later in his life known for his "eagerness to consign the morally perverse and socially inadequate to the asylum," as has been pointed out by Andrew Scull.[82] It is surprising to learn that Conolly constantly argued for widening the definition of madness in the cases in which he was involved from the late 1840s to early 1850s—in the illegal confinement case of *Nottidge v.*

Ripley, the commission of lunacy against Ruck, and several others.[83] One cannot tell for certain whether this drastic change of attitude resulted from a switch of political allegiance or from his growing more conservative with age. The most likely explanation may be, however, that Conolly in 1830 was largely an outsider to psychiatric practice in the metropolis. His contact with the clientele asking for psychiatric help seems to have been very limited and sporadic, if there was any at all. Somewhat like Charles Dunne, Conolly in his *Indications* could afford to ignore the family, whose presence and constant pressure for conformity to *their* ethos he must have hardly felt. Thus Conolly could, at least in the pages of his book, express opinions congruent less with the demands of practice than with his political and ideological sympathies. Moreover, by doing so, he also served to defend his patron who was under attack from many other medical practitioners. Fifteen years later, at the time of the case of *Nottidge v. Ripley,* Conolly found himself in a very different situation in terms of practice. His reputation as a leading psychiatrist was confirmed after his successful implementation of nonrestraint at the Hanwell Asylum, and he subsequently assumed the position of being the authority on mental diseases. All these successes, as well as his ownership of a private licensed house for wealthy ladies whose ailments were euphemistically termed "nervous," brought him into extensive contact with families with property who sought his help in cases of insanity, sometimes dubious ones. *Mutatis mutandis,* this was exactly the same situation in which G. M. Burrows had found himself before 1829. In all probability, ironically, though not surprisingly, the now successful and eminent Conolly fell into the grip of the family-centered model of psychiatry.

FOUR

Managing Lunatics within the Domestic Sphere

THE PREVIOUS TWO CHAPTERS ANALYZED the primacy of the family in psychiatric practice. Practicing psychiatrists were often integrated into family affairs, largely playing an ancillary, if not always subordinate, part. Their more or less dependent position vis-à-vis the family marks a strong contrast to their claims to professional autonomy based on scientific medical expertise, so much trumpeted in the pages of medical treatises and articles. Psychiatrists could not live up to their scientific aspirations for several reasons. One reason was the obvious advantage enjoyed by the family because of their intimate knowledge of the insane family member. Another reason was the absence of any neat medical definition and criteria of madness. Yet another was the economic dependence of the doctors on the fees paid by the family. Perhaps the most important factor was that psychiatric practitioners shared a belief in family integrity with their clients, who were anxious to protect their property and reputations. There existed a close alliance between the doctor and the family in practical, economic, and ideological terms. This is why many practice-conscious doctors leaned toward the protection of family property rather than the protection of personal liberty and individual rights, when these two grave issues were in conflict. Although there existed significant dissenting views, many psychiatrists who made their living through the business of mad-doctoring had to conform to the conventional pattern of practice. The priority of personal liberty, legal authority, or of medico-scientific authority was advocated by peripheral practitioners—the few who had to do so to conform with the views of their patrons, or who had nothing to lose by expressing such radical views.

Moreover, families at that time possessed one fundamental advantage vis-à-vis alienists: a powerful cultural framework for understanding madness. In other words, the family had something to pit, if necessary, against the medical-scientific framework for understanding mental disease. The families' framework was sometimes contradictory to medical-professional ones, but often the framework held by clients and that held by psychiatric practitioners were symbiotic and mutually reinforcing. Families were able to understand, care for, control, and treat—or at least direct the treatment of—insane family members on the basis of their own framework. If doctors dared to insist on medical interpretations of madness, they had to compete with the other set of interpretations, originating from a cogent fabric of values and ideas. The richness and resourcefulness of this lay framework, as well as its origins independent of medical psychiatry, allow it to be called "domestic psychiatry."

Some research has already indicated the important roles played by lay psychiatric culture in the nineteenth century.[1] Historians agree that it was patients' families who made the initial diagnosis of madness.[2] We have already seen in previous chapters how easily the initial diagnoses made by families found their way into medical diagnoses. In the eighteenth century, the practice of lay diagnosis received implicit endorsement from medical writers, even in medical texts. Eighteenth-century popular medical books, which were generally keen to impose medical learning on their readers, expressed the idea that diagnosis of madness was not a problem that required medical expertise but rather was everybody's business, tacitly encouraging lay diagnosis of madness.[3] Although from the late eighteenth century on there were increasingly visible efforts made by medically qualified men to medicalize the act of diagnosing insanity, their attempts did not convince laypeople to let doctors monopolize the act.

Indeed, in the early nineteenth century, the practice of looking into the healthy or morbid psyche from outward signs became more widespread among laypeople, best exemplified by the enormous popularity of phrenology and physiognomy.[4] As Roger Cooter and others have pointed out, the phrenology of Franz Joseph Gull was transformed from an esoteric medical doctrine into a body of popular knowledge. By the vigorous activities of Johann Gaspar Spurzheim in London and George Combe in Edinburgh, phrenology spread into the British middle class and the upper sectors of the working class, providing them with a means to know their hidden selves and the characters of others.[5] Alison Winter has demonstrated the survival of mesmerism in London and provincial cities, emanating from the wards of teaching hospitals to Victorian sickrooms, salons, and theaters.[6] Around the same time, knowledge of physiognomy made its way to the British reading public through the works of John Caspar Lavater and others. Using the novels of Charlotte Brontë, Sally Shuttleworth has shown that both the author and her readers were well versed in the new technique of depicting and decoding human interiority from the outlook of the individual.[7] Moving from literary to pictorial material, Mary Cowling has maintained that mid- and late-Victorian painters such as W. P. Frith were able to depict enormous varieties of "characters" in their panorama of contemporary social life, and that the educated public were able to understand their subtle meanings.[8] These studies have revealed that the means to decode human psyches were widely shared by nineteenth-century doctors and laypersons.[9]

Although the works of Cooter, Shuttleworth, and others are immensely valuable in illuminating the widespread influence of medical ideas on the general culture of the nineteenth century, my approach to the internal dynamics of domestic psychiatry is different from theirs. Cooter and others have largely used the framework of the influence of scientifically developed ideas (phrenology and physiognomy) on laypeople in forming a background culture. My emphasis is, on the other hand, on the *primacy* of the lay over the medical, or the *independence* of domestic psychiatry from the psychiatry practiced by doctors.[10] In this chapter, I argue that the practice of domestic psychiatry, or understanding and caring for the insane in domestic settings by family members, was less a product of the influence of professional psychiatry than a self-generated cultural framework. I show that the source of domestic psychiatry lay not so much in the realm of science per se as in the domestic sphere. Instead of being subservient to the dictates of learned medicine, laypersons employed their own cultural framework to understand, treat, and cope with the madness of their family members.

In so arguing, I follow the lead of some recent works in the social history of medicine "from below." In recent years, many works on the social history of patients' experience of illness have revealed that laypersons in the early modern period possessed their own rich cultural resources through which to understand their own illnesses.[11] Historians such as Michael MacDonald, Roy and Dorothy Porter, Mary Fissell, and Barbara Duden have uncovered powerful lay cultural frameworks for understanding and coping with various diseases that were not necessarily drawn from learned medicine. This was particularly the case with madness, which was (and still is) a disease heavily loaded with cultural meanings, be they religious, supernatural, emotional, or moral. The failure of Enlightenment scientific psychiatry to fully address those issues also created a discursive vacuum that was filled by lay and homespun interpretations. As a place in which the meanings of madness have been decoded, the family has been recognized as a particularly important locus. As MacDonald has shown, the family was such a fundamental social unit that its norms were important measures by which to define madness, and people's understanding of insanity was interwoven with their experience of their own personal domestic lives.[12]

I am, however, going to dissent from the above-mentioned historians of the lay understanding of disease, especially MacDonald, Fissell, and Duden, in one important point: the chronology of the decline of the lay frameworks. MacDonald, Fissell, and Duden concur on one point: that lay medical culture declined during the eighteenth century. They differ in their assessment of the exact timing of the decline: MacDonald finds it at the beginning of the eighteenth century, whereas Fissell and Duden assert that decline started toward the end of the century. They also differ in their attributions of the causes of the decline, MacDonald attributing it to secularization, Fissell and Duden to the rise of hospital medicine, which enabled doctors to localize disease and to objectify patients. The chronologies and the causal attributions suggested by MacDonald, Fissell, and Duden do not, however, apply to the history of the lay cultural framework for interpreting madness. In the first half of the nineteenth century, numerous pieces of evidence suggest the continuing strength and resourcefulness of lay frameworks for understanding the madness of a family member. Thus, my chronology supports the Porters' claims about the survival of lay medical culture well into the nineteenth century. Far from suffering a decline, interpretations and judgments emanating from domestic psychiatry continued to be expressed with visible confidence throughout the period under consideration. They were often imposed on the psychiatric practitioners involved. Indeed, there are circumstantial reasons to believe that domestic psychiatry became stronger and acquired more resources and relevance in the early nineteenth century. My aim in this chapter is to demonstrate the existence of what I have chosen to call domestic psychiatry, to examine its internal characteristics, and to investigate its social and cultural basis. I first examine the letters of one London banker, in which his responses to the mental disease of his mother in 1816 were recorded in exceptional detail and with remarkable candidness. Then I contextualize this evidence, mainly using records from commission of lunacy cases. I also investigate the social and cultural background of domestic psychiatry, linking it to the development of the ideal of domesticity in England in the late eighteenth and early nineteenth centuries. Here I rely on recent works on the history of upper- and middle-class families in Britain by Leonore Davidoff, Catherine Hall, Amanda Vickery, and others. I conclude this chapter by providing a revisionist assessment of the rise of moral treatment, the cornerstone of nineteenth-century psychiatry.

BANKRUPT BROTHER, ELOPED SISTER, AND MAD MOTHER: THE "DOMESTIC PSYCHIATRY" OF H.N. MIDDLETON

The practice of "domestic psychiatry" was often unrecorded in historical sources easily accessible to medical historians. Layers of secrecy that surrounded a lunatic in the family have hindered research. Fortunately, one detailed and extremely candid account has survived: the account of the madness of Anne Frances Middleton by her son Hastings Nathaniel Middleton, a banker in London.[13] I first examine the practice of domestic psychiatry expressed in Middleton's private letters. As is often the case with lay understanding of illness, a family's understanding of insanity was not a systematized body of knowledge but rather a flexible fabric of strategies for dealing with lunatics.[14] It is thus somewhat misleading to impose on it the structure of medical learning, neatly laid out in psychiatric textbooks at that time. For convenience's sake, I use here medical terms such as *diagnosis, prognosis,* and *etiology* for domestic understanding, treatment, and control of the insane.

Hastings Nathaniel Middleton was the eldest son of Nathaniel Middleton, who made a fortune in India and set up a partnership to establish a bank in London after returning to England.[15] The father died in 1807, and Hastings succeeded his father as a partner in the bank, then Alexander Davison & Co. In the financial turmoil caused by the French Revolution and the Napoleonic Wars, the bank did not prosper, and in 1816 it was finally taken over by Thomas Coutts & Co. Middleton's house in London and some other property of his were assigned to creditors. The family, consisting of his wife, Emilia, and five children, was reduced to living in Tunbridge Wells on the income from his wife's property.[16]

At this point, Middleton received another blow: his mother—then living in Bath with her widowed sister Sarah (Aunt Cator to Middleton) and one Mrs. Baynes, perhaps their companion—developed mental illness. Middleton was first informed of his mother's mental disturbance by his aunt toward the end of August 1816. Subsequent letters from Bath to Tunbridge Wells told that his mother was getting worse despite medical treatment. In one letter, he was informed that "she sits absorbed, and seldom speaks, but raises her eyes to Heaven, in prayer, goes out daily in a carriage and wheel-chair, is blooded, and blistered to quell the irritability." Another letter informed him that "the mind [was] infinitely more diseased than the body."[17] Initially, Middleton indulged in wishful thinking and remained optimistic about his mother's prognosis, believing that the reports from Bath were exaggerated. Letters in early October, however, made him recognize the painful fact that his mother was suffering from serious mental illness. When her friends brought her to London "for further and more competent [medical] advice," Middleton decided to see his disturbed mother.

He explained that the purpose of seeing his mother was "to form my opinion of my parent's state, and of [its] probable duration."[18] This suggests that his aim was to make *his own* observations, on the basis of which he was to form his own judgment about the state of the patient. Middleton's subsequent letters show his ample capacity to do so. His observation of her symptoms was vivid and detailed: "a restlessness of manner, perpetually picking, and searching as it were, for pins, round her person, biting her fingers, almost to the drawing of blood, and, of late, employing her nails about her neck, to a degree provoking an appearance of rash—sitting athwart her chair, instead of straight upon it, with her head, and looks, eternally down-cast."[19] Middleton's account also included the physiognomy of madness: "Her countenance too, is a sad index of her perturbed condition of mind, there is a pitiful lack-lustre in her eye, the mouth is pursed, and her whole features haggard, and elongated."[20] These observations of the patient's behavior and outlook, expressed in short passages and punctuated by commas, display substantial similarities to clinical case histories published by contemporary doctors.[21] Moreover, his emphasis on the countenance and especially on the eye was shared by medical writers of his time.

Besides examining his mother's bodily posture and countenance, he extended his observation to her social behavior. He was shocked at the way his mother behaved in terms of her finances—an oscillation between meanness and profligate waste of money:

> [She] is observed wringing her hands, in all the anguish of the most abject poverty, and privation; the next, making disbursements, as profuse, as they are unnecessary, now, her sister refuses her adequate sustenance, then is charged with exercising undue influence, in restraining her wishes, and withholding her funds *for her own particular purposes!* To day, she is purchasing quantities of useless pills, tomorrow, would, if not prevented, procure as many dresses, giving alms of shillings to passing mendicants, as she walks along, throwing up the sash sometimes, to do so, to street-minstrels, and hurdy-gurdy-players, and after all, frequently reverting to the primitive declaration, that she is entirely ruined, and no longer mistress of a single guinea![22]

This account reveals that he was greatly alarmed at his mother's impulsive disposal of her money, coupled with her apparent inability to correctly assess her own financial status. In short, she could not manage her own property.

What unsettled him most was his mother's attitude to himself, especially her failure to show any affection toward him: "she betrayed no emotion" when he embraced her; she shed no tears; when he asked whether she was glad to see him and his family, she gave "the monosyllable 'yes'."[23] She did not respond to his displays of affective concern. Middleton's narrative of his observation of the mental disease of his mother thus consists in the description of her body, her irrational disposal of her money, her interpersonal behavior, and her specific relation to himself. Note that Middleton's major concerns were economic and emotional—his mother's reckless expenditure and her lack of affection toward him—which fit in well with the concept of moral insanity I examined in chapter 3.

On the basis of these observations, he formed his "prognosis" very quickly. He almost immediately gave up hope of her recovery, which he had entertained before the interview. He informed his friend of his despair: "This is indeed, a case of the most awful, and serious description—and her advanced period of life, and various harassing family occurrences taken into the estimate, frustrated hopes, infelicitous marriages, to wit, &c &c. No very sanguine expectation ought, I think, reasonably to be indulged, of her ever being restored to sound, and pristine health."[24] Although John Latham, a prestigious Fellow and President of the Royal College of Physicians, was present when Middleton saw his mother, it is likely that he formed this prognosis mainly by himself. The day after the interview with his mother, he wrote that he had formed "an opinion *for myself*." He congratulated himself on his own observations as "the most accurate."[25] When he was informed by Aunt Cator of the poor prognosis formed at a consultation with Matthew Bailie, another prosperous London physician, he replied that "his opinion of her unhappy case . . . quite corroborate[s] my anticipation."[26] These remarks of his do not, of course, mean that he did not respect the opinion of medical men: in fact, he was keen to secure the advice and judgment of a specialist in psychiatry.[27] Nevertheless, he did not give up the act of decoding the mental illness of his mother. For him, understanding the disease was never the business of an expert or a specialist in which he should not meddle.

Once having formed his prognosis, he stuck to it. When in 1820 his mother was moved to Brighton for a change of air at the initiative of his married sister, Louisa Herbert, he was suspicious of the effect of the scheme, describing it as "so hopeless an experiment."[28] Indeed, he expressed his determination to oppose any new attempt at a cure suggested by other family members:

> I personally beg to protest against any fresh one being made with our wretched parent, either in the form of *new* medical advice, change of residence, or any thing else, beyond what we already see and know to be most conductive to the palliation, for there can be no cure, of her sufferings. To harass, alarm, and worry her by new speculative arrangements, and from whence it is more than ten thousand to one, not a particle of advantage can accrue, is what I never can consent to. And if under such conviction of sentiment, I shall be found to stand alone, or even in a minority in our family[,] the majority declaring in favour of further trials of her temper and constitution, I hereby renounce such portion of responsibility as devolves upon me individually.[29]

Likewise, when in 1821 George Man Burrows proposed to the family that they should try a fresh course of medical treatment, Middleton was extremely skeptical, and the proposal seems to have been dropped.[30]

One of the reasons for this pessimism was Christian resignation, which was no doubt strengthened by Middleton's recent experience of the reversal of financial fortune. He continually referred to his virtual bankruptcy as God's will and as out of his control, and he saw his mother's insanity in the same light: "God's will be done! My cup cannot be much more charged with bitters, than it already is, and, out of many apparent evils, and mortifications, arising from his late severe dispensations towards me—this good at least, has resulted, namely, an entire resignation to his will, on my part, and a confident reliance on his mercy, and omniscience, that it is for some all-wise though occult purposes, that He has been pleased lately to put me to so many severe trials."[31] It is, however, misleading to emphasize Middleton's Christian resignation too much, because he did not regard his mother's insanity as a mysterious visitation of God beyond his understanding. He judged his mother to be incurable because he thought he knew the causes of the disease. In other words, he based his prognosis on his own understanding of the "etiology" of his mother's insanity.

Middleton's etiology was tightly framed around domestic circumstances and events. Although domestic anxiety was often listed in medical lists of causes of madness, Middleton's lay psychiatric etiology was different from medical discourse in its specificity: although medical writers were often vague about the circumstance that might have caused the disease of any individual, Middleton pointed his finger to a specific individual's specific act. In his opinion, the person to blame was his sister Louisa, who had eloped with Charles John Herbert. Immediately after his personal interview with his mother, he wrote to a friend: "[it] is quite needless, just now, to go into the causes, forming the origin of her melancholy fatuity—suspicion with me, I own strongly points at the H——t [Herbert?] marriage, and its infelicitous consequences."[32] Middleton also differed from the doctor in the priority he gave to the domestic cause of madness. Whereas contemporary doctors were eager to find factors directly or vaguely related to the patient's body, Middleton was firm in putting the domestic factor first: he wrote that the disease rose from "a combination of untoward circumstances, at the top of which catalogue, I must ever place Louisa's marriage."[33] This lay etiology of insanity had a very strong imprint of the ideal of domesticity. As people's expectations of the family as the source of happiness and emotional satisfaction rose, any breach of domestic harmony could be severely blamed as a source of misfortunes or evils.[34]

It was obvious to everyone, including Middleton himself, that his blaming his sister served the purpose of exonerating himself. It was commonplace both in medical and lay discourse to attribute madness to economic mishaps and consequent anxieties. Indeed, some of the symptoms exhibited by his mother lead me to believe that she was anxious about the recent financial disaster that had befallen her son's family. Middleton was aware that there might be a link between the failure of his bank and his mother's madness, and he was extremely candid about the relief he felt when he concluded that his sister was primarily to blame: "[I] derive abstract consolation from such conviction, that my own reverses have had little, or nothing, to do with it—They have unavoidably hopped the cup, and rendered it rather more bitter to [my mother's] palate—but the foundation-stone of the Babel-tower, was, long since, laid."[35] If one considers Middleton's uncertainty about whether Louisa or himself was to be held the more responsible, it is no wonder that he opposed the therapeutic experiment of having Louisa and his mother see each other, and that he insisted on stopping the experiment as soon as possible. If Louisa's presence had *improved* his mother's state, that would have spoiled his self-serving etiology. After knowing that cohabitation with Louisa did not improve his mother's state, he wrote, with a sense of relief visible between lines, that "the great trump card, the interview with her favorite child [Louisa], on which so much stress seems to have been placed having failed, the game, I consider, irremediably lost," and he recommended that "not an instant should be lost in procuring her emancipation from so unwise, but self-inflicted a trial."[36] In order to exonerate himself and to keep the blame placed on his sister, Middleton needed to prevent his sister from demonstrating her curative power.

However, the person Middleton blamed the most was the patient herself. His relationship with his mother before her illness had never been good, and he particularly disliked her secrecy over her own financial matters.[37] He directly projected his discontent with this aspect of his mother's behavior onto his etiology of her insanity:

> She was ere, and at the best of times, of a most uncommunicative turn, and always too confident in her own powers of intellect, and *presumed* knowledge of business. . . . One knows that she has securities for money in this place, another in that, and so on, but no individual can state fairly, that he is wholly my mother's *charge d'affaires,* thus she has been acting for years, in a spider-like capacity, insensibly, but fatally, spinning a web, which has now become so perplexed and entangled, that even her own, naturally penetrating sensorium, yields to the herculean task of attempting to unravel it.[38]

In painting a very unkind picture of the patient being caught in the spiderweb of anxieties that she herself had generated, Middleton was saying that it was her secretive personality that was to blame, as well as recent misfortunes that had befallen her. In other words, the disease "arises from a continuation, and succession, of adverse occurrences, operating upon a nature, at best too apt to conceal, and brood over, rather than impart its sorrows."[39] It is, therefore, obvious that the core of his etiology was framed around his unsuccessful personal relationship with his mother.

Middleton also thought that his mother was responsible for developing the disease into a confirmed one: she let the disease occupy her mind, without exercising much resistance. From the early stage of the disease, his account was strongly colored by religion: "Oh, may my loved parent be persuaded, ere it be too late, to resist the admission of this colossal, this Aaron's serpent, into her bosom! since once suffered to shelter, and establish itself there, like its great prototype of old, 'twill swallow all the rest, and she, be lost to us."[40] Later his account became explicitly demonological: he found that "the demon band, anarchy, confusion, and self-abandonment" took possession of her.[41] Like evil demons, madness was something one should resist, using one's willpower. If she had exercised her own personal resistance to the disease at an early stage, he implied, the disease would not have fully developed. Although this observation of Middleton's squared with the often-expressed medical opinion that the earlier the intervention, the more likely the cure, Middleton's viewpoint was explicitly nonmedical. He wrote that "her own personal exertion" was the key to a cure, adding, "without her own co-operation, *medical skill*, affectionate solicitude, and friendly counsel, will alike to [be] applied in vain."[42] Or, in other words, "unless she can be prevailed upon to make such an effort, no benefit could possibly result to her, 'though the whole College of Physicians were to take her in hand."[43] The crux of the problem was her defective personality. Middleton held his mother herself responsible for the disease that had befallen her.

Middleton's etiology thus centered on the patient's domestic circumstances, the interpersonal relationships between the patient and her family members, and the personality of the patient herself. His "therapeutics" was conceived along a similar line. As shown earlier, Middleton thought that his mother's secretiveness was the major cause of the disease. The cure was conceived in the same light. At an early stage, he thought that his family's cohabitation with his mother would contribute to her cure, and that his writing of his and his wife's sympathy would console and soothe his mother's afflictions.[44] When he met his mother, he attempted to make her open her heart to him, hoping that he could find a clue to disentangle the suffering of her psyche. He had a conversation with her "on the various family topics which I conceived likely to have produced such inquietude," hoping that would break her psychic enclosure in herself, "but failed in making the slightest impression." She did not emotionally respond to his appeal or to her sister's: "neither does she, at any time, drop a tear—utterly indifferent to the torrents her sister is perpetually shedding at her elbow." The key to her recovery was, he thought, to make her open her heart: "There is no getting her to unbosom herself, upon any matter whatever. [C]ould she be brought to do so, her supposed gigantic difficulties might be met, palliated, and I repeat, the most sanguine hope then entertained of substantial, and permanent amendment."[45] Even after he had confirmed the status of her mental disease, Middleton thought of its cure in terms of establishing mental correspondence with his mother. Whether she was willfully persevering in her refusal to start restorative communication or was unable to do so seems to have been irrelevant to her son. Middleton was at best half-hearted in conferring the status of the "sick role" or of patienthood on his mother. His attempt at making her open her heart was radically ambiguous—whether it was a medical treatment of madness or psychological counseling of an unhappy person.

This ambiguity is evident also in another design Middleton proposed to cure or relieve his mother's distress, a plan for his family to live with her. As I have suggested, Middleton had been optimistic about his mother's state until he actually met with her. Before his interview with his mother, he wrote that she would benefit from living with his family, with his children at his own house: "[the] seeing and cohabiting with our darling children might successfully tend to stimulate her depressed sensibilities, and the known disposition of the two elder gentle creatures [his wife and himself], to sympathise with, and soothe those they see in affliction, will be pleasing, & comfortable to her."[46] He also wrote to his mother directly that he was ready to "receive you under our roof."[47] As soon as he saw his mother's actual state, however, the "known disposition of the two elder gentle creatures" disappeared instantly. Just after he saw her, he wrote that no benefit could be expected from "receiving her into our family, or even having her near us," because she was totally incapable of appreciating the tenderness and attention of his sympathetic and kind family.[48]

His true motive for dropping his plan of cohabitation was his fear that rumors would spread among his neighbors. A few days later, he wrote very candidly as follows:

> With respect to an asylum for my severely-visited parent, I conceive that [his house in] Brighton should be the *last* place proposed—she would not be there twenty-four hours, before, busy slander, ever mischievously inclined, would noise throughout the whole town, that Mrs Middleton,

> once so provident, and highly-gifted, was under surveillance & incompetent to the management of her own affairs, and thus a stigma would be thrown upon herself and family, and a publicity given to the occurrence which would aggravate our misfortunes, and render her return to the world, and to her friends, doubly difficult.[49]

Instead, he proposed that his mother might be better placed in "a small house in an open situation, on the sunny side of London, somewhere about Clapham or Stockwell."[50] His fear of gossip made him give up living with and providing care to his mad mother. Keeping an insane family member away from one's home turf was not uncommon. The genteel suburbs of London, which combined anonymity and easy access to medical services, became the favorite choice: St. John's Wood was immortalized by Wilkie Collins in *The Woman in White.* Some availed themselves of the service of French or Swiss private asylums—small, exclusive, and invisible, combining the merit of secrecy and the therapeutic effect of a change of air. Lord Shaftesbury sent Maurice, his epileptic third son, to Lausanne, and a private asylum in the outskirts of Paris advertised in English and had an agent at Oxford Street.[51] Middleton was doing what many others did.

There is no evidence in Middleton's letters to document what happened to his plan. The only clue is a short reference in the list of commissions of lunacy in the Public Record Office, which states "Middleton, Ann Frances, commissioned 19 Dec 1818, late of Holles Street Cavendish Square but now residing at the House of Alexander Amyor Gentleman in Fulham Road Little Chelsea." Judging from this, it is reasonable to guess that Middleton had gotten what he wished. Not exactly Clapham or Stockwell, but his mother resided at the time of the commission neither in Bath nor in Tunbridge Wells, places where Middleton feared the curious eyes of the family's acquaintances. Moreover, with the commission and the announcement that she was not fit to manage her own affairs, her property must have come under the control of Middleton. His frustration at his mother's secrecy must have come to an end. He did not, however, live long to enjoy his final victory over his mother. He himself died in Paris in 1821, outlived by his mother by two years.

DOMESTIC PSYCHIATRY AND ITS RESOURCES

Middleton's letters reveal that his domestic world provided rich resources for lay psychiatry. Insanity was neither an unfathomable mystery to him nor an esoteric subject beyond his reach. He did not assume a subservient attitude toward the eminent practitioners of the metropolis. He was confident that he had found out by himself the nature of his mother's affliction, as well as its cause and the means of its cure. He declined a proposal of a cure made by Burrows, then one of the most eminent psychiatric practitioners. Most important, both etiology and therapeutics were firmly placed in the context of personal relationships within the family: he was able to find tools for understanding madness always at hand, in his domestic situation. With its rich resources for psychiatric discourse, Middleton's home was almost a self-contained and independent psychiatric regime. It is important to note that he was not alone among his relatives in attempting to cure his mother by establishing successful interpersonal relationships with her. His sister, Louisa, made an effort at a cure by arranging an interview with their mother. Without question, his sister had her own domestic interpretation of her mother's disease, which was significantly different from her brother's. To cite just one parallel instance, Thomas Campbell, a poet, and his wife disagreed over how to manage their insane son: the father wanting to have his son kept in an asylum, the mother preferring to keep him at home under a keeper.[52] Even after the confinement of the son, they continued to disagree over the arrangement. The mother devised a plan of constant and regular visiting, in which she and her three sisters went to the asylum. The father, however, did not approve of this scheme, calling the plan an "injudicious espionage" of visiting ladies. Family feuds were such a common feature that Bucknill and Tuke's *Manual of Psychological Medicine* warned psychiatrists of the dangers of getting involved in them.[53] With no systematized framework imposed from above, domestic psychiatry differed considerably from one family to another, and from one member of the family to another member.

However variable, domestic psychiatry was practiced in numerous instances. Abundant evidence confirms that many families did believe that they clearly understood the nature of their family members' mental diseases and they did not hesitate to force their own ideas on the doctors. The case of the sister of Mary M——, discussed at the beginning of chapter 2, is a polite, discreet, but firm statement of the family's own preferred arrangement. After seventeen years of treatment of the insane Mary at various institutions away from home, her sister still thought that the key to Mary's improvement was proper understanding of her personality, which was the lever the sister used to challenge the present medical regime. She criticized Dr. Stewart, the doctor then in charge, for failing to grasp Mary's personality. Even after Mary's long mental illness, her sister did not think Mary had ceased to be the person that she had been. Her letter implied her belief that her knowledge of Mary's early personality made her a better judge of the way to cure or improve Mary's mental state than any doctor. Likewise, Dominique Dupont, a French immigrant to London, wrote a long and detailed letter to the Colney Hatch Asylum in which he explained the situation of his institutionalized wife. In the letter he specified the ways in which she should be cured and treated: first, she should be assured of her security and that of her husband; second, she should be drawn out of her belief in magnetism and sorcery; and last, no straps, chains, or manacles should be used. Despite his poor English, his instructions were given with visible confidence.[54] These cases show that a family with an insane member did not necessarily panic and desperately ask for psychiatric help. They might be very much alarmed at the first manifestation of the disease, but the chronic nature of the disease must have given time for the family to recover from its initial shock and to think about strategies for coping with the problem. In so doing, they relied no less on their own cultural framework than on professional service.

The cases of Middleton and others all suggest that domestic psychiatry was a homespun product of personal relationships. Unlike medical or professional psychiatry, it was not self-consciously systematized knowledge. Variety well might be a hallmark of domestic psychiatry. Nevertheless, one may infer certain overall characteristics from the diverse patterns found often in fragmentary ways.

The most important feature is that domestic psychiatry was framed around the issue of a personal relationship constructed around the patient. The crucial part of the domestic regime for the care of a mentally disordered patient was to find a suitable person, preferably in the family, who could communicate with the patient and exercise control over him or her. Instead of mechanical or chemical devices, domestic psychiatry's major means to control the insane was a person with a suitable personality.

The sister of Mary M—— indicated that by acting firmly, a suitable person could control the patient in a proper way. Although the sister did not specify who the suitable person was, such a belief in personal power was expressed regularly in the context of domestic psychiatric control. Finding who could best communicate with, pacify, and control the lunatic was a crucial part of the management of the insane at home. Ideally, the person was one of the members of the family. Middleton initially thought that his mother might benefit from cohabiting with his family, believing in the curative power of the affections of his wife, his children, and himself. William Callow, a retired whip maker in Regent Street, was placed under the care of the family of his eldest daughter by other members of the family, as he was "extremely partial" to the daughter and her family.[55] In the case of John Brome, the key person was his mother: his sister, Mrs. Bashford, testified that "his mother was the only person who could have any control over him," and that he allowed only his mother to speak to him.[56] Alexander Stevenson wrote to the doctor of the asylum where his insane brother, James, stayed that "he [James] has manifested a great regard to me since this illness came upon him and was always willing to do whatever I wished him."[57]

One could also send a patient to another household of extended kin or an intimate friend of the family, combining a change of air and a salubrious arrangement of personalities. When W. M. Thackeray's wife, Isabella, became melancholic in early 1840, the novelist and his mad wife moved to Cork to live with Mrs. Thackeray's mother, believing that "female companionship w[ould] be the best thing for her."[58] When James King, the younger son of a successful wholesale butcher in Newgate Market, became insane, another family, "who had been very old friends of the family," invited the patient to come and stay at their house.[59] Persons in the close circle of the family were crucial to psychiatric therapeutics and/or management, and these human arrangements were the key in producing a successful regime to care for the disturbed mind of the patient. This practice was extended easily to sending a patient into a medical practitioner's household and incorporating him or her into the doctor's family: Henry Robert Pearce, "a gentleman of property," was removed from Sutherland's Blackland House in Chelsea to "the house of Mr. Blood, a medical gentleman of some eminence, residing in North Audley-street, Grosvenor-square, of whose family circle he became a member."[60] Similarly, one John Brome, a graduate of Trinity College, Cambridge, who became a subject of a commission of lunacy in 1842, was "removed to the residence and the care of Sir Charles Aldis."[61]

Sometimes it was essential to remove certain persons from the scene, when interaction with them harmed the mental health of the patient. Mary M——'s sister pointed her finger of blame at the indulgent servant, who had been making the disease worse for years. When, in 1825, Lady Caroline Lamb's eccentricities and violent mood swings raised serious doubt about her sanity, one Dr. Goddard, the family physician, reported back to her husband (the future prime minister Lord Melbourne) that the situation was not very urgent: the doctor wrote that she would not need restraint ("positive coercion") and would improve with "kind treatment and occasional restraint." Still, the doctor was rather firm in pruning bad friends from her personal circle: "But there are friends who *must* be removed from her . . . and some situation must be chosen for her where she can be governed with every appearance of favouring herself."[62] The business of designing a curative environment was a matter of finding a suitable personality match, and of removing unsuitable ones from around the patient.

In several cases, the family recruited a suitable person and gave him or her membership in the household or the family. A particularly conspicuous form of this psychiatric recruiting business was to arrange a marriage for the purpose of taking care of a lunatic. As far as I have found, this "psychiatric arranged marriage" seems to have been mainly practiced by aristocratic families. Their wealth and powerful resources, as well as their prioritizing the family property over individual sentiment, enabled them to arrange a marriage between a weak-minded or lunatic lord and a nursing and controlling woman. The first marriage of the third Earl of Portsmouth, whose commission of lunacy case was examined at the beginning of chapter 1, was an obvious example of this type of arranged marriage. Lord Portsmouth, who had been weak-minded from his youth, was in 1799 married to Miss Grace Norton, the sister of one of the four trustees who effectively controlled His Lordship's vast property. Lord Portsmouth was then just come of age, and the bride was in her early to mid-forties. The principal function of this newlywed middle-aged wife was to conceal "his infirmities from the eye of the world" and to prevent his oddities "from exhibiting any of that ungovernable conduct which required medical aid." It seems that she was a competent manager of her husband, with the assistance of her father (Lord Gantley) and mother-in-law.[63] Likewise, Hon. Jervis Jervis, a lunatic son of the second Viscount St. Vincent, was in 1815 married to Sophia Vincent, a distant relative, who "had a great power over him, and kept him out of scrapes." When Sophia died in 1828, the family thought it necessary to replace the former wife-as-nurse with yet another wife-as-nurse, or, to put it in their own words, "to introduce a respectable female into the family, to protect Mr. Jervis from imposition." The commission against Jervis requested in 1829 is likely to have been an alternative to an arranged marriage for the protection of his property.[64] For both Portsmouth and Jervis, however, the major aim of their marriages was the prevention of marriage contracted on the spur of the moment. A lunatic lord who was neither married nor put under a commission of lunacy was a great financial hazard, because any person who obtained his "consent" could marry him and gain control over his huge property. Lady Portsmouth and Lady Jervis played the double roles of matron and legal safeguard.[65] They were given membership in the respective families by those who were concerned with the property of the insane lords.

The situation of Lord Portsmouth took a new turn in 1808, and the family had to readjust itself to cope with it. Perhaps because of her age, Lady Portsmouth, who was then almost sixty years old, was apparently no longer able to control her husband: one witness recalled that she "had not then sufficient influence over him to restrain his Lordship."[66] She solved the problem by inviting one Dr. John Combe, a medical man, into the household. This does not, however, mean the end of the domestic management and the beginning of a new medical regime. An important fact was that this medical man was a relative of Lady Portsmouth, and thus already belonged to an extended kin-group, which made it relatively easy for him to assume a new membership in the family. Combe's qualification for household membership was thus less professional than familial. Moreover, Combe's role was clearly more managerial than medical, and he was described as an "efficient manager," whose power lay in his personal influence more than in a depersonalized medical professional skill: "his management had been successful by that *personal controul, which arose out of the influence he possessed over him*—by this skill with which he performed the office of a curator, he preserved [the Lord] in a state of tranquillity."[67] Lord Portsmouth was thus under the control of a succession of two persons who lived with him and exercised their influence over him. Both were given membership in the family or household for the purpose of controlling His Lordship. The wife assumed the role of matron, the doctor that of steward. Both fulfilled their duties effectively through their *personal* influence.

In middle-class families, one might expect that their relatively limited resources and their belief in companionate marriage and romantic love would have more or less excluded the option of arranging a marriage for establishing a psychiatric regime. Somewhat surprisingly, however, there is one case in which such a marriage was planned by a middle-class family.[68] Middle-class families, too, were flexible in terms of their human arrangements for the sake of creating a suitable psychiatric regime, as I shall shortly discuss. Nevertheless, an arranged marriage for the sake of psychiatric control seems to have been too radical a defiance of the middle-class value of affectionate matrimony. Few, if any, were ready to practice it.

Perhaps the most common method along this line of domestic psychiatric regimes was to hire a special keeper.[69] Upper- and middle-class households were fluid and flexible in terms of the constant flow of employed labor forces within them. For both upper- and middle-class families, recruiting servants for special purposes was an important part of family life. Hiring a person whose specific function was to control an insane member of the family was thus a natural choice. If a family employed a cook for preparing meals or a groom for taking care of the horses, a keeper for taking care of the lunatic seems to have been a natural extension.[70]

To employ a "keeper" for controlling and caring for an insane person in his or her own house was widespread. Particularly in London, where the service industry was highly developed and specialized, it was possible to find plenty of servants specializing in the care of lunatics. The abundance of private licensed madhouses in London—there were about forty of them in the 1830s—facilitated a constant supply of keepers who had had experience in the care of rich lunatics at one of those places. Many of these private licensed houses were small in capacity and ideal training places for the care of the insane in a domestic setting.[71] Private families could hire experienced psychiatric keepers from several major private madhouses—Warburton's, Sir John Wells's establishment at Hoxton, and George Man Burrows's Clapham Retreat. Warburton had a royal and aristocratic clientele, sending four to five attendants when King George III relapsed in 1801, as well as offering similar services to insane aristocrats. The Royal Appointment must have been a huge boost to the upmarket sector of his business.[72] They offered discreet service, sending an attendant who gave the semblance of being a normal servant. Such an arrangement was also frequently mentioned during the course of the examination of witnesses in commissions of lunacy. For instance, Sarah Eliason was taken care of by a young female nurse "who was engaged from the service of Dr. Warburton."[73] Some of those keepers sent to private houses cut impressive figures during the examination of the commission of lunacy. Jane Prithenden, who called herself "a nurse in the employ of Dr. Monroe," showed that she was very experienced in treating insane patients in their own houses:

> On the 18th of December, I went to Miss White's, and told her that I had come from Dr. Monroe's to which she replied that she did not want a keeper but a servant. Upon one occasion she was cleaning a bird, and I asked her for a knife which she placed under her pillow of a night, and she told me that I should not have it. I attempted to obtain possession of it, and she said "You take it at your peril. You shall only have it with your blood." I was compelled, upon that occasion, to place a strait-

waistcoat upon her, and keep her under restraint the whole of the night and half the next day.[74]

Although her true function was deliberately made somewhat ambiguous, her vigilance over the person she was in charge of and her quick, firm, and apparently appropriate decision to put her mistress into a straitjacket testifies to her experience.

An even more discreet service was offered by perhaps a handful of persons, who were not formally affiliated with any madhouse but still claimed experience and expertise in the care of the insane at their own homes. For example, Frances Backler, one of the witnesses in the commission of lunacy against Lady Kirkwell, stated that she "had been in the habit of waiting on insane ladies. Had made their state her study. Knows the theory of it. Expected such an occupation at Lady Kirkwell's. Was prepared to find her in that state of mind." Confidence in her own experience in the specialist trade is clearly discernible in her statement. She might have even treated the occasion of her legal deposition as a chance for advertisement.

Further up in the scale of service, we encounter an impressive figure: one Arabella Norford, who acted in the 1820s as a matron to the household of William Robinson, an insane nephew of Edward Clive, the first Earl of Powis. Norford's letter to Lord Powis in 1826 has survived, in which she reported on the arrangement of care for Robinson.[75] Norford had recently assumed responsibility for the care of Robinson and she experienced considerable conflict with the person who had done the job before her. One of the bones of contention was their disagreement over the use of restraint. Norford presented an articulate principle of moral treatment and fiercely opposed the use of restraint, whereas a Mr. Smith, who had apparently been in charge of the patient previously, thought restraint was necessary:

> On the subject of Mr Smith, my Lord, as you have honored me with your entire confidence & have to observe that were you to see poor William in his present helpless emaciated state, tortured with a mind sensitive beyond description—your Lordship *would not, could not* for a moment harbour the thought of *"coercion"*, or *"Restraint"* as well might you think of using it toward a *dying infant,* because it pined & moaned in its last agony. Nothing but the most conciliating soothing measures must be adopted and I have no hesitation in asserting, that the return of Mr Smith would prove of the most fatal consequence, and such as I could not remain here to witness—and I am convinced your Lordship *need only see* poor William, to think & feel upon the subject.[76]

This letter shows Norford in a very impressive light. She was an employee of considerable stature, who could confront others over the treatment of her patients based on principled rejection of the use of coercion and restraint. Her authority seems to have been above that of a medical attendant, one Mr. Miles, "a person experienced in the treatment of [the] peculiar malady."[77]

My characterization of persons who were recruited into a family for the care of a lunatic thus differs considerably from the accepted images of "keepers" of lunatics. Decidedly negative images of psychiatric keepers at private (noninstitutional) settings were first established by Lunacy Commissioners in the mid-nineteenth century. In the 1850s, the investigation of "single lunatics" by Lunacy Commissioners revealed that the business of attending insane persons at home was alarmingly large and well established. There was even an association of private psychiatric keepers, calling itself "The Lisson Grove Association of Attendants on Persons Bodily and Mentally Afflicted." As might be expected, the commissioners were extremely hostile to its members, calling them mercenary and "disreputable characters" who were prone to put the patients under excessive restraint in order to lessen their workload.[78] No doubt such unprofessional conduct did exist and may even have been common among the keepers under investigation. The Lunacy Commissioners' characterization of the conduct of the managers of the insane in private homes, however, tells us more about their prejudices and frustrations than about reality. At least in the 1820s and 1830s, this small business sector of psychiatric services at home contained within itself a considerable range and diversity. Perhaps in accordance with the size of the purse of the employing family and with the degree of their interest in the welfare of the patient, there existed a variety of levels of service, from indifferent and coarse administrators of the straitjacket to skilled and experienced psychiatric home nurses, with the figure of Norford as the manager of the household on the principle of moral treatment perhaps at its apex.

The domestic psychiatric regime was thus centered on the issue of finding an individual who could design and establish a suitable regime and exercise control over the patient. Ideally, this person belonged to the family of the lunatic itself or was a close relative. If not, one could recruit a person and introduce him or her into the family or the household. The membership given to him or her differed: a spouse, a member of the kin group, a manager of the household, or an attendant. Despite these differences, the important point is the *personal nature* of domestic psychiatry. It was conceived as an enterprise to conduct a person-to-person relationship of a special kind: the personality of the patient should be grasped, controlled, and manipulated by a person with a suitable personality to do so.

Such an emphasis on personal nature as the key to controlling an insane family member may have a timeless aspect. Long cohabitation naturally leads to a surer grasp of behavioral patterns of a family member, and perhaps in every culture intimate knowledge generated in the most basic social unit must play some role in coping with disruptive behavior. I suggest, however, that there is considerable historicity in those elements of domestic psychiatry that I have just described, because they were interwoven with the emphasis on domestic life in England in the early nineteenth century.

The history of the family in England from the sixteenth century on suggests that it constituted a particularly favorable site for developing intimate personal relationships. Lawrence Stone has argued that the eighteenth century witnessed "the rise of affective individualism" in upper- and upper-middle-class families, in which a family member was viewed less as an occupant of a particular familial status than as a unique individual with a special character or personality. Attacking Stone's chronology, Keith Wrightson and others have conclusively demonstrated that strong emotional ties between family members can be traced back to the sixteenth and seventeenth centuries.[79] Despite their difference in chronology and causal attributions, Stone, Wrightson, and many other historians concur that the early modern English family put stress on personal attachment among its members conceived as individuals.

The early nineteenth century saw further developments of family ties. In the period that Eric Hobsbawm termed the Age of the Dual Revolution, the family was placed at center stage of the contemporary ideology of social cohesion. The religiously oriented middle class set up the family as a bulwark in the fight against the radical tide stimulated by the French Revolution and as a refuge from the massive social disruptions caused by the Industrial Revolution.[80] By strengthening relationships within the family and infusing them with the revived Christianity of the heart, the turn-of-the-century middle-class reformers attempted to put a stop to the spread of atheism, immorality, the disintegration of society, and, above all, the revolution *à la* Jacobins. The recommendation to remold the family into a place in which mutual love, affection, and companionship should reign had an enormous ideological urgency. The family should not be a puppetry of role-playing or a businesslike transaction of formalities, but a haven in which a true communion of the heart took place.

At the basis of such domestic companionship lay the key ritual of opening one's heart to other family members. A vital part of establishing such ideal human relationships was to recognize, understand, and share other family members' anxieties or concerns. The inward-looking nature of Evangelicalism and its encouragement of close examination of one's own sins and faults provided favorable circumstances for grasping the character traits of other family members as well as one's own. The inspection of the self was not only conducted in diaries and journals, but also supported and shared by the family. One historian has observed: "[as] the religious household gathered each day to pray, they would act as checks and guides to each other, discussing the details of individual falls from grace, taking comfort together in Christ's capacity to understand and forgive."[81] A person who was chronically sullen, irascible, discontented, or withdrawn should be drawn into a community of mutual love, first by disclosing his or her inner agonies to other family members and then by opening a channel for communication.

This ideal of domestic counseling was exactly the process of "unbosoming," a practice attempted by both Middleton and his sister as they tried to cope with the problem of their insane mother. A mentally or emotionally troubled person, who was breaching the ideal of the domestic enjoyment of mutual affection, should be encouraged to open up his or her heart and impart hidden anxieties, fears, and other morbid feelings. This was the first step toward establishing trust between him or her and other members of the family. The suffering person should then be integrated into the sweet delights of home. Quite common was the use of the word *unbosom* in the context of bringing back a mentally distressed or otherwise troubled person into a normal family relationship. In 1838, Lady Sarah Seymour, a subject of commission of lunacy then confined in Norman-house at Fulham, wished to see her sister, Mrs. Sophia Harriet Ramsden, "in order that she might unbosom herself." She also testified about her own situation as follows: "I was frightened at the time; I felt nervous from an occurrence only known to myself, as I have no friend to unbosom myself to."[82] The phrase was used also in a medical work. Sir Henry Halford wrote that "unbosoming" oneself was a key therapeutic action: "[If], at this auspicious moment, the intercourse of a discreet friend be permitted, he will cheer his heart, and kindness and attention easily get possession of his confidence; and induce him to unbosom himself of the distempered notion which haunts him."[83] The use of "unbosoming" was thus recognized by the patient, the family, and the doctor as a crucial step in the cure of madness or in the healing of the troubled mind. All these actors believed in the therapeutic power of opening one's heart and imparting its anxieties to family members, relatives, or close friends. This important piece in the therapeutics of domestic psychiatry was intertwined with the Evangelical belief in the role of the family as a place where each member's true self should be mutually understood, shared, and taken care of. Domestic psychiatry in the early nineteenth century drew its strength from the concept of the family as a community of hearts.

As is evident from the examples discussed here, a suitable person who could make the troubled patient "unbosom" and could exercise control over him or her did not always come from the cohabiting nuclear core of the family, but often hailed from an extended kin-group, many of whom had lived separately. This suggests that, in search of a proper person, the family activated strong networks of their kin-group. In the eighteenth and nineteenth centuries, upper- and middle-class families forged tightly knit networks through intermarriages, religious associations, and business partnerships.[84] They visited each other, wrote letters, exchanged gifts, and enhanced their group solidarity, which was facilitated by the development of the postal service and improved means of transportation. Moreover, members of the group frequently offered mutual help and support in times of other members' practical, financial, spiritual, or emotional difficulty. Attempting to establish communication with a mentally disordered member of the group must scarcely have been different from their routine bonding, at least while the manifestations of the disease were relatively mild. Friends and relatives were sought after through the network, in the expectation of finding one whose personality matched the task of making the patient open his or her heart, establishing communication with him or her, and exercising domestic psychiatric control. If necessary, they were given temporary membership in the family, or the patient stayed in a household where he or she could live with such a suitable person. Even when one could not find a suitable individual within the lunatic's own family or relatives, one could adjust the family or household personnel for the sake of creating a suitable psychiatric regime with relative ease. Domestic psychiatry drew its strength from the elasticity of the family/household membership, which made the family network a very versatile means to cope with the problem of lunacy at home.

Domestic psychiatry was thus interwoven with the very ethos of the nineteenth-century wealthy family, as well as with the structure of intra- and interfamilial relationships at that time. The ideal of the family as an emotional haven and the Evangelical stress on opening one's heart underlay the therapeutic technique of finding a person with suitable character to make the patient "unbosom" himself or herself. Moreover, the fluidity of households and the extended networks among families, linking members of the kin-group, in-laws, and friends, meant flexibility in domestic psychiatry—it could be practiced either at home by one who was not a member of a direct family, and also practiced away from home by a relative or a close friend. Considerable flexibility and expansiveness thus characterized domestic psychiatry, which compels us to modify our concept of the neat dichotomy and stark contrast between home and psychiatric institution. Even away from home, there existed fine grades of domestic psychiatry.

THE DOMESTIC ORIGIN OF MORAL TREATMENT?

We should reconceptualize the rise of "moral treatment" in the light of the domestic psychiatric regime and its resonance with the early nineteenth-century sociocultural emphasis on the family. Moral treatment was one of the most important features of psychiatry in the early nineteenth century, and is one of the subjects whose place in the history of psychiatry has been most hotly debated.[85] Starting around the late eighteenth century, more or less simultaneously in England and France, there emerged "new" therapeutic or managerial techniques for coping with the insane. Samuel Tuke's *Description of the Retreat* (1813), as well as Philippe Pinel's *Traité médico-philosophique* (English translation in 1806), established the viability of moral treatment in England. In the 1810s, moral treatment became one of the guiding principles that inspired the reform in lunacy, starting from the 1815–16 Parliamentary Inquiry into Bethlem and the York Asylum.[86] Although traditionally hailed as a humanitarian breakthrough that introduced modernity to psychiatry, moral treatment's status in the history of psychiatry has become a subject of intense debate in the last couple of generations. Michel Foucault famously debunked it by revealing the invisible internalization of norms achieved through the moral treatment of Tuke and Pinel. Andrew Scull largely followed Foucault's interpretation of the nature of the practice and related it to the new code of behavior in industrial society.[87] Largely based on French examples, Jan Goldstein argued that moral treatment provided a set of core therapeutic techniques for the new profession of alienists around which they were able to construct their new professional identity.[88] Roy Porter has argued for a more gradualist development of the practice of moral management, finding turn-of-the-century moral treatment as a development, not a rupture, from the practice of Francis Willis, William Pargeter, and other owners of the private madhouses.[89] I should like to conclude this chapter by looking at another dimension of moral treatment, namely its resonance with the practice of controlling lunatics at home.

Moral treatment, especially as practiced at the York Retreat, had obvious resonance with those instances of domestic psychiatry that have been analyzed in this chapter. They both share a strong emphasis on the power of personal influence on the patient. They both attempted to go beyond mere surface manifestations, to reach the depth of the mad mind and to establish a channel of communication with the patient ("unbosoming"). Both at the York Retreat and in the domestic psychiatric regime, patients were persuaded to behave themselves without recourse to physical coercion or the threat of violence. Moreover, at least one English doctor explicitly called psychological healing practiced at home by family members "moral treatment," and that is Sir Henry Halford, whose emphasis on "unbosoming" was quoted earlier. This leader of the metropolitan elite physicians identified moral treatment as introducing an intimate friend who could unbosom the patient and establish the basis of communication, persuasion, and control. Note that Halford adopted a technique well-established in domestic psychiatry and called it "moral treatment," conceptualizing his version of moral treatment after the model of domestic psychiatry. The influence flowed from lay psychiatric practice to medical, not the other way round.

Moral treatment thus had multiple origins. No doubt, moral treatment for the poor, practiced in the Bicêtre or Salpêtrière or English county asylums, derived its inspiration from the humanitarian enterprise to alleviate the plight of the depraved, as well as from the desire to mold the character of the lower class into an orderly and self-governing cast. It was a form of compassion of the elite for the poor, and contained within itself the power structure of the class society, as has been analyzed by Foucault and Scull. Porter's psychological entrepreneurs based in private madhouses were a different kind of practitioner of moral treatment. They developed highly theatrical and self-dramatizing manipulation of their patients, which was very different from the sobriety of the moral treatment of the York Retreat. In addition to such institutional settings, homes of the wealthy were another locus where a prototype of moral treatment was developed in the late eighteenth and early nineteenth century. It is thus only natural that the first generation of practitioners of institutional moral treatment tried to re-create a sense of family within institutional walls: they imported a practice well-established, if not clearly articulated, at home.

Since all my examples examined in this chapter, except that of Lord Portsmouth, came after the wide publicity given to moral treatment by the Parliamentary Inquiry in 1814–15, one cannot exclude the possibility that the influence flowed from institutional moral treatment to domestic. My own interpretation is, however, the other way round: the institutional practice of moral treatment grew out of domestic interpersonal psychiatric techniques. In other words, a prototype of "moral treatment" had been practiced in the family before it was articulated, developed, and adjusted to institutional use by innovative asylum doctors, hospital superintendents, and lunacy reformers. The ease with which the Middletons and others delineated their belief in the personality-centered therapeutics and controlling of insanity indicates that they did not learn this technique as something new or borrowed. The confidence with which Middleton expressed his views on his mother's insanity suggests that they were a part of his own cultural framework, not somebody else's. The case of Lord Portsmouth is particularly suggestive. When a doctor was introduced into the household, it was only as a supplement to, and the reproduction of, the control that had been previously exercised by his wife. In other words, the doctor had a concrete model to follow. Likewise, when the sister of Mary M—— asked the psychiatrist to be firm with the patient, she was telling him to follow the family's own way of managing their troublesome sister. All these pieces of evidence suggest that a prototype of moral treatment as personal control without recourse to the infliction of physical pain or the threat of its use, had been first exercised in the domestic and private sphere, and was then transplanted to psychiatric practice and institutions.

If my interpretation is correct, what happened around the late eighteenth and early nineteenth centuries in "the rise of moral treatment" was, therefore, the boundary-crossing of a species of psychological technique from the domestic realm to the realm of institutions. This could be seen as an appropriation of lay technique for medical use. It could also been seen as a domestication of institutional practice, as Andrew Scull has pointed out.[90] This boundary-crossing enabled psychiatric entrepreneurs to treat the patient, who was a stranger to them, as an individual on intimate terms, as if he or she were their own family member. Moral treatment allowed the institutional doctor to see a patient not as a remote, alien, strange "other," but as one who had a unique personality. Seen from another perspective, due to the transplantation, the lay notion of control through personality matches was transformed into that of personal charisma or special expertise, on the basis of which one could create a business, design an institutional regime, or even build the credentials of an entire branch of medicine. The rise of moral treatment thus represents the interweaving and amalgamation of domestic psychiatry and institutional psychiatry, the family and medicine.[91] Institutional psychiatry drew its cultural relevancy from the family; the family was able to colonize yet another locus, that of the institution.

FIVE

Destabilizing the Domestic Psychiatric Regime

CHAPTER 4 EXAMINED THE POWERFUL resources of domestic psychiatry. Centered on the notion of the family as a close-knit community of individual personalities bound together by mutual affection, a framework emerged for decoding and understanding insanity, as well as a set of strategies for the management of lunacy at home. Both the framework and the strategies were constructed around the power of personal influence exercised by those who knew the patient intimately and who could inspire the patient to "unbosom" his or her internal sufferings. This confessional practice was modeled after Evangelical family gatherings. Perhaps it became a prototype of moral treatment. The practice of domestic psychiatry was thus interwoven with the fundamental building blocks of nineteenth-century domestic ideology, which hailed the family as the most important anchor of a society in turmoil and in danger of disintegration. Faced with such a coherent and socially powerful set of interpretations, it is no wonder that "professional" doctors dared not compete with them, but rather adapted themselves to the domestic psychiatric regime. Moreover, domestic psychiatry was not limited to home, nor were its practitioners limited to the members of the immediate family. It was flexible and expansive; it could be practiced away from home and by a person who was incorporated into the household for the special purpose of taking care of the patient. Indeed, the expansiveness of domestic psychiatry fostered an environment that was favorable to the growth of psychiatric institutions, so long as they emphasized their intimate or homelike atmosphere. The family and institutional psychiatry were not antagonistic, but symbiotic.

So far, my emphasis has been put on the power and integrity of domestic psychiatry and its relevance to the wider cultural context. Now I turn to an explanation of its limits, weak points, and the factors that destabilized its reign at home. First, both common sense and historical evidence from diverse areas and time periods suggest that managing madness at home is a difficult task.[1] Not surprisingly, nineteenth-century families were often at great pains to prevent the lunatic from doing mischief and to make him or her obey orders. In one case, the lunatic in question was so fiercely mad, violently destructive, or even homicidal that the family gave up any hope of controlling him and arranged to dispatch him to a foreign country.[2] In many cases, families routinely asked for "keepers" with special equipment from private madhouse, which was no doubt the sign of the difficulty they experienced. Chains, manacles, cords, and other devices for restraint were a staple part of the management of mental patients. Quite often the availability of these special kinds of equipment was the major raison d'être of institutions for the insane.[3] Even Victorian asylums where the belief in "nonrestraint" was exceptionally strong provided themselves with special rooms for secluding particularly violent patients. Controlling a mental patient was and is never an easy task, whether at home or in specialist institutions. The difficulty may well be timeless.

I propose here, however, to examine the difficulties of domestic psychiatry in a *historical* context. In so doing, I am not suggesting any variations in the pathological manifestation of the disease. Instead, I argue that practicing domestic psychiatry in the early nineteenth century presented historically specific difficulties. I propose to analyze those aspects of the difficulty of domestic psychiatry that were conditioned by social and cultural forces then present. By close examination of the sources, one can uncover a certain historicity in the hardship experienced by the family in coping with an insane member.

In this chapter, I argue that there were two major concerns for the family that wanted to control a lunatic at home: the first was the danger posed to the family's property; the second was the lunatic's behavior in public. Families were worried about lunatics' mismanagement of their property and the possibility of their being taken advantage of by unscrupulous persons. Depriving lunatics of their civil rights and protecting their property were the reasons for seeking commissions of lunacy. Such concerns were particularly intense when the family faced the insanity of an adult male with full property rights, but even families with female lunatics were not exempt from such worries. Although female rights were quite limited during the period under review, that did not mean that women were barred from engaging in every type of property transaction. Single women, widows, and (although few in number) divorced women had considerable civil rights: they could own property and they could marry of their own accord.[4]

Also evident in those sources I have consulted is the embarrassment and sense of shame caused by strange behaviors of the lunatic outside the walls of the home or in public places. Despite the Victorian myth of the family as a place completely distinct and separated from the external world, the family was always open to the external world. An ordinary family member, either man or woman, had to live in two realms, private and public.[5] Both men and women showed their physical presence in public spaces, on the street, at church, at public dinners, or in the theater. From the family's viewpoint, the lunatic's physical presence in such public places represented a constant source of trouble and embarrassment. Family members felt intense shame when lunatics "exposed themselves" in public places. They tried to enclose madness within the private sphere and to put the lunatic's behavior in the public space under tight control. Perhaps no other case illuminates so well those two kinds of concerns than that of Rosa Bagster, who became the subject of a gigantic commission of lunacy in 1832. I first examine the Bagster case in detail, and then draw some general observations about the difficulties the family had to face when attempting to contain an insane family member within the private sphere. Here, I emphasize the threat to the domestic regime perceived as coming from outside.

On the other hand, one should not assume that the world outside the home was the only force that threatened and destabilized a domestic psychiatric regime. There were many cases in which the family with a lunatic was threatened *from inside*. The Victorian emphasis on home as a place of solidarity and of high standards of morality led some family members or relatives to label certain behaviors as insanity. They often appealed to the outer world to help them to solve the problem inside the family. The cases of Edward Frank (1825), George Davenport (1838), and Lawrence Ruck (1858) suggest that the very beliefs that created mental and spiritual solidarity within the family turned out to be the force that eroded the internal containment of the problem of lunacy. In short, a tightly knit family generated a dynamic that externalized the problem of lunacy. In the latter part of this chapter, I analyze the dynamic through which the domestic psychiatric regime was challenged, focusing on the ambivalent role of the domestic ideology that was then prevalent.

CONTROLLING A WEAK-MINDED HEIRESS: THE CASE OF ROSA BAGSTER

In July 1832, readers of the *Times* were again inundated with detailed reports of a high-profile commission of lunacy. Succeeding the cases of Lord Portsmouth, Edward Frank, and Edward Davies, this was the fourth commission that deserves to be called genuinely sensational. The case of Lord Portsmouth in 1823 and that of Edward Frank in 1825 were pornographic in its historical sense, exposing sexual misdemeanors of elite members of society. The case of Edward Davies at the end of 1829 was turned into a morality play depicting the triumph of liberty against mad-doctors. This time, the drama of the commission was centered around Rosa Bagster, whose story looks remarkably similar to a work of popular domestic fiction. A rich heiress fell in love with a suitor of whom her parent disapproved; the couple eloped and contracted a clandestine marriage; the parent did not give up and asked for a commission to annul the marriage on the basis of the heroine's lunacy, a legal maneuver that the new husband adamantly opposed. A gigantic lawsuit followed, which lasted for fourteen days, during which the *Times* covered the story daily at considerable length. The excitement of the paper and the public reached its climax on 10 July, when Rosa Bagster herself was examined. She testified about the consummation of the marriage in front of a large audience.[6] Toward the end of the examination, evidence for and against her sanity was evenly matched. Testimony was given to show her weak-mindedness. On the other side, medical witnesses disclosed dirty tricks played by the family to dupe Rosa, and testified to her sanity. John Haslam gave arguably the most remarkable performance in his long career in support of Rosa. On 16 July, the verdict was read. Everybody held their breath, including the reporter for the *Times,* who wrote: "The most deathlike silence pervaded the entire body of spectators, who filled every corner and avenue of the court." The jury was split, 20 to 2, and returned a verdict of unsoundness of mind, at which the audience was visibly astonished.[7] By any standard, this was the most dramatic commission of lunacy of its era. Apart from its dramatic merits and human poignancy, the Bagster case is quite revealing and deserves close analysis of its background.

Rosa Bagster was born in 1810 to a wealthy family in London. Her grandfather, John Crowder, was a successful printer in the City of London and served as alderman of the Ward of Farrington Within from 1800, and subsequently as Lord Mayor of the City of London from 1829 until his death in December 1830.[8] Her mother, Crowder's daughter, was Rosetta Bagster. In her youth, Rosetta had run away with one Richard Bagster, who was probably related to the Bagster family, another successful printer in London. Rosetta Bagster gave birth to Rosa soon after their marriage. For reasons that are unclear, the runaway couple lived together for less than a year, and Rosa was Rosetta's only child and the only grandchild of John Crowder.[9] Rosa was brought up by her mother and a series of governesses, but they lived with Crowder, who exercised considerable influence on the family. It is obvious that Crowder never pardoned his disobedient daughter and, perhaps in compensation, doted on his granddaughter. The mother was naturally unhappy at the grandfather's intrusions into the domestic regime. Peter Laurie, a close friend of Rosetta and the governor of Bethlem Hospital, testified that "Mrs. Bagster has told me that in any differences between her daughter and herself the late Alderman Crowder always leaned to the side of his grand-daughter."[10]

From her early childhood, Rosa had difficulty with learning, and exhibited emotional problems. At boarding school, she did not make any progress in arithmetic, reading, grammar, and the like, and she was occasionally violent toward other pupils. She was soon forced to leave the school, and later was instructed at home by a succession of governesses, who did not improve either her learning or her behavior. At the time of the commission, when she had just come of age, she could answer how much twice ten was, but could not add ten and ten.[11] The family was divided on how to treat this weak-minded girl. The mother and governesses, who were responsible for Rosa's day-to-day management and were often the target of her violence, repeatedly asked Crowder to hire a special keeper and to sanction the use of a straitjacket. However, Crowder continued to refuse these pleas until his death.[12] From Crowder's viewpoint, the weak-minded, irritable, and difficult Rosa was a victim of Rosetta's imprudent elopement. When he was appointed Lord Mayor, Crowder imparted to Rev. Samuel Smith, the chaplain to the Lord Mayor, his opinion that the mental weakness of his granddaughter originated from the tumultuous excitement of her pregnant mother. "Shortly before Mr. Alderman Crowder came to the Mansion-house, he communicated the whole history of the unfortunate union of Mrs. Bagster with her husband, and of which marriage Miss Bagster is the issue. He informed me that Mr. and Mrs. Bagster had not lived together for more than a year; and that during that period Mrs. Bagster was in a high state of excitement, mental and otherwise, and for a portion of the time in prison;

and that the consequence of this excitement had descended to the child."[13] Crowder's etiology of Rosa's illness implied that Rosa was suffering the consequences of her mother's impudent disobedience and subsequent morbid excitement. His decoding of his granddaughter's mental weakness squared with the ways in which Crowder behaved toward Rosa and her mother: Rosa deserved sympathy, her mother was to blame. Note that Crowder's framework for understanding his granddaughter's mental disorder was firmly embedded in the family history, sharing a basic characteristic with Middleton's understanding of his mother's disease, discussed in chapter 4.

The deep division within the family, with an indulgent grandfather at its head, made consistent and firm personal control of Rosa impossible. As Laurie's remark suggests, the authority of her mother over Rosa was significantly weakened by the frequent intervention of Crowder on Rosa's behalf. Miss Clayton, one of the governesses, testified that "she was much indulged by her grandfather. She is not afraid of her mother. . . . She is not afraid of me."[14] It also seems that Rosa's mother herself failed to act on any firm principle. Several witnesses told the court that they did not entirely approve of the mother's treatment of her daughter. One of them, Thomas Kelly, another alderman and later Lord Mayor, and a close business friend of Crowder, candidly maintained that "I should expect she would correct her daughter when she has omitted to do so, and not caressed her at the time she has done so."[15] Even Rosa herself was aware of the situation in a more or less articulated way: she once said, "I know that my grandpapa's fondness spoiled me; he told me he would leave me a fortune, and I am sensible that I have neglected my learning," which implies that Rosa knew she was taking advantage of her grandfather's partiality toward her to escape the discipline of her governesses and her mother.[16]

The death of Crowder in December 1830 could have made the situation easier for Rosa's mother: the situation of the multiple and conflicting authorities within the family finally came to an end, and there was no longer a family member who opposed getting a keeper. Unfortunately for Rosetta, however, that was not the case. As soon as the internal difficulty appeared to be over, a more serious problem arose, which came from outside the family. In 1831, Rosa came of age and inherited a vast amount of property: £4,000 per annum from her late grandfather and a deceased uncle. (Doubtless, Crowder disinherited his daughter as punishment for her disobedience.) The new situation instantly made Rosa a target of numerous approaches from young men in London looking for a rich heiress.[17] To the alarm of those concerned, Rosa was "very susceptible of partialities for young gentleman she happened to see who pretended to be in love with [her]."[18] Moreover, imbibing the notion of romantic love and marriage from reading novels, as well as wishing to escape from the control of her mother, Rosa developed a longing for elopement: later Rosa testified that "she had read novels, and a great deal about elopements, and always had a notion that she should like to run away with some one."[19] Her mother (who had herself eloped, of course) naturally became alarmed at the romantic advances from a variety of young men, Rosa's positive response to them, and her longing to elope. Consequently, she tightened her control over Rosa, intercepting letters sent to her, forcing her to write a letter rejecting a certain suitor, and preventing her from going out alone.[20] To her mother's tighter control over her courtship, Rosa protested by increasing her physical violence toward her mother and her governess.[21]

That the family was keen to curb Rosa's association with men is exemplified by an episode that one Mr. Windus, a family friend, later recounted in court. During Crowder's mayoralty, a public dinner was held at the Mansion House, and Mr. Windus took a seat next to Rosa. He did not know her before, and he paid her the usual courtesy of inviting her to take wine. At that moment, "she turned round and looked at me very full in the face," which was a serious breach of the decorous behavior expected of upper-class women. In a few minutes, the breach became even more grave. She started to narrate her love life to the man, who was almost a stranger to her: "she said she was in love" and then told him that she was going to be married to Mr. Jupp. Mr. Windus was astonished at the conduct of Rosa toward him, which he communicated to Crowder's family and the chaplain. He was concerned not only about Rosa's breach of decorum at the dinner table, but also about her overfamiliarity, her inappropriately intimate conversation, and her lack of the invisible self-protection that a girl of respectable family was expected to build up around herself. Mr. Windus, therefore, advised that "she ought not be sent into company without being 'fenced in' . . . by female friends on each side."[22] He clearly thought that the family should create the barrier of women against members of the opposite sex and prohibit Rosa's unsupervised association with men. This was, so to speak, one variation of a human arrangement for the control of the insane, discussed in chapter 4.

The family had recourse to more direct methods to control Rosa's marriage, namely finding a suitable match in order to protect the property. When Mr. Jupp made a romantic advance toward Rosa, her mother spoke to a family friend about him, and said "she had hoped the time will arrive when she should see her daughter comfortably settled in life." She made an inquiry into Mr. Jupp's character, but found it "objectionable." She told Mr. Jupp "in the presence of his brother, that she disapproved of his paying his addresses to her daughter. She said that she was sure that money was his object, and that her child, he must be aware, was different to other girls."[23] While rejecting Mr. Jupp, Mrs. Bagster was trying to arrange a marriage for her daughter. Rosa recalled, "[there] was Mr. Howell, who lived in Warwick Square for a week, he wished me to marry him, and I think my mother also wished him, but I did not like Mr. Howell at all, and was very happy when he left the house."[24] Just as Lord Portsmouth was married to a wife whose major function was to nurse the lord, to control his affairs, and to maintain the lord's property in a way that would satisfy the family, Mrs. Bagster was looking for a suitable match between her weak-minded daughter and a trustworthy man, whom she expected to care for her daughter and to protect her property.[25] It is at least mildly surprising to know that this typical middle-class family attempted an arranged marriage, especially when the mother herself had defied her father's wishes in the most spectacular way by eloping.

Rosa did not submissively accept the arranged match. It is not clear whether this was owing to the notion of romantic marriage she had imbibed from reading novels, or to her longing to liberate herself from the tight regime constructed by her mother, or to her desire to emulate her mother by running away with a man of whom her parent disapproved. In any event, the family's vigilance and marriage plans were set at naught by a tour de force of Rosa and her secret fiancé, Raymond Newton. On Saturday, 21 April 1832, Rosa and her governess visited the Zoological Gardens with three members of the Newton family, Raymond and two sisters of his.[26] In fact, this was a plan prepared by Rosa and Raymond, who had proposed marriage to her about a year before.[27] The governess had been holding Rosa so fast that Rosa almost gave up on the plan, but, in the end, Rosa invented an excuse for leaving the governess and slipped into Newton's carriage. Together they ran away across the northern border to Gretna Green, where one could still make legally valid (if often contested) marriages without church banns.[28] They exchanged vows at Gretna Green before a smith, and that night they consummated the marriage at an inn at Keswick. Excited and agitated at what she had done, Rosa played the part of a heroine in a romantic novel and told people at the inn that she was stolen from a boarding school and that she was anxious whether her mamma would forgive such a naughty girl.[29] The mamma did not forgive. On receiving letters asking for pardon from the newly married couple, the mother had two police officers take her away by force and bring her back to London, to start a gigantic legal procedure to nullify the marriage on the basis of Rosa's "unsoundness of mind."[30] This started a new phase of control over Rosa: the resort to private and domestic control ended, and the attempt to employ public and legal means started. Subsequently, another drama unfolded in the courtroom, which will not be discussed here.

PATROLLING THE BORDER OF THE PRIVATE AND PUBLIC SPHERES

The case of Rosa Bagster shows that the business of controlling a lunatic within the domestic sphere was riddled with severe difficulties for the family, and the family had to employ more forceful means to curb their troublesome member's disturbing behavior. Especially difficult and crucial problems were, first, how to control the lunatic's economic activities, most especially property transactions; and second, how to control the lunatic's behavior in public spaces. Next I examine these two kinds of problems and the family's struggles at the boundary of the private and public spheres.

Controlling Property Transaction of Lunatics

Rosa Bagster's commission of lunacy highlights the fact that the exercise of her civil rights—contracting a marriage—was the legal core of her family's concern. Other cases confirm that the major source of difficulty for families with a lunatic was the lunatic's economic activity, ranging from simple purchases and signing of small checks to the transaction of an estate. There was a variety of means to achieve some control on this front. The most primitive but effective one was not to give any pocket money to the lunatic. Mather R. Ebbing, formerly a prosperous merchant, had lived with his sister before he was put in a private madhouse. (Note again that this is a practice of domestic psychiatry discussed in chapter 4.) A servant to the family testified: "His sister took his purse. He used not to pay his own bills when I knew him, but his sister discharged them."[31] Likewise, Lord Portsmouth did not have the command of money. His first wife gave him pocket money only when necessary, and his second wife does not seem to have allowed him any money at all. Richard Jones, a gardener to Lord Portsmouth, testified that this nobleman with an annual income of £20,000 was badly in want of pocket money: "I never saw any money with his lordship; he has borrowed money of me."[32] Another simple solution was to deprive the lunatic of access to shops. Keeping a lunatic in a private madhouse served that purpose, as well as many others. Lady Charlotte Sherard was kept in a private asylum but does not seem to have been particularly violent or dangerous. When she wished to walk about, however, the medical attendant did not allow her to do so, "as she was so extravagantly disposed of money."[33] Confinement also could protect alleged lunatics from those who would have taken advantage of their incapacity. Richard Taylor explained that he removed his demented father "to prevent the persons about him from obtaining possession of his property."[34]

Yet another primitive but often vital means was the exercise of personal vigilance regarding the lunatic, especially over his or her economic activity. Rosa was said to have "never made a single purchase" during the whole course of her life and one of the governesses recalled that Rosa was so ignorant of the value of money that she would have paid a shilling or a sovereign for a yard of two-penny ribbon at a shop, if the governess had not been with her.[35] When Barbara White went to an ironmonger's shop in Oxford Street and wanted to purchase an iron bath to prevent people from seeing her, her clerk "motioned to the shopman not to serve her."[36] Although these examples sound rather minor, for the family they were ominous signs of more serious damage to the property. When Miss Louisa Ridge was found to have paid her poulterer's bill without inquiring the price of the articles she had purchased, one Mrs. Whitehead expressed her fear: "she was very imprudent in her domestic concerns, and it is my opinion that any designing person could have easily duped her out of property."[37] Minor lack of discipline in economic matters here suggested the possibility of disaster on a larger scale. Anxiety over possible huge damage to the property hovered over a lunatic at home.

In the case of Rosa Bagster, her daydreaming of elopement was far from the innocent fantasy of a young girl, for her romantic life was inseparably tied up with a property transaction that would accompany her marriage. As I suggested in chapter 4 using the cases of the Portsmouth family and the Jervis family, unmarried lunatics with large property that was unprotected by a commission of lunacy were a great hazard for their families. Such examples abounded. Sons of John Taylor requested a commission against their father, fearing, as one of them stated, that "his father might be prevailed upon to make a dozen wills in a day, or to sign any document."[38] The father's indiscriminate proposals of marriage to women he met alarmed the sons so much that they removed the father to a private madhouse (where he continued to be romantically inclined and made offers of marriage to the female superintendent on several occasions).[39] Young and weak-minded heiresses must have required particular attention lest they should be taken advantage of. A weak-minded heiress named Mary Hoy, who became the subject of a commission of lunacy in 1843, was forcefully abducted and "prevailed upon to execute some deed or marriage settlement" while detained.[40] In the case of commission of lunacy of Princess Bariatinski, another weak-minded heiress, a love-letter written by the princess to one Mr. Newman and her all-but-explicit proposal of marriage or sexual intercourse alarmed her family very much.[41] Rosa Bagster's mother was thus far from unique. Her anxiety to curb her weak-minded daughter's association with members of the opposite sex was shared by many who were in a similar situation.[42] Any hint of Rosa's unsupervised association with members of the opposite sex thus alarmed her mother. When Rosa expressed fondness for jewels and dresses or showed interest in how she looked or whether she was attractive to men, these apparently innocent and natural concerns were not just indications of Rosa's frivolity, but ominous signs of trouble for the family.[43] The hypersensitivity detected here reveals a kind of "siege mentality" held by the family. The world outside was full of danger and sources of financial peril: the lunatic might make extravagant purchases, or might make damaging property transactions, or he or she might be duped by unscrupulous persons into disasters. The home was regarded as the only safe place, within which the family entrenched itself. Home was not just an emotional haven, but the only secure place the family had in which to securely contain a lunatic.[44]

Families thus had to prevent a lunatic from being engaged in economic activities, from making relatively minor purchases to effecting large-scale property transactions. In some cases, however, they had to do the opposite: efforts were made to make the lunatic sign a check, execute a deed, and so on. In some cases, the family went so far as to force the lunatic to remain within the household to sign documents, for smooth running of the individual's or the family's business. One such case is that of John Peter Robinson, a large shareholder and the director of a number of commercial companies who became the subject of a commission in 1840.[45] At the time of the commission Robinson was seventy and married to a much younger wife. Owing to senile infirmity, Robinson could not manage his own affairs, and Mrs. Robinson did so on his behalf. Some of his relatives, who were also his business partners, did not welcome the marriage and the control exercised by Mrs. Robinson and sought a commission of lunacy against Robinson to overturn the arrangement set up by his wife. The manner in which Mrs. Robinson managed her husband's affairs was described by Alexander Morison as follows:

> Mrs. Robinson said to him . . . "you had better fill up a check to pay an account for wine for £14 odd shillings." At first Mr. Robinson did not do so, but on being again persuaded by Mrs. Robinson, he did so. . . . Mr. Robinson did not appear to understand what he was doing. When he had signed it I said to him "For what did you give the check?" He said "Oh for some charity—some business of Mrs. Robinson." This question was put to him about five minutes after the check was given.[46]

Obviously, he was "under the influence of" his young wife, as one of the counsels in support of the commission implied.[47]

Robinson was not an exceptional example. Robert Clement, a partner in the bank of Tugwell & Co., became old, senile, and incapable of carrying out the business. Like Mr. Robinson, he came under the care and control of other partners at the bank and of his wife at home. He was made to stay away from the bank; at the bank he issued instructions that were not followed; the clerks were told to ignore his orders and they put an old banking book before Clement "to amuse him."[48] One relative recalled that "he was so childish that we thought no more of him than a chair in the room."[49] Sometimes he was dictated to perform a particular piece of business when the family found it necessary. When people visited his home to do business with him, Mrs. Clement settled it and obtained her husband's signature when necessary. A niece of Clement recalled:

> I was directed by Mrs. Clement always to take care of Mr. Clement, and if any paper was to be signed, I had to tutor him for one hour previously, and particularly to tell him not to say any thing when the parties came; and with this tutoring we had great difficulty to get him to do it. I have known him to refuse for half an hour, and say he did not know what it was all about. This occurred from time to time during the whole time I lived with Mr. and Mrs. Clement. He signed several papers, the contents of which I did not know, nor did he. Mrs. Clement used to say to him, "Mr. Clement, when Mr. Mackenzie or Mr. Gunter comes with the papers, don't you ask questions as to what they are about? They are merely papers which require your signature, and you will only expose yourself." His general remark was, "What's all this about? I dare say it's all right."[50]

To treat him as if he were a chair in the room seems to have presented less trouble than to make the chair into an automaton that could sign business documents. Lunatics at home were not just confined or taken care of, but sometimes they were required to engage with the outside world. The difficulties experienced by Mrs. Robinson and Mrs. Clement in making their husbands transact business highlight the economic aspects of the problems faced by families that had to contain lunatics.

The manners in which Mrs. Robinson and Mrs. Clement instructed their respective mentally incapacitated husbands must have been fairly common at that time. Actually, there existed a word, *tutoring,* to describe the practice of instructing the lunatic what to do. What the two wives did was a typical example of tutoring. The tutoring was done through the power of one person over the patient: the use of personal influence to make the patient tractable and obedient. (Thus it had a clear resemblance to moral treatment.) Lady Portsmouth and Dr. Combe, the able domestic managers of lunatics I described in chapter 4, were good at tutoring. At the beginning of the twenty-first century, we naturally look askance at this practice of tutoring: tutoring weak-minded persons into signing checks seems ethically dubious, at the very least. The key question here is not what we think of the act, but whether the early Victorian family and its contemporaries saw their act of tutoring in that light. Indeed, there existed a significant overlap between tutoring and the personal control of the insane. Their boundaries seem to have been very ambiguous. Much praise was given to the first Lady Portsmouth and John Combe for exercising personal control over the affairs of the weak-minded lord, including his financial affairs. Likewise, when the second Earl of Eldon had become incapable of managing his own affairs due to old age, his wife "had managed the property of her husband, and had also managed him with great affection and tact."[51] The death of his wife deprived Eldon of the protection of personal control and necessitated a commission of lunacy. The irony is that the second Earl of Eldon was himself a lawyer and a grandson of the first Earl of Eldon, who had occupied the office of Lord Chancellor and had presided over numerous commissions of lunacy. Personal control and informal tutoring, rather than obtaining a commission, was the measure adopted by the family at the pinnacle of the legal profession in England.[52] Moreover, R. A. Houston has pointed out that in eighteenth-century Scotland, it was regarded as a duty of a wife to conceal her husband's incapacity. Alexander Monro Primus, the first of the medical dynasty of Edinburgh, wrote: "The woman who sordidly marries a fool ought never to be guilty of the gross folly of shewing him away in his proper character. It is her duty and interest to conceal his weakness."[53] The tutoring of Robinson and Clement shared the same pattern of the wife attempting to contain the damage caused by the husband's insanity and controlling his property transactions.

The wives of Robinson and Clement were performing their duty of preventing their husbands from "exposing themselves" and carrying on the business for their incapacitated husbands. What was wrong, in the view of their contemporaries, was the ways in which they tutored their respective husbands. Mrs. Clement's obvious lack of tact and some cruel remarks and coarse behavior directed against her husband shocked many of his relatives: asking for powerful medicines for her husband without letting a surgeon see the patient, making him sign a contract without explaining the content to him, and openly calling her husband "a great fool"—these must have seemed a tactless and overly coarse way to tutor the insane patient.[54] The major fault of Mrs. Clement seems to have been that she exposed her husband's lunacy in an unacceptable way: she almost insulted her lunatic husband in public. It was not her tutoring itself, but her indiscreet and clumsy ways of handling the business of tutoring that was criticized. What was of utmost importance was to maintain a decent appearance and achieve a semblance of normality. The strange behavior or inability of the person in question should be controlled, but it should be done in a discreet way. Too direct or too forceful a control would actually expose the mental disease. The rules of the game were subtle indeed.

The Perils of Public Space

Breaches of ordinary standards of behavior by a lunatic in public spaces were liable to cause serious embarrassment for the family. Serious misconduct at church, one of the most important public places at that time, was especially likely to embarrass the family.[55] The family of Solomon Cohen thought that his serious departure from a rule of Jewish religious ritual was "the first positive indication of his insanity."[56] The family of Lord Suffolk, who took care of Princess Bariatinski, were so shocked when the weak-minded princess laughed, put out her tongue, and made faces at church, that they stopped allowing her to attend services. Likewise, they were deeply embarrassed when the princess tied up her garters and pulled up her skirt in the street.[57]

The family's embarrassment at people's attention to the antics of lunatics had a very concrete form—a crowd. The antics of the insane on the street attracted people, who gathered to form a "crowd" to watch the lunatic. People stopped to look at Princess Bariatinski tying up her garter. Andrew Mitchell Campbell, who became the subject of a commission in 1842, went to Oxford Street wearing only his pantaloon, and a crowd gathered around him.[58] Miss Clayton, a governess of Rosa Bagster, remembered that her charge's violent and strange behavior assembled a crowd everywhere they went:

> I accompanied Mrs. and Miss Bagster, in August last, on a tour to the West of England. . . . In the course of this tour, Miss Bagster conducted herself very violently; and at Lauceston, she tore her mother's bonnet, also Mrs. Horn's bonnet and dress, and threw the reticule, and her mother's watch, out of the carriage window. We were not got out of the town at the time, and a crowd assembled. . . . It was 9 o'clock when we got to Holdsworthy, and it was past 11 before we could get her into the inn. Miss Bagster attempted to kick [the] witness, but was restrained by some persons in the crowd which had assembled. Miss Bagster laughed at the crowd, and asked what they were staring at her for. . . . When we were about to leave, a great crowd of persons had assembled to see her, in consequence of her conduct on the preceding evening. . . . [In Dover, she] suddenly rushed upon her mother, tore her hair, and threw her shoes and other articles out of the window into the street. On the quays also she behaved and conducted herself in a most violent manner before all the spectators. . . . At New Romney, I believe, she behaved in a most childish manner, and the passengers laughed at her, and inquired if she was in her senses.[59]

Through these repeated embarrassments, the governess was painfully aware that outside the protected private space of a carriage or a room in the inn, there existed an open public space with curious people who would quickly assemble to look and laugh at the lunatic.

As is suggested in the passage just quoted ("We were not got out of the town at the time . . ."), urban spaces were particularly full of curious people. In such situations, cabs or carriages provided a haven of privacy. When John Brome insulted and struck women at York Place and Bond Street and collected a crowd around him, Sir Charles Aldis, his relative and medical attendant, "had to get him into a cab and took him home."[60] The private space of a carriage or a cab was precarious, however. When in a commission of lunacy the commissioners examined an alleged lunatic in her carriage, "the circumstance soon attracted a crowd, to know 'the rights' of the matter."[61] When Princess Bariatinski misbehaved on the street, she was put in a carriage but would "laugh out of the windows in such a manner that people would frequently stop to look at her"[62] Even a private house circumscribed by its walls had windows, which were open to the world outside. Mrs. Catherine Jennings, a lunatic widow with a large property, lived in Windsor. When the castle was illuminated in honor of the marriage of Queen Victoria, she "got out of bed, and remained an hour and a-half standing at the window looking into the street, causing a mob of 200 or 300 persons to assemble, with nothing on but her night chemise."[63] The regularity with which references to the assembling of curious people appear in statements testifies to the feelings of shame and embarrassment these attentions evoked. As is evident in Middleton's attempt at keeping his mad mother as remote as possible from those who knew him and his family, the family lived in dread lest their insane member be seen *in their presence.* The extent to which they would go in an attempt to prevent their insane or weak-minded member from attracting attention was often staggering. The family of George Smith, a wealthy farmer near Birmingham, moved to a remoter part of the village in search of invisibility. There the family literally bricked up the window of the room in which George was kept. George Booth was a weak-minded eldest son of a well-known and opulent distiller in Cow Cross Street, and the heir to property to the amount of between £300,000 and £400,000. The clerk to his father's distilling company stated, "he was not allowed to go out alone, and perhaps he had never walked 10 rods [i.e., approx. fifty meters] about the streets of London in his life."

When there was no attempt by the family to contain the lunatic's behavior within private spaces and curb its exhibition, chaos could ensue. Such was the case with Daniel Gundry, an insane gentleman of means living in Albany. He had long been a notoriously tumultuous person, "whose name has so frequently figured before the public in the police reports."[64] When his wife, who had been continually abused and tortured by him since marriage, finally left him, he was left entirely on his own: "[he] sat upon the [horse] opposite the door for an hour and a quarter, making the most extraordinary gesticulations all the time. He collected a crowd of about 200 persons round him, and it was eventually found necessary to send for the police to disperse them. . . . Latterly, whenever he went out on horseback, he was followed by a mob calling after him, 'There goes mad Gundry.'"[65] A similar situation took place in the case of Miss Caney, who was a spinster older than eighty, came from a highly respectable family, and possessed considerable property. Because of her inability to manage her own affairs, she was without any regular servant, and left completely to the mercy of the crowd. The counsel for the commission stated: "[From] the state in which she permits her house to be, she has become the object of daring cupidity, so much so, that the police felt it necessary to be doubly vigilant in respect to her residence. . . . In consequence of the extraordinary mode of life adopted by the poor lady, the house was constantly beset by all the idle vagabonds of the neighborhood, and she was caricatured as 'the old miser,' 'the old witch,' etc." A woman who resided nearby and took occasional care of her reported the horrible state she was put into: "Mobs have for the last two years continually assembled and pelted both Miss Caney and [the] witness. Miss Caney fancies that the people come out of respect to her."[66]

The mobs and crowds mentioned in the testimonies were highly and openly interested in watching lunatics, unlike most of us, who, when passing by a lunatic on the street, try our best to ignore him or her or to assume indifference. Lunatics' antic and eccentric behavior easily became the talk of the town. One Captain Baker, who became the subject of a commission in Cheltenham in 1837, was reported "to have for some time [become a subject of] much notice and observation in that town and also in Bath."[67] Actually, the court of the commission of lunacy itself was often crowded with curious members of the public who wanted to watch the alleged lunatic. Whether the show was on the street or in the courtroom, the public enjoyed the sight of lunatics.[68] Indeed, the very source this book relies on—the newspaper reports of commissions of lunacy—draws on the curiosity about lunacy among the nineteenth-century British public, as well as on a more sober sympathy for a victim of a dreaded disease.

The crowd was, however, far from just curious, searching for the entertainment of a freak show. As the social history of the "mob" and popular movements has clarified, the crowd in the eighteenth and nineteenth centuries had its own sense of justice and morality. Assemblies around a lunatic often mobilized themselves into a defense of the rights of a free-born Englishman.[69] Accordingly, when they believed that a wrongful confinement was going to take place, they actively frustrated the attempt. G. M. Burrows explained as follows: "It frequently happens, in removing a lunatic from one place to another, that he is very violent, or endeavours, by making artful appeals to those near him, to attract their attention, and raise a feeling to rescue him. In such a case, the populace are almost always sure to side with the lunatic, and sometimes liberate him."[70] It is almost certain that Burrows had frequently experienced the crowd's intervention. When keepers of his asylum attempted to move Edward Davies from Furnival's Inn Coffee House to Davies's own house at the request of Davies's mother, the coach was stopped by people at the coffeehouse, and only by producing a faked certificate of lunacy signed by Burrows could the coach go on.[71] Similar scenes appeared also in fiction. In *The Mysteries of the Madhouse,* an anonymous work of fiction published in 1847 that dealt with the wrongful confinement of a young gentleman, such an action by a crowd was depicted: a coach arrived at an inn; an appeal was made by the alleged lunatic to people around him; people assembled, interrogated the situation, and showed their readiness to rescue the alleged lunatic, who was about to be wrongfully confined.[72] In the early nineteenth-century landscape of psychiatry, an alleged lunatic often appealed for help to strangers in public places, and the people on the street often intervened on behalf of the lunatic. From the viewpoint of the family (and the doctor), therefore, there existed in public spaces the danger of the disruption and frustration of their control over the lunatic. On the other hand, seen from the lunatic's viewpoint, a public space meant a greater chance to escape the family's control, for strangers around might come to rescue him or her from the grip of the family. When faced with the threat of confinement by the keepers sent by Burrows, Freeman Anderdon sought the help of his neighbors, and Edward Davies acted similarly: both of them had an intuitive trust in the sense of justice of the crowd. Perhaps the protesting Rosa Bagster might have been vaguely aware of the vulnerability of her family in public places, sensing that she could embarrass the family more effectively by carrying on her struggle in the open. She might even have understood that the crowd was a potential enemy of her family's and a potential ally of hers. In short, the crowd assembling around lunatics in public places exacerbated the family's trouble, either by deepening its embarrassment or by frustrating its attempt to control the lunatic. Public places presented multiple perils to the family.

Those expressions of deep embarrassment and the resulting "siege mentality" are telling evidence of the keen sense of boundaries between the public and the private spheres. Strange behavior within the private sphere of a home, a carriage, or a room in an inn were tolerated to a certain extent, whereas similar behavior in public places caused deep embarrassment to the family. Figures of lunacy should be seen only by members of the direct family, relatives, and perhaps close friends, but not by strangers. The *Times* wrote in an editorial in 1867 that "[the] strange humours and escapades of such [eccentric] persons are usually screened by the kindly instinct of relations from the notice of strangers."[73]

The major difficulty was thus that of keeping up the semblance of normality to the world outside. The families attempted to contain the disorder caused by their lunatic members within the domain of the private, trying to prevent the disturbances from being *noticed* by the public. They were thus engaged on two fronts simultaneously: internally, intensely policing the mad behavior of their insane members; and externally, pretending that there was no problem within. The "fencing" of Rosa Bagster by putting women connected to her family on each side of her epitomizes this duplicity. The granddaughter of the Lord Mayor should be present at the dinner table, keeping what must already have been a slim pretension that she was normal. At the same time, she had to be prevented from exposing herself in socially unacceptable ways to members of the opposite sex. Similar examples abound. The "tutoring" wives of the senile bankers discussed earlier were keeping up the slim pretence of normalcy of their husbands. As the case of Barbara White shows, when a lunatic was about to make an extravagant purchase in a shop, the attendant should motion to the shopkeeper not to serve him or her: a straightforward indication that the person was a lunatic was not to be made. When a young epileptic man had a fit in a park, his accompanying father was worried "lest a vast crowd should be gathered" and pretended "as though we were lying on the grass." This father was no other than the seventh Earl of Shaftesbury, who insisted that every lunatic should be put under the public eye of the Lunacy Commissioners.[74] The means to reconcile the two opposite demands of normal appearance and effective coercion were quite limited, and the room for maneuver for the family was equally small. The tension of coping with the disorder and coercion inside and sustaining the pretence of normalcy outside must often have been great, and sometimes unbearable, even to the controlling families themselves.

The lengths to which a family with an insane member went in its attempt to hide the problems away from public view and to maintain a fiction of normalcy is eloquent evidence of the strength of the Victorian myth of the family as a private haven of free individuals. As D. A. Miller has argued, the liberal myth of the family as the sphere of freedom and spontaneous feeling was maintained at considerable cost, and its public survival was made possible only by the close surveillance of the signs of transgression of the individuals and by the coarse suppression of attempts at rebellion.[75] Controlling lunatics within the family meant not just the intense policing of the domestic sphere, but the simultaneous pretence of the *absence* of such policing directed toward the world outside. The dramatis personae of the cases analyzed in this chapter were essentially playing this double game of control and its denial. The recurrence of the same pattern of this paradoxical—or even impossible—enterprise of the domestic psychiatric regime reminds us how pervasive the myth of the free private sphere was and how high a price families were willing to pay to keep the myth intact.

For many of us, this sounds like a typically Victorian form of hypocrisy, a blatant inability to accept things as they really were.[76] One might even be tempted to accuse the family of sinister control: the web it spun around its mentally disabled member, inside and outside of the home, was all the more effective and hard to point out because it was discreet and all but invisible. And there is, to be sure, some truth to this argument. Most important, this argument reminds us of how pervasive the control of lunatics was in early nineteenth-century England. Some historians, inspired with the fervent naiveté of the radicalism of the 1960s and 1970s, came to regard institutions—asylums, hospitals, and private madhouses—as places of psychiatric management, coercion, and suppression. Such a historiography tacitly assumes that the world outside the walls of institutions was a land of freedom. This view is grossly simplistic. As I have been emphasizing in this and previous chapters, there existed another form of control over the insane *outside* the walls of the asylum. Unlike the power of psychiatrists, the controlling practices exercised by the family have largely escaped the attention of historians, just as they were hidden from contemporaries. This was so exactly because they were meant to be so. Concealing both the embarrassing antics of lunatics and the ugly sight of coercion was the basic rule of the game. The family did not trumpet its ingenious ways of containing the insane in published monographs and articles, nor did the family's power of managing the mad mind take the visible form of the high walls and brick and mortar of the institutions. Nudging gently (or not so gently) a senile husband into signing a check, nodding meaningfully to a clerk in a shop, putting a girl between two women at a dinner party—they were all subtle, makeshift, fragile, but effective means of containing the disruptive behavior of insanity. To put it another way, when sent to an asylum, the patient was transplanted from one form of control to another form, from a discreet and invisible one to an obvious and solid one.

The examples I have analyzed in this chapter also compel us to rethink, if not reject, the view that emphasizes increasing intolerance of disruptive behavior within the domestic sphere as the driving force that lay behind the rise of the asylum. Inspired by Norbert Elias, many historians have seen the rise of psychiatric institutions in the light of the "civilizing process," which commanded people to suppress their instincts and behave in polite ways.[77] As the code of behavior became more stringent, the argument goes, people became increasingly intolerant toward the family member's strange behaviors that were induced by mental disease. Nancy Tomes has presented the most recent and sophisticated application of this model to her study of the Pennsylvania Hospital for the Insane in the nineteenth century. Tomes has linked the committal of a patient to the asylum with heightened expectations for the emotional satisfaction the family was to give: "[as] more significance came to be attached to the quality of emotional relationships, the 'perversions' of familial affections found in insanity became more ominous."[78] This is certainly an important point, which is, at the very least, plausible.

My examples suggest, however, a more complicated picture: not the disruptive behavior per se, but the *exposure* of such behavior to the eyes of the public, troubled the family most acutely.[79] They tolerated, to a considerable extent, the antic and violent behavior of an insane member of the family so long as such behavior was contained within the private sphere. On the other hand, the level of their tolerance in the public sphere seems to have been considerably lower. The family's tolerance toward the insanity of its member was thus conditioned by its desire to present to the world outside a façade of normalcy, domestic peace, and the lack of coercion within. The high expectations for the emotional integrity of the home, which Tomes has regarded as the key factor in psychiatric committal, were only one component of the dynamic lowering the tolerance of the family. In the final analysis, hypocrisy, not domestic affection per se, loomed large in my research findings as the major source of trouble that befell the family.

So long as the family deliberately tried to make its difficulties invisible, it might justly be charged with hypocrisy. We can look at the situation from a different angle, however. All the personal vigilance, restrictive means, and small tricks were indeed constraining, but they all enabled the lunatics to achieve a semblance of normality, without drastically changing their status. With some help, the subnormal could assume the appearance of a normal life, and the defenders of the family might plausibly claim that what was provided was exactly the help that was necessary: protection from possible dangers, either external or self-inflicted. In the process, the family blurred the distinction between the normal and the subnormal. The neat distinction of sanity and insanity, epitomized in institutionalization, the certificate of lunacy, or the commission of lunacy, was not the logic that was exercised in the world of domestic psychiatry. The family employed an elastic measure of normalcy.

DOMESTICITY AS THE SOURCE OF DESTABILIZATION

So far in this chapter I have followed a framework that posits a dichotomy: the threat of exposure in the public sphere and the logic of containment in the private sphere. The family had to be vigilant vis-à-vis the world outside, whether this amounted to the intrusion of the curious public or the possible damage caused by an infelicitous business transaction. The boundary between inside and outside was, in an important sense, the major line of defense of the domestic psychiatric regime. Now I turn to an examination of the threat to the self-contained domestic psychiatric regime that came *from within.* The cases I have chosen to allow us to examine such dynamics are those of Edward Frank, George Davenport, and Lawrence Ruck, all of whom were the heads of their households or the masters of their houses at the time of their respective commissions. The following cases thus could be read as evidence of how the new Victorian ideal made the head of the family vulnerable to a charge of insanity.

The Case of Edward Frank

The commission of lunacy against Edward Frank, a clergyman of the Church of England in Yorkshire, highlights some key problems associated with the lunacy of the master of the household. Certainly by Victorian standards, Frank was an epitome of perverse debauchery. Reports of his case sound exactly like a contemporary pornographic novel: the clergyman knowingly let an itinerant rupture doctor live and sleep with his wife, while Frank was indulging himself with a succession of prostitutes.[80] Even worse, these acts were barely hidden from the clergymen's children, or even from the public.[81] The huge commission, with its salacious details of the shocking debauchery and perversity of a clergyman of the Established Church with an income of £8,000 a year from his estate, provided a nonfictional pornography, echoing the case of Lord Portsmouth, which had taken place only two years before.

The process by which the problem of this wayward clergyman was drawn into the world outside his family circle illuminates both the strength and the vulnerability of the master of the house. Relatives of Frank tried to intervene soon after they heard rumors of adultery and debauchery. One Captain Mainwaring, Frank's brother-in-law, tried to put an end to the situation, which he found "of so disgusting nature and so ruinous and destructive to his family." However, Captain Mainwaring had a very difficult mission. As the head of the family, legally speaking Frank had every right to manage his own affairs and those of his family exactly as he wished. There was no easy or routine way to intervene in the domestic problems of a family, even when the master's behavior deviated from accepted norms. The captain thus tried personal and informal intervention first. After having talked separately with Frank and his wife in 1816, he succeeded in making Frank promise to divorce his wife and never to see her again; a deed of separation was signed in January 1817.[82] The testimony of Mainwaring suggests abundant use of coaxing, confrontation, bullying, and intimidation to achieve this end. When it turned out that Frank, his wife, and the rupture doctor carried on just as before, a commission of lunacy was requested.[83] Nine years had passed between the captain's initial intervention and the beginning of the commission. There must have been many moral, psychological, and legal barriers to be overcome before Frank's relatives finally decided to go to the extreme length of a commission of lunacy. This time they had to wash the dirty family linen in front of a national audience, instead of just those in the immediate locality.

During the commission, Frank's relatives faced another potential difficulty: the lack of any hard evidence of "lunacy." This aspect of the case will be dealt with more fully in the next chapter. Here I would simply emphasize that the counsel for the commission laid great stress on Frank's failure to act as a master of the household should. The crux of the problem was, as the counsel stated, that Frank let his wife's lover "get complete control over Mr. Frank, his wife, children, and even his property."[84] The adulterous affair of Mrs. Frank was represented not just as a breach of sexual morality but as the husband's abandoning of his patriarchal authority over his wife's body. Letting his wife commit adultery also signaled the abandonment of the patriarchal responsibility to ensure the transmission of the family property along the legitimate line. The fact that the couple did not hide their debaucheries from their children was frequently mentioned as evidence of Frank's inability to act as a patriarchal guide to his children. Such demonstrable inability to act as a patriarch amounted, or so the logic went, to lunacy or unsoundness of mind. No doubt, sheer visceral disgust toward this libertine clergyman must have been the major reason for the unanimous verdict of lunacy against Frank. It is important to note, nonetheless, that the logic for the commission was constructed along the lines of his failure to act as a proper patriarch.

The Case of George Davenport

The commission of lunacy against George Davenport presents a logic very different from that employed in the commission against Edward Frank. Once more, an outsider intervened in the family to argue that its head was incapable of managing his own affairs. This time, however, the bone of contention was whether the subject of the commission treated his wife with due affection.

George Davenport inherited a sum of £20,000 from his father in 1834.[85]

He had been an active member of the Society for Promoting Christian Knowledge at Stoke Newington, where he met Frances, a daughter of a laceman. Frances's father apparently did not give any fortune to his daughter, which suggests that the wife's social status was much lower than the husband's.[86] They married in May 1837, and for a few months the marriage was a happy one. In July, however, Davenport's religious interests started to became excessive: he heard a voice from heaven; he planned to build at his cost an inn in Scotland to prevent drunkenness and Sabbath-breaking; he donated to the Bishop of Sodor and Man a sum of £6,000. Within a few months, his property was reduced to £10,000, half of what he had inherited.[87] His exorbitant activity was accompanied by a zealous denunciation of personal property. He started to break his furniture and belongings, such as a dessert service and ornaments of painted glass: "He turned round, and taking two ornaments of painted glass which were on the mantleshelf in his hands, he said—'Now, these are my property,' and, breaking them, added 'Now they are God's.'"[88] Reading a passage from the twenty-third chapter of Deuteronomy, he looked up and said, "It most forcibly strikes me that a water-closet in a house is an abomination to the Lord," and later made a plumber tear out the bathroom in his house.[89]

Mrs. Davenport was not entirely happy about the religious zeal exhibited by her husband, while he in turn regarded her unwillingness to follow his example as the sign of her vanity. In the house, he put up a large board on which was written, "Christ says except ye repent, ye shall all likewise perish. . . . Sinner! dost thou repent thee of thy sin?"—which was almost certainly intended for his wife. He complained that his wife "was looking too much after things of this world, and instead of going to Canaan, they were all going back to Egypt." At a family prayer, he said "I am surrounded by evil spirits. I cannot love my wife—she is proud."[90] His wife's family was alarmed at his excessive zeal and his antagonistic attitude to her, and tried to intervene on her behalf. Davenport did not give in, and prohibited his wife from associating with her friends, whom he thought were tempting her to sin.[91] A niece of Mrs. Davenport described what she called the husband's "extraordinary conduct towards his wife": "when she was lying on the sofa very ill, he made her get up and walk to a chapel at Islington, a distance of two miles."[92] When his wife was unwell and near her confinement, the husband did not call medical advice, because physicians, like water-closets, were "an abomination to the Lord" in Mr. Davenport's mind. Learning this, Ann Mason, who was Mrs. Davenport's sister, confronted George Davenport forcefully and insisted that Mrs. Davenport should have medical advice. Davenport, however, was adamant in his belief that his wife's ill health was caused by her own intemperance and sin.[93] After these attempts at private dealing had failed, Mrs. Davenport's father finally petitioned for a commission of lunacy. Legal details for this action are not available, but in some respects it may have been similar to that of Rosa Bagster, a commission to dissolve the marriage by proving that the subject was *non compos mentis* at the time of the marriage. The son of the late Bishop of Sodor and Man, who had received £6,000 from Davenport after the marriage, opposed the commission, because its success meant that the transaction could be nullified.

In his personal examination, Davenport did not exhibit any symptoms that were even remotely similar to a delusion. He was just firm in his belief that he had acted according to the teachings of the Bible when he destroyed the dessert-service and the water-closet in his house, and when he made a large donation to the Bishop of Sodor and Man. Nevertheless, the jury in the end concluded that Davenport was of unsound mind. Quite understandably, the success of the commission of lunacy against Davenport was narrow—the verdict of unsoundness was made only on a vote of fourteen of twenty jurors. This case must have posed particular difficulty, even with the employment of a flexible criterion of "unsound mind." Davenport did not show any signs of immorality, nor had he done any harm to others in an irresponsible way. The motives for his unusual behavior, as he proclaimed them, were religion, philanthropy, and a fervent desire to follow the will of God, all of which were highly regarded principles at that time. Nor did he display any signs of hysterical or enthusiastic religiosity. Most important, unlike the Frank case, the Davenport case did not fit into the pattern of failure in patriarchal authority. Actually, the crux of this case involved a wife who was not following the guidance of her husband. Admittedly, the husband was trying to guide his wife into an extremely narrow and difficult path of the strict renunciation of everything that he thought was a disgrace to God. But there was no stereotypical physical cruelty to the wife. Davenport did reproach his wife, but it is questionable whether that amounted to mental cruelty, which was to become a valid reason for separation and divorce after the crucial case of *Kelly v. Kelly* in 1870.[94]

Against all these odds, the commission was successful. Many witnesses' emphasis on Davenport's stern attitude toward his wife certainly contributed to the decision by showing that Davenport did not obey the ethos of companionate marriage as a contract for mutual comfort and domestic happiness.[95] It shows that the legal machinery provided by a commission of lunacy could enable people outside the family to challenge the authority of a husband over his wife, *when the husband did not treat the wife with due affection.* It is also important to note that the commission of lunacy against Davenport was requested for in order to obtain a divorce by proving the insanity of the husband. In at least three other cases I have found, the commission was closely linked to the purpose of divorce: the case of Lord Portsmouth in 1823, the case of Edward Frank in 1825 (as mentioned earlier), and perhaps the case of Daniel Gundry in 1842.[96] Although they differed considerably from each other with respect to the nature of the domestic troubles and the motives of the petitioners, they all testify to the role played by an allegation of lunacy in achieving the difficult goal of securing an annulment of marriage before the Divorce Act in 1858.

The Case of Lawrence Ruck

The connection between the decision to seek a commission of lunacy and an attempt to secure a divorce is even more striking in the commission of lunacy against Lawrence Ruck in 1858, which lasted for five days, with extensive coverage in the *Times.*[97] Whereas the commission against Frank was requested by his heirs and that against Davenport was sought by his father-in-law, the Ruck case was initiated by his wife herself. The Ruck case was remarkable also because the alleged damages arising from his lunacy were visited only upon his wife. The core part of Mrs. Ruck's petition for the commission consisted in complaints about her husband's defamation of her character. Ruck believed, without any evidence or reason, that his wife had committed adultery with numerous men, and he made slanderous (and totally groundless) claims to his relatives and friends about his wife's conduct.[98] At the very moment when he started to slander his wife, it transpired that Ruck himself had entered into a long-term adulterous relationship with one Mary Jones, a cousin of Mrs. Ruck, an affair that resulted in the birth of two illegitimate children. Although the episode of Mary Jones was never made the central part of the allegation that Ruck was mad, the very frequent mention witnesses made of Jones during the course of their testimony suggests that the (actual) adultery between her husband and Jones played a major role in motivating Mrs. Ruck to ask for the commission.

The problem for Mrs. Ruck was that the basis for her allegation of her husband's unsoundness of mind was very slim. Its core argument was that her husband's slanders were the products of delusion. In all other respects, he was only mildly disruptive and threatening. The greatest obstacle to the success of the commission was that he was at the time of the hearing completely composed and sober, and, when he appeared in court, exhibited no symptoms of lunacy or unsoundness of mind. There could be little doubt in the mind of the jury about his sanity at the time of the commission. Numerous doctors who had been sent by the commissioner to examine him stated their full conviction of his sanity. Virtually the only exception to the consensus was John Conolly, who articulated an intricate argument about his mental state and testified for a still hidden trace of lunacy in him.[99] When the jury returned the verdict, twelve voted for Ruck's sanity, and the remaining six dissented.[100]

Thus, on the surface, the wife's attempt to prove her husband's insanity and to annul the marriage failed. One should not assume, however, that the cause of the wronged wife was dismissed outright. It is noteworthy that six out of eighteen jurymen did not support the husband's sanity. This is even more remarkable when one considers that the commissioner repeatedly insisted that the jury's verdict should be based solely on the present state of Ruck, whose sanity was convincingly established by his own performance at court, as well as through the testimony of the majority of the medical witnesses. Moreover, the commissioner himself expressed almost unconditional sympathy for Ruck's wife and urged the jurymen to do the same: "He could not help thinking that, whatever the verdict of the jury might be, they must feel deep sympathy with the petitioner. Few cases in his (the Commissioner's) experience had appeared to him so painful as that of this lady, Mrs. Ruck. Evidence the most ample had been given in her behalf to show that she was an affectionate wife."[101] This remark of the commissioner, as well as numerous other aspects of the proceedings, shows that the possibility or desirability of declaring Ruck of unsound mind was seriously contemplated. Moreover, the commissioner acknowledged that Ruck's violent slandering of his wife was undoubtedly a product of a delusion. If the commission had been sought at that moment, Ruck would have certainly been declared insane. Or, if the commissioner had asked the jury to judge Ruck's state of mind in the past, the commission would almost certainly have been successful.[102] Ruck escaped that verdict only through his subsequent recovery, and, perhaps, the repentant attitude he assumed in court. When a man breached the domestic code of behavior and acted toward his wife in a way that was intolerable to her, he put himself in serious danger of being declared unable to manage his own affairs.

All the cases of Frank, Davenport, and Ruck attest to the importance of domestic behavior in decisions about someone's sanity. Note that the witnesses testifying in Frank's commission repeatedly emphasized his complete lack of concern about the influence of his and his wife's conduct on the morality of their children. The clergyman's inability to perform a father's duty of supervising the moral education of his children was represented as evidence of his insanity. His letting his wife conduct adultery with the rupture doctor was used as evidence of his inability to perform a husband's duty to exercise control over his wife. (Following the typical double standard of the time, his own debauchery—openly sleeping with prostitutes—received only a passing mention during the commission.) Witnesses emphasized that Frank let the rupture doctor usurp the place of the master of the house, both sexually and financially. In short, Frank's sexual misconduct was represented not as a type of sexual perversity but as his failure to perform the master's duty within his family. He should be deemed a lunatic, the argument went, not because of the sexual misconduct per se, but because of his failure to play the proper role of father and husband.

In the Davenport case, the importance of domestic virtues as the measure of sanity was even greater. The emphasis has shifted, however, from patriarchal authority to affective attitude in companionate marriage. Davenport's "lunacy" consisted almost solely in his failure to treat his wife with due affection. In the representations made in court, his exorbitant charity and excessive religiosity were given less emphasis, while witnesses focused on his "cruelty" toward his wife. Although the success of the commission was a narrow one, Davenport was declared to be a lunatic essentially because he did not behave toward his wife as the Victorian domestic code expected a husband to do. As for the case of Ruck, his escape from the verdict of insanity was as narrow as Davenport's failure to do so. His grave insults directed toward his wife almost cost him his civil rights, and certainly would have done so if the commission had been sought earlier.

While the commission of lunacy of Edward Frank reiterates the importance of the old code of patriarchal responsibility, those of George Davenport and Lawrence Ruck thus reveal the new vulnerability of the head of a household: even if he did not show stereotypical symptoms of madness, he could be held to be of unsound mind and of being incapable of managing his own affairs on the basis of his inability to act as an affectionate husband should. The cases of Davenport and Ruck also show that a commission of lunacy gave the wife and her sympathizers an option to solve the problems she confronted through declaring her husband to be insane. This was also the case with William Augustus Newton, a successful solicitor who became the subject of a commission in 1841. His wife asked for the commission partly because "he conducted himself with considerable violence towards his wife without apparent cause."[103] A glaring failure to show affection towards his wife when it was due was a symptom of insanity frequently alluded to by the witnesses in the case. The evidence for the insanity of James Smith included his treatment of his wife "with great insult and indignity" and his false accusations of her infidelity. William Bartlett's malady was first noticed when he paid no attention to his wife's pregnancy but "became sulky and appeared to be in a state of perfect apathy and ignorance of what was going forward at the time of her accouchement." One witness testified that "[This] naturally excited alarm in the breasts of his friends," and medical assistance was called.[104] Likewise, lack of paternal affection toward one's children was often regarded as a sign of insanity. Such was the case of H. Mayo, who treated his children with utmost cruelty. Particularly alarming to the family members was his assistance at the post-mortem examination of his own children.[105] One's attitudes toward servants and animals of the household also were used as a yardstick of one's sanity. As I discussed in chapter 1, Lord Portsmouth's morbid cruelty toward the servants and horses was emphasized during the course of the trial. Likewise, James King's disease was noticed when his conduct toward the inferior beings in the household changed: "[before] this illness, he had been . . . peculiarly kind to his servants, and humane to his horses; but since his illness he had been directly the reverse of this."[106]

These cases thus confirm some recent arguments about the nature of Victorian masculinity. John Tosh and A. James Hammerton have argued that the establishment of the notion of the separate spheres put strong demands on men as well as women. With the Evangelical emphasis on the domestic haven as the bastion of morality and a safeguard against social dislocation, rigorous codes of behavior were imposed on *both* men *and* women. From the early nineteenth century on, domestic behavior—attitudes toward one's wife and one's children—became another important part of the middle-class masculine identity. Tosh summarizes the change succinctly: "The Victorians articulated an ideal of home against which men's conduct has been measured ever since."[107] In such circumstances, male as well as female domestic behavior came under close scrutiny by other family members and outsiders. If it fell short of now heightened expectations, there was a danger that a man might be declared insane and lose his civil rights.

The link between the cultivation of private virtues and qualification for public roles was as old as the Greeks and the Romans, and was revived by humanists during the Renaissance. Stoics and Neo-Stoics maintained that the cultivation of private virtues was a prerequisite for a man's claim to public recognition.[108] What seems to be novel in the nineteenth century is the intensity with which the private behavior of the male head of the family was scrutinized by *others,* not just by himself. Wives, children, relatives, in-laws, and outsiders, as well as the man himself, were now measuring his behavior against the standard of a domestic ideal. If they were dissatisfied, they could take some measures to change the situation. Undoubtedly they took recourse to more informal means—gently soliciting a husband to change his behavior. Admittedly, cases that ended in a commission of lunacy were very rare. One should keep in mind that Mrs. Davenport and Mrs. Ruck must have been only the tip of a huge iceberg of women who suffered under husbands whose cruelty approached or even constituted insanity, without any means of legal redress. Nevertheless, these cases reveal men's new vulnerability, as well as a hitherto little noticed role for psychiatric labeling, where it was employed for a wife's benefit.

To conclude this chapter, I should like to pick up one thread that I have not sufficiently emphasized in my argument earlier: both the presence and the absence of gender differences in the construction of madness within domestic settings. First, the cases I have analyzed in this chapter should remind us that the madness of both males and females was a gendered cultural construct, as has been pointed out by numerous feminist historians and literary critics who have studied the "female malady" in the past.[109] The nineteenth-century "female malady," particularly in the form of hysteria, has been the subject of extensive research. The parallel construction of male hysteria in the nineteenth and twentieth centuries has been examined as well.[110] Emphasis has been laid on the exploration of the influence of the idea of the separate spheres on male and female madness. Historians of psychiatry largely concur that mental diseases or behavioral disorders in the nineteenth century were deeply embedded in the culture of the separate spheres. In Mark Micale's words, "[hysterical] women suffered from an excess of 'feminine' behaviours, hysterical men an excess of 'masculine' behaviours."[111]

At one level, my account in this chapter confirms the relevance of the notion of the separate spheres as the fundamental component of the construction of the madness of men and women in the early nineteenth century: the lunacy of males and females was understood in different ways. Female virtues such as submission were a measure for decoding female madness; masculine ones were the yardstick of male sanity. One of the major problems of Rosa Bagster was her behaviors that did not fit feminine roles in family and society.[112] She did not follow the feminine decorum of demure gentility, in which nineteenth-century women of her class were expected to cocoon themselves. She was aggressive, used physical violence against other members of her household, and did not *obey* the instructions of her governess and her mother. There was a certain, if small and unconscious, amount of rebellion against the accepted feminine code of behavior in Rosa Bagster. Similarly, Mary Hartley, who became the subject of a complicated commission in 1843, was said to have "exhibited self-will and eccentricity."[113] Comparably, the language of the petitioners for commissions against men was saturated with concern about failure in manly activities. Edward Frank's failure to prevent his wife from engaging in adultery was one of the major reasons why the commission of lunacy was sought. Guarding one's spouse's chastity was a man's duty, not a woman's. In numerous commissions, the male subject's misconduct of his business was cited as evidence of his insanity.[114] The ideal of feminine docility was invoked as a yardstick to measure female sanity, whereas those of masculine authority and business prowess were invoked for assessing the male mind.

On the other hand, there are hazards of thinking in dichotomies: my sources compel us to rethink or at least modify the simplistic framework of the separate spheres in madness. Significant overlaps existed in the ways in which female madness and male madness were discovered and defined. Instead of always employing different sets of assumptions to judge the sanity of women and men, people often used a set of common rules for both women and men. Most significantly, there were cases in which female madness was understood in terms of the propriety of women's behavior and acts in the public sphere, and male madness was recognized with respect to the propriety of men's behavior in the private sphere. Such criss-crossing of gendered construction of insanity vis-à-vis the separate spheres occurred fairly often, as may be already evident from my account of the cases in this chapter. What worried the Bagster family most and, in the end, what brought them to ask for a commission was Rosa's act of property transaction through a marriage contract, not the numerous troubles Rosa posed within the family. Families were naturally anxious about unmarried (both single and widowed) women's civil rights, because single or widowed women had much more occasion to exercise their civil rights than married women did. About one-third of commissions of lunacy (614 out of 1813 cases) were sought for female lunatics between 1800 and 1852, and the overwhelming majority of women who became subjects of commissions were spinsters and widows, respectively comprising 57 percent and 29 percent of the female total. When a widowed woman ran an independent household, she was expected to act as its head, and failure in this role constituted evidence of inability to manage her own affairs.[115] Such examples suggest that we should understand female madness, particularly that of single and widowed women, in a framework that incorporated their activities in the public sphere, as well as those in the private sphere, not solely in terms of their failure to conform to feminine roles. My analysis of the commissions of lunacy against women thus confirms the points reiterated by recent feminist historians of medicine, calling for a more nuanced approach to understanding the construction of female maladies.[116] Instead of talking about *the* "female malady," we should explore variations in the construction of female madness, conditioned by marital status, age, and other situations of the subject. Moreover, cases of commission of lunacy against women compel us to relocate female madness from exclusively domestic parameters to those that encompass both the private and public spheres, as feminist historians of the last generations have emphasized in their search to understand various activities of eighteenth- and nineteenth-century women.[117]

Such criss-crossing is equally observable in delineations of male madness found in the reports of commissions of lunacy. The cases of Frank, Davenport, and Ruck evidently show that men's sanity was gauged against the code of male domesticity. Judging sanity in terms of the male head's behavior in his own home seems to be a new development, or an enlargement of the interpretation of the phrase *managing one's own affairs.* Behavior toward nominally subordinate members of the household was also scrutinized and judged. If a man was deemed short of "soundness" in that aspect of his existence, he was to be declared of unsound mind. Placing these cases in the context of studies on the conflicts over male authority within the family by A. James Hammerton and John Tosh, cases such as Davenport's and Ruck's seem to be an index of a new ethos that became visible in the letter of the law from the late 1850s on. The autocratic power of the master of the castle was denied. The family was no longer his possession or fiefdom, but a measure against which his conduct should be judged. The judgment was not confined narrowly to the realm of morality. When the breach of the male domestic code was serious, it could result in a legal deprivation of his civil rights on the basis of his unsoundness of mind. The observance of social and cultural norms expected from the male head became so much higher that its breach could form a part of the legal definition of unsoundness of mind and sanction the intervention of the public authorities.

SIX

Public Authorities and the Ambiguities of the Lunatic at Home

IN CHAPTER 5, I EXAMINED those cases that reveal the limits of domestic measures to control lunatics. Families' attempts at containing the mentally disturbed were often seriously undermined and threatened by a multitude of factors: by the unruly behavior of the lunatics themselves; by internal discord among the family; by the intrusion of a curious crowd in public spaces; by the protest of lunatics who sought to free themselves from domestic surveillance and control; and by the actions of interested outsiders who wanted to take advantage of the incapacity of the lunatics. To cope with these problems, the family had to police the behavior of the lunatic and use a variety of tactics to achieve some semblance of normality. Such a game of duplicity, so to speak, put an enormous strain on the family, which tried to patrol the border of the private and the public spheres, fending off intrusions. On the other hand, the private sphere itself generated a hazard for containing the problem of lunacy within the family walls. The new demand that husbands display kindness and affection toward their wives led to the redefinition of soundness of mind in men. The early Victorian transformation of the ideal of masculinity had two contradictory effects: increasing a man's authority within his family as a virtuous paterfamilias, and making him more vulnerable to the charge of incompetence when he failed to live up to that ideal. When he fell sufficiently short of the ideal, he might be charged with unsoundness of mind and deprived of his civil rights. This is resonant with the paradox in the forging of Victorian domesticity: domestic virtues should be the ultimate basis of the claim to public respect.

Throughout this book, I have been investigating how the private sphere of the family negotiated its boundaries with the world outside: the world of medicine, law, crowds, and the like. In this final chapter, I turn to the investigation of the relationship between the family and public authorities, particularly those of the state. My question is: How were the tenuous boundaries between the family and public authorities drawn when the family had to cope with an insane family member?

I have emphasized that the primary role of commissions of lunacy was to deprive a person of power over his or her own person or property, and to establish a guardianship for that purpose. As might be expected, the most common pattern was that of the lunatic's immediate family requesting a commission. These commissions were routinely sought and routinely granted. Numerous cases were more concerned with "deviancy," such as immorality, sexual misconduct, or aberrant behavior. The wife and the daughter of John Norris, a former surgeon in the East India Company, sought a commission to stop him from living with and making a bigamous marriage with a woman he had picked up in the streets.[1] Joseph Balden possessed a freehold estate worth £400 a year and was addicted to drinking and gambling. After one particularly bad episode of drinking and extravagant spending, his friends had a deed drawn up, placing the management of his property in the hands of trustees, fearing "that he might become the victim of an improvident marriage, or squander his property."[2] The commission of lunacy against James King, a son of a wealthy wholesale butcher, was almost certainly sought by the family to dissolve his marriage with "an obscure female, [with whom he had lived] for a month or six weeks in a small inn."[3] The case of Rosa Bagster was slightly complicated, because in strict legal terms Rosa was the lawful wife of Raymond Newton at the time of the commission, but still it was essentially a case of her family's use of the state's legal apparatus to recover its stray lamb and the immense wealth she carried with her.

In such cases, the family asked the state for help in forcing its wayward family member to return to a proper path. The interests of the propertied family and those of the state converged, and they joined forces to suppress the "insane" individual, who may have been merely eccentric or rebellious. Such cases lend support to an interpretative model that has been long established in the historiography of nineteenth-century psychiatry, seeing the rise of psychiatry in terms of an alliance, or even a conspiracy, between the family and the state. The most forceful proponent of this view is Robert Castel, who has argued that modern psychiatric power beginning in the early nineteenth century was a medical replacement for *lettres de cachet:* a device through which the French absolutist regal power had enabled the family to correct, punish, and confine troublesome family members without trial or tribunal.[4] Indeed, the rhetoric linking the French ancien régime to psychiatric power or its abuse was quite common in English criticisms of psychiatric incarceration from the early nineteenth century on. Many authors, in their angry criticism of the abuse of power by psychiatrists, compared certificates of lunacy to *lettres de cachet.* Commenting on *Anderdon v. Burrows* in 1829, one James Wells wrote to Robert Peel, then the Home Secretary, "What is, or wherein does lay, the difference between a 'Lettre de Cachet' and a 'Certificate of Lunacy'?" Louisa Lowe in 1883 equated the certificate of lunacy with the "French letter de cachet," and compared "English houses licensed for lunatics" to "Bastilles of pre-revolutionary France."[5] A. L. Wigan conceptualized *lettres de cachet* in a more benign light and proposed that this power should be expanded in order to help the family. Likewise, J. C. Prichard, J. A. Symonds, and others cast the psychiatrist in the role of an intermediary aid to the family vis-à-vis the state. Whether one characterized it as sinister or benign, psychiatry has long been understood as a mediator between the family and the state. Castel's thesis, despite its theoretical sophistication, derives from this long tradition beginning in the early nineteenth century.

This interpretative model certainly applies to some extent to English commissions of lunacy in the early and mid-nineteenth century. The state sometimes *did* intend to help the family control its insane member and protect its property. However, I suggest that this classic framework fails to capture many important aspects of the legal procedure of commission of lunacy, and it oversimplifies the wider issue of the relationship between the family and public authorities. First, it should be emphasized that although in all probability numerically predominant in my sample, the cases brought by the immediate family do not cover the entire spectrum of commissions. There were many commissions sought by those outside the immediate family. Indeed, there existed significant exceptions, which served the diametrically opposite purpose: to use the state's legal apparatus to challenge the family's control over the lunatic. The cases of Lord Portsmouth, Edward Frank, and George Davenport are obvious examples of this pattern. The cases of commission of lunacy against Robinson and Clemens, two senile lunatics, examined in chapter 5, fall in that pattern, too. Technically, the case of Rosa Bagster is another, because at the time of her commission she was the lawful wife of Raymond Newton.[6] Such cases were possible because the right to petition for a commission was by no means limited to the immediate family or the relatives of the insane. Anyone could request a commission so long as notice was given to the nearest kin of the person in question. *Pace* the classic model advocated by Castel, there did exist many commissions in which the protective barrier set up by the family around a lunatic was broken by outsiders with the aid of the state. The state's legal machinery of the commission of lunacy was sometimes used to undermine the family's power. This suggests that a much more nuanced approach is necessary to understand the nature of the commission of lunacy as it bore upon the relationship between the family and the state.

Second, one should not look only at cases of commission of lunacy when one discusses the relationship between the family and public authorities or the state. There existed several distinct layers of public authorities dealing with the problem of lunatics: parishes, county magistrates, and the central government.[7] Even within the administrative machinery of the central government, there were two authorities whose interests often clashed: the Lord Chancellor, who was responsible for commissions of lunacy; and the (confusingly named) Commissioners in Lunacy, who, after the 1845 Lunacy Act, were empowered to visit and inspect all lunatics held in county asylums, licensed houses, and subscription and charity hospitals for the insane. These two authorities were the most obviously competing state entities. Examining some of these complexities will help us to move away from a naive picture of a simple alliance between the family and the public authorities resulting in the social control of lunatics. Instead, I suggest that through negotiations on many fronts, the boundaries between the private and the public in terms of lunacy were drawn and redrawn.

In this chapter I spin out some of these complexities and ambiguities over the varied relationships between the family and public authorities, who sometimes collaborated and sometimes opposed each other. First, I examine the changing relationships between the state and the family in terms of commissions of lunacy, and discuss the background and the impact of some legal changes during the period under consideration. Then I proceed to show that there existed deep ambiguities about the extent of the power of public authorities, using the case of George Smith as an example. I conclude this chapter by examining the conflicting approaches within the central government to the question of lunacy and privacy.

The early nineteenth century was a crucial period in the history of forensic psychiatry in the context of criminal responsibility. Calling medical witnesses to testify about the mental state of the defendant was increasingly common in court. Major precedents, such as the M'Naghten Rules, were established, and concepts of lunacy and criminal responsibility became a focus of medico-legal debates. These developments with respect to criminal lunacy have been carefully studied, particularly by Joel Eigen and Roger Smith.[8] Similarly, the question of lunacy and personal liberty was fervently discussed at the time and has become the subject of a large body of historical work, as I discussed in chapter 2.

Such "reform in lunacy" extended to the realm of commissions of lunacy. The early part of the nineteenth century witnessed major attempts to transform the commission of lunacy as a means of depriving a person of his or her civil rights.[9] Although no concrete evidence is available that demonstrates that such changes were related to the new developments in criminal law, they largely concurred in one respect—the expansion of the legal definition of madness or unsoundness of mind, which resulted in the application of the status of lunacy to a larger number of subjects.

One of the new moves in civil law was a significant expansion of the definition of "lunacy" and a more liberal use of legal machinery. The era following the Glorious Revolution was sensitive to the issue of the Crown's infringement on the liberty of the subject. A landmark ruling that established the limit of the commission of lunacy was made by Lord Hardwicke, then Lord Chancellor, in the case of the commission of lunacy against the fourth Earl of Donegal in 1750–51. Lord Donegal exhibited ambiguous symptoms. He could answer rationally questions related to his estates, but not questions touching on figures.[10] This incapacity was sufficient to term him weak-minded, but not to confer the diagnosis of idiocy, because the latter referred to a congenital incapacity of the mind. Commenting on this case, Lord Hardwicke stated that a commission of lunacy should be strictly limited to cases in which the subject was proved to be suffering from either idiocy or lunacy, or was found to be *non compos mentis* (of unsound mind). Mere incapacity did not justify the granting of a commission; in other words, "though a jury finds, that one is incapable of managing his affairs, yet such a finding is not sufficient, but they must expressly find him to be of unsound mind." In his speech, Lord Hardwicke made it clear that he placed such a restriction in order to protect the individual's freedom: "though he

[Lord Hardwicke] was desirous of maintaining the prerogative of the Crown in its just and proper limits, yet, at the same time, he must take care not to make a precedent of extending the authority of the Crown, so as to restrain the liberty of the subject, and his power over his own person and estate, further than the law would allow."[11] Hardwicke's words carried considerable weight. In the mid-eighteenth century, official guidelines dictated a very cautious use of legal machinery and deliberately limited its scope.

The early years of the nineteenth century saw a major change in this respect. Hardewicke's ruling was challenged in 1802 by Lord Eldon, in his first term as Lord Chancellor. A commission of lunacy was issued against Miss Ann Kendrick, who was in "a state of imbecility of mind in a great degree, proceeding from epilepsy."[12] Finding that her case was not "a case of actual insanity," the jury returned a verdict of "not a lunatic." Her relatives were not satisfied with this result and petitioned the Lord Chancellor to reconsider the case. Hearing the petition and studying precedents, Eldon declared that he would depart from Hardwicke's ruling to expand the scope of commission of lunacy. He ruled that "the commission of lunacy is not confined to strict insanity; but is applied to cases of imbecility of mind, to the extent of incapacity, from any cause; as disease, age, or habitual intoxication." In so doing, he was clearly aware that he was making a new precedent that was at odds with Hardwicke's ruling in 1751, stating, "I am pretty confident Lord Hardwicke would not have [us] go so far." The reason he gave for his new ruling was twofold: precedents and protection. Eldon found that Hardwicke's strict limit had often been violated in many cases of commission. Though Eldon granted that the question of liberty was a grave concern, nonetheless he proposed to deviate from Hardwicke's ruling:

> The court in Lord Hardwicke's time did not grant a commission of lunacy in case[s] in which it has been since granted. Of late the question has not been whether the party is absolutely insane; but the court has thought itself authorized (though certainly many difficult and delicate cases with regard to the liberty of the subject occur upon that), to issue the commission, provided it is made out, that the party is unable to act with any proper and provident management . . . under that imbecility of mind, not strictly insanity, but as to the mischief calling for as much protection as actual insanity.[13]

To put it differently, Eldon thought that there were cases in which something should be done, even if one could not prove the "lunacy" of the subject in question. Commenting on the case of Miss Kendrick, Eldon noted that "[no] one can look at this case without seeing, that every person about this lady is satisfied, that some care [should] be thrown round her." In other words, where "every person about" the subject of a commission agreed that legal intervention was necessary, the state should grant a commission, even if no hard evidence of lunacy was available.[14] Eldon proposed, in short, the priority of the family's interests over the individual's liberty.

Eldon's ruling in 1802 was confirmed and firmly established in Lord Erskine's ruling in the case of Henry Cranmer in 1806.[15] The importance of Erskine's ruling in this case was that he established a standard verdict for such situations: a person was "of unsound mind, so that he is not sufficient for the government of himself and his affairs." Erskine thus indicated a way in which a commission in such an ambiguous case could be issued routinely. Before, one had to prove incapacity *and* unsoundness of mind for a petition for a commission to be successful. Now, one only had to prove that the incapacity *amounted to* unsoundness of mind. The lawyers involved in the case of Henry Cranmer were fully aware of the importance of the case, writing "this is a subject of great importance with reference to future cases."[16] And they were quite right in thinking so. In his *Treatise on the Law of Idiocy and Lunacy,* published in 1807, Anthony Highmore quickly incorporated the implications of the ruling. Highmore maintained that although the personal rights and liberty of an alleged lunatic must be protected with peculiar attention, "the interests of their family at the same time [must be] preserved." At the court of a commission of lunacy, Highmore proposed, "the severity of the principles of courts of law is mitigated and relaxed, and a more liberal and expanded judgment is pronounced upon a cool investigation of all the circumstances of the case."[17] The contrast is very clear. Both the mid-eighteenth century and the early nineteenth century faced the same dilemma of individual liberty and the protection of the family. The eighteenth century prioritized liberty and the individual; the nineteenth century chose the protection of the family's property.

A change of great importance thus took place in the criteria for granting a commission of lunacy in the early nineteenth century. Instead of a rigid criterion of "lunacy," a more flexible criterion was established, which was a vague combination of "unsoundness of mind" and "the incapacity to manage one's own affairs." Without question, this flexible criterion facilitated the granting of a commission. On the other hand, many lawyers sensed the danger of an infringement on personal liberty in this very loose criterion for the award of a commission of lunacy. Eldon's careful wording in the passage quoted earlier suggests that he himself was well aware of this danger. In 1847, Leonard Shelford, a barrister at law at Middle Temple, criticized Eldon for giving "so much latitude and uncertainty" to the category of "unsound mind." Shelford accused Eldon of "[opening] a door to invade the liberty of the subject and the rights of property" by departing from long-established notions of idiocy and lunacy.[18] Shelford's criticism was well founded. It turned out that one could encompass a great deal with terms such as *incapacity to manage one's own affairs* and *unsoundness of mind.* In many cases in which there was no concrete evidence of either idiocy or lunacy, the language of the lawyers representing the petitioner for the commission blurred the distinction between insanity and immorality. Many commissions of lunacy became a tool to punish, suppress, and control deviant behavior. The cases of Lord Portsmouth, Edward Frank, George Davenport, and Rosa Bagster were the most glaring examples of this trend.

Concern about the danger of the loose definition of *unsoundness of mind* was most clearly expressed in the case of Edward Frank. As we have seen in chapter 5, the behavior of Edward Frank, his wife, and her lover sounds much like a caricature of the worst sexual license of Regency aristocrats.[19] Particularly Frank had deviated from the contemporary moral standard in a most glaring way. The problem, from a legal point of view, was that he did not show any obvious sign of lunacy or delusion. Two medical authorities of the caliber of John Haslam and George Man Burrows were summoned to the court to state that they believed Frank to be sane.[20] The opening remark of the counsel for the commission betrayed the risky grounds on which this legal action was brought: "He [the counsel] would not say that because a man was profligate he was therefore mad; for a man might be of the most abandoned, loose, and profligate character, and yet be not of unsound mind. . . . But here there was a man conducting himself, and suffering others to conduct him, in a manner totally unbecoming the character of a man, a Christian, and a clergyman—in fact, in a manner proving himself to be quite deranged."[21] Here the legal counsel tacitly admitted that ordinary definitions of lunacy or madness did not apply to this case, and stated that Frank's total disregard of sexual morality qualified him for being declared insane in legal terms. In this legal legerdemain, the counsel was helped by the new criterion of unsoundness of mind established by Eldon and Erskine. He started his account of the case with an explicit reference to Erskine, and concluded his summary speech with a rather free interpretation of Eldon's words: "insanity was not actually necessary to be proved to induce the court to interfere, provided that the conduct were of a character utterly senseless, improvident, and destructive of the immediate property and enjoyments of the party."[22]

To this argument, Henry Brougham, the counsel against the commission, answered that however grossly immoral a man might be, that did not mean he was of unsound mind in the English legal system. Invoking such an august authority as Blackstone, Brougham reiterated that Frank should not be deemed insane under the laws of England: "however prodigal a man might be—however much his prodigality might tend to the ruin of his family—the [English] law took no notice of it."[23] In the end, however, neither Brougham's speech nor the medical witnesses' testimony did more than delay the procedure. The jury returned a unanimous verdict of unsoundness of mind. Clearly, the jury could not swallow the "bare-faced adultery" between the wife of an Anglican clergyman and a lowly rupture doctor, who completely usurped the husband's authority over his household and his wife's body. They saw the commission as an expedient means for the enforcement of morality on this completely wayward clergyman. Frank's commission of lunacy well exemplifies that moral expediency had become an integral part of some commissions of lunacy in the early nineteenth century, a development made possible by the rulings of Eldon and Erskine.

Generally speaking, the lack of strict legal criteria worked in favor of those who sought commissions by reducing the onus of proof. Probably more petitioners were encouraged to apply because they were given a greater hope of success in cases for which only vague evidence of lunacy was available. Eldon himself thought his ruling made people more ready to request commissions. In 1831, he recalled that the number of the petitions "had greatly increased since he had taken the Seal" and declared somewhat apologetically that his conduct was "influenced solely by an anxious desire to benefit the parties laboring under such a state of affliction."[24] Eldon is right in recognizing that his term as Lord Chancellor *coincided with* a period when the number of commissions rose rapidly. There is no proof, however, of a *causal* relationship: that the rise in the number of commissions in the early nineteenth century was actually a consequence of Eldon's ruling.

It might look significant that Eldon, the ultra-Tory, departed from the ruling by Hardwicke, whose major aim was the protection of liberty.[25] The fact that Eldon's ruling was made during the exceptional period of the war with France, when habeas corpus was suspended, might appear to have significance, too. Likewise, in the case of Edward Frank, Henry Brougham, a rising star in the Whig Party, attempted a full-frontal attack on the assumption that lay behind Eldon's ruling, advocating liberty as the chief value to be protected in the English legal system. This picture might reinforce the dichotomy between a political ideology that put a premium on individual liberty and another ideology that was more concerned with the protection of the interests of the family. Such a Whig interpretation of the history of the commission of lunacy, however, does not stand up under scrutiny. Brougham himself, when he received the Great Seal in 1830, started to expand the range of circumstances in which a commission could be issued. The fervent champion of liberty in the cases of Edward Frank and Edward Davies started a legal reform the announced purpose of which was to encourage people to seek commissions more frequently, whereas the ruling of Eldon in 1802, which coincided with the beginning of the increase in the number of commissions in the first three decades of the nineteenth century, did not express such a goal.

During his first Lord Chancellorship, Brougham made a series of efforts to pass a new Act of Parliament to reduce the cost of obtaining a commission of lunacy. His primary concern was the complexities of the process for issuing a commission and the high costs that resulted. The cost of a commission could be astronomical, especially when it was contested. As Michael Angelo Taylor revealed in a motion in the House of Commons in 1830, in the case of the commission against Lord Portsmouth in 1823, the cost was about £25,000, and in the case of Edward Davies in 1829, costs amounted to about £4,000, which was one-fourth of the entire value of his property.[26] Under Brougham's initiative, several bills were offered to simplify the legal proceedings and to cut costs. These efforts bore their first fruit in "An Act to Diminish the Inconvenience and Expense of Commissions in the Nature of Writs De Lunatico Inquirendo," passed in 1833.[27] Despite the Act, the cost for a commission still could become astronomical, as is exemplified in the commission of lunacy against John Taylor in 1839, which was reported to have cost £300 a day and lasted eleven days.[28] Subsequently, the pressure to simplify and lower the cost of the proceedings continued, chiefly under Lord Lyndhurst, and in 1842 another Act was passed, which created two full-time commissioners.[29] In 1853, the Lunacy Regulation Act, a major midcentury legislative reform in commission of lunacy, passed under the Chancellorship of Lord Cranworth.[30] Its aim was once more to cut the cost and the length of time it took to secure a commission, as discussed in the introduction to this book. Under the terms of this Act, the title of the commissioners was changed to "Masters in Lunacy," each of whom was empowered to issue a commission individually. The new

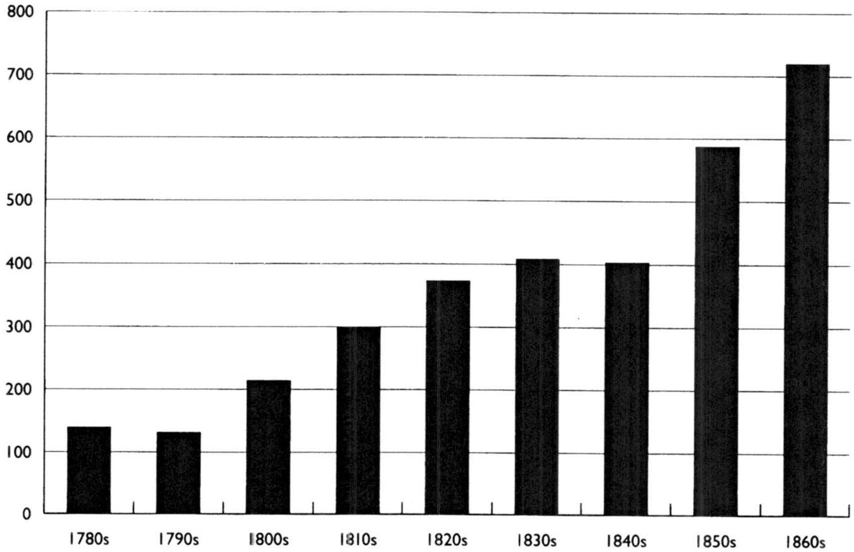

Figure 3. Numbers of Commissions of Lunacy Aggregated by Decade, 1780s—1860s

Masters were paid the handsome salary of £2,000 a year for their full-time service. These measures thus bore the familiar hallmark of early nineteenth-century professionalization of the government. The 1853 Act introduced another major change, allowing the Masters in Lunacy to hear cases directly, instead of empanelling a jury. Because the members of a special jury were paid one guinea per day and members of a common jury half a guinea, this new arrangement cut costs further.[31] Even still, one medical practitioner remarked in 1859 that "under the most favourable circumstance, [the commission] cost not less than £40."[32] Under the new rules, however, families were finally spared the pain of exhibiting their insane family members before the gaze of the curious public.

In theory, the attempts from the 1830s on to reduce the cost by simplifying the process must have encouraged more families to apply for commissions. Figure 3 shows that the number of commissions sharply increased in the first decade of the nineteenth century, and continued to do so for the following three decades. Numbers, however, stagnated in the 1840s, just when the legal reforms were made to simplify commissions of lunacy. The number of commissions again increased rapidly during the 1850s, which was without question a result of the 1853 Act. Brougham's reforms in the

TABLE 4

Income Levels of Those under Commissions of Lunacy, 1839–1859

	1839		*1852–1853*		*1856*		*1859*	
Income per Annum	Number	Percentage of Total	Number	Percentage of Total	Number	Percentage of Total	Number	Percentage of Total
0–100	86	17.4	99	19.3	127	23.0	140	26.0
100–200	83	16.8	117	22.8	129	23.4	139	25.8
200–400	98	19.8	94	18.3	100	18.1	113	21.0
400–600	49	9.9	56	10.9	58	10.5	55	10.2
600–1,000	46	9.3	47	9.1	40	7.3	36	6.7
1,000+	71	14.4	65	12.6	51	9.3	56	10.4
Unknown	61	12.3	36	7.0	46	8.3	—	—
Total	494	100.0	514	100.0	551	100.0	539	100.0

SOURCE: *British Parliamentary Papers* 1839 XLIV; 1852–53 LXXVIII; 1856 LII; 1859 Session I, XXII.

1830s were, however, not without effect, though they did not lead to an increase in the overall number of commissions. As table 4 indicates, the 1840s and 1850s witnessed a proportional increase of commissions among those who possessed income of £400 per year or less, with a corresponding decline in the proportion of those with income of more than £600. Table 4 is compiled from several reports about the Chancery published in *British Parliamentary Papers.* Apart from reiterating a very strong bias toward the wealthy section of the population, this establishes the growing representation of those people with (relatively speaking) smaller incomes. In 1839, those with income of less than £200 per annum comprised only about one-third (34.2 percent) of the total of people under commissions. By 1859, this had increased to more than half (51.8 percent). During these two decades, the commission was extended to those with "modest" income.[33] Comparison of the data for 1839 with those for 1852–53 establishes that this trend started before 1853 and continued after the passage of the new Act. These pieces of evidence together suggest that the reforms in the 1830s and 1840s democratized the process of securing a commission of lunacy and this democratizing trend was furthered and confirmed by the legislation of 1853. Nonetheless, reliance on commissions of lunacy remained very much the prerogative of the very rich sector of the population.

The provision of the 1853 Act that permitted a commission of lunacy without requiring a jury seems to have been a great blessing for families. Although direct evidence is lacking on this point, for the family who petitioned for a commission, proceedings in open court and trial by jury must have been an ordeal. As I showed in chapter 5, families felt great shame when the lunacy of a family member was exposed in public and made enormous efforts to maintain the appearance of normality. It must have been a nightmare for them to have the person of the lunatic and his or her antics exposed before a jury and a larger audience in the courtroom. Even worse, such proceedings were reported in the national press. Understandably, the use of juries thus acted as a deterrent for families, adding shame and embarrassment to the considerable financial costs. The sharp increase in the number of commissions requested after the passage of the 1853 Act, together with the decline in the cases reported in the *Times* around the same time, suggests that the newly simplified procedures acted as a strong incentive for families to apply for the protection it offered.

There is, however, no evidence to suggest that under the new arrangements the family was disproportionately advantaged. At least in theory, those outside the immediate family must have reaped the same benefit from cheaper commissions. These outsiders often intervened when they feared that the trouble caused by a lunatic was getting out of control. As we have seen, the sister of Mrs. Davenport had appealed to the alleged lunatic to change the way he treated his wife. When this meeting failed to achieve the desired end, the wife's family requested a commission. Other cases, too, suggest that the new legislation opened up opportunities to intervene for those who had little to do directly with the family. One is the case of Solomon Cohen. Cohen did not hail from a wealthy family; on the contrary, he was an inmate of the county pauper lunatic asylum at Hanwell. The novelty of this commission was noted and explained at the beginning of the proceedings: "The circumstances which gave rise to this proceeding were of a novel character, and it was stated to be the first inquiry of the kind that had occurred in this country. The commission was taken out at the instance of the parish authorities of St. Luke's, to which parish Mr. Cohen was chargeable, upon their discovering that a share of 1,663l.3s.4d. 3 per cent consolidated bank annuities had been bequeathed him by the late Mr. Cohen, of Great Prescott-street, Goodman's-fields."[34] The legal proceedings thus were undertaken to allow the parish authorities to make use of Cohen's relatively modest property to support him at the county asylum (or at another suitable place). Unquestionably, this commission became feasible only because of the lowered cost. Perhaps encouraged by the success of this commission, three years later, in 1844, the parish authorities of St. Luke's again asked for a commission, this time against Brent Spencer.[35] The commission took place in an even humbler abode, the boardroom of the St. Luke's workhouse in Chelsea. On this second occasion, the commission was explicitly sought against the interests of the family of the person in question. The commission was sought to remove him from the control of his natural mother, Harriet Pelham. Although she did not formally oppose the commission, Mrs. Pelham was present at the court, and interrupted and obstructed the proceedings, for which she was chastised by the commissioner. Admittedly, these cases of the parish authorities requesting commissions were exceptional. Nevertheless, they reinforce the point that a commission of lunacy could be sought by non–family members, and, occasionally, by public authorities, against the interests of the immediate family.

The reform in matters related to Chancery lunatics thus shared some characteristics with the concept of early and mid-nineteenth-century English government. Instead of the early tunnel-visioned model of progress from laissez-faire to state intervention or of the "Victorian Revolution in government" enabling collectivistic state intervention, recent scholarship has emphasized more gradual and nuanced changes, with the central assumptions of state action largely remaining the same during most of the nineteenth century.[36] Also recent historiography has taken a more cautious attitude toward the earlier emphasis on the impact of "isms" or clearly formulated ideologies on the formation of social or economic policies.[37] Reforms in the area of commissions of lunacy did not fit well into those frameworks that used to dominate historians' discussions of the role of the public authority and the state vis-à-vis the initiatives held by the individual, which were mainly centered on questions of economic policy. Taken in the widest sense, in the realm of lunacy, "state intervention" against "laissez-faire" approaches began as early as 1774, when the Act for the Regulation of Private Madhouses secured public authorities' powers over the private business through inspection and licensing. In the mid-nineteenth century, the alleged heyday of laissez-faire policy, the state increased and firmly consolidated its oversight of the places where lunatics were held. This increase in state power and responsibility culminated in the Act of 1845, which some psychiatrists dubbed the "Magna Carta" of English psychiatry.[38] David Wright has succinctly phrased the anomalous position occupied by reform in lunacy in the general history of the development of the welfare state: "[The Act of 1845 established] a system of public mental hospitals one hundred years before the creation of the National Health Service."[39] Of course, it is absolutely correct to say that reform in lunacy from the late eighteenth century to the mid-nineteenth century was anomalous in the development of major economic and social policies in England. Much of the pressure for lunacy reform was philanthropic and Evangelical in its inspiration, and these were ideologies that often had uneasy, if not hostile, relationships with the spirit of laissez-faire.[40] Historians' emphasis on the early establishment of state intervention in the area of lunacy has somewhat isolated the historiography of nineteenth-century lunacy from the rest of historical scholarship.[41]

Perceptions are now changing, however, about the role of nineteenth-century government in general. The reform in Chancery lunatics fits in well with this new model. The assumption is, according to Pat Thane: "[The] government's role was at most strictly limited, that it not only should not but could not determine the structure and working of society. Rather its role was to provide a firmly established and clearly understood framework within which society could very largely run itself."[42] The developments in the state's treatment of Chancery lunatics can be seen in this light. Neither Eldon nor Brougham attempted to achieve their aim through active intervention in the affairs of the families of alleged lunatics. Instead, the government encouraged more people to seek commissions, by lowering the onus of proof and by reducing the cost, both financial and psychological. The outcome of the commission was to be determined by the contest between the two parties, whose testimonies were weighed, with the final decision to be reached by the jury. The threshold for granting a commission should become lower, and the door should be opened wider through which more commissions should be requested by petitioners, or opposed by those against the commission. The matter should be settled between these contestants, with the state providing the framework in which the contest should take place. In short, the state designed a suitable framework for a legal procedure: the decisions of whether and how to use the machinery was largely left to the society.

The protection offered by the state to those of unsound mind expanded dramatically during the first half of the nineteenth century, and the second half witnessed even more rapid growth. Both Eldon and Brougham, two Lord Chancellors whose political views were diametrically opposed, intended to expand this sort of legal machinery, although the intentions of the latter were much more clearly spelled out.[43] They shared the assumption that the state should be responsible for the protection of the person and property of lunatics. Lord Lyndhurst, another Lord Chancellor, stated succinctly in 1841, "law should provide for the safe management [of the property of a lunatic], instead of leaving it to the voluntary assistance of friends and relations."[44] Without directly intervening in the realm of the family, the state effected a momentous change in the way in which the family controlled the person and the property of a lunatic. The autonomous running of society in terms of the control of the property of lunatics increasingly took place within the legal framework provided by the state. In short, private agents were encouraged to employ public measures. In that sense, the Lunacy Regulation Act of 1853 commands particular attention. The 1853 Act had a far greater impact on the social practice of the management of the insane than the previous Acts of 1833 and 1842, which entertained the same goal. The exponential increase in the number of commissions after 1853 dwarfed the changes effected by the two previous Acts. In the latter half of the nineteenth century, legislation by the state provided a framework that brought management of lunacy firmly under the state's regulation.

CHALLENGING THE DOMESTIC BARRIER: THE CASES OF BRENT SPENCER AND GEORGE SMITH

The case of Brent Spencer, in which the parish authorities asked for a commission of lunacy, had an interesting twist. It was sought by the parish in order to remove the lunatic from his family. Spencer's was a case of glaring abuse and neglect at his own house.[45] On 18 May 1844, the magistrate was informed of the maltreatment of a lunatic and sent three policemen to the house of Mrs. Harriet Eleanor Pelham in Chelsea. There they found Spencer, who turned out to be a thirty-four-year-old illegitimate son of the late general Sir Brent Spencer, confined in a single room in her house. The policemen found the room in a filthy and horrid state: the mattress on which Spencer lay was full of vermin, wood lice, and maggots; the window was barred outside and secured on the inside by a wire guard; the door was lined with sheet iron and covered with green baize inside. One witness stated that the patient had not been out of that room for four or five years. On the basis of these findings, he was removed to St. Luke's workhouse, where a commission of lunacy was granted in favor of the parish authorities.

The case of Spencer ended well from the viewpoint of the public authorities: he was rescued from wretched conditions by the forceful intervention of police, and he was declared to be of unsound mind, which meant that he could be extracted from his mother's grip. The problem was that this raid or forceful breaking into a private house had only a shaky legal basis. Quite simply, there was no legislation that permitted an authority to behave in this fashion. By an Act in 1744 (17 Geo.II.c.5) magistrates were empowered to remove wandering lunatics into safe places of custody, but not lunatics kept in their own homes. The statute, which empowered magistrates to confine wandering and dangerous lunatics, "does not extend to persons of rank and condition, whose relations can take care of them properly," as Anthony Highmore stressed.[46] Not until the Lunatic Asylums Act in 1853 were justices of the peace empowered to examine and institutionalize lunatics who were not wandering about and who were taken care of by their relatives.[47] Accordingly, the story of Spencer and Pelham had a disappointing anticlimax on another front. Pelham was indicted for ill-treating the lunatic, but was not convicted because no evidence had been produced to prove that the patient's suffering was at all connected with his mother's misconduct.[48]

The same ambiguities revealed themselves in a more intense way in the case of George Smith in 1826. The Smith case was not primarily a commission of lunacy but rather an action for libel. Because it reveals so much about the tension between the public authorities and the family over the question of keeping a lunatic at home, the case deserves close scrutiny. George Smith was born around 1785 into the family of a wealthy farmer in the county of Stafford. He had been feeble-minded from his early childhood, and grew worse as he became older.[49] His mother, who had mainly taken care of him, died in 1807, and his father's death followed in 1812. After their deaths, the major responsibility for taking care of him fell on the shoulders of Sarah, the eldest daughter of the family. When their mother died, she wished Sarah "to take charge of him in the same manner as she [the mother] had herself," and his father had the same request on his deathbed.[50] Sarah was to perform the role of a full-time house-nurse for George, a role she performed with great dedication. Numerous witnesses testified about the admirable care of George by Sarah and her self-sacrifice. In order to take care of George, she "had more than once refused advantageous offers of marriage"; "[George] was constantly falling into fits, and his sister . . . used to stand by him and often cry"; "[she] repeatedly sat up with him, and never went to bed, without first seeing after him, and mostly praying by his side, during his suffering."[51]

There is no reason to doubt these accounts of the sister's devotion. The problem was, however, that all these acts of familial love, affection, and tenderness went on behind a strictly closed door. Soon after their mother's death, George and Sarah's father moved the family to a new farm in Mucklestone Wood and kept George in a separate room in the house. The window of the room where he was kept was bricked up, allegedly because they found that the light tended to irritate George and to throw him into fits, and because George broke the glass with his fists.[52] One major purpose of their doing so was, however, to hide George from the sight of other people. George was hidden even from the sight of visitors to the house: although Martha Haskett described herself as having "an intimate knowledge of Mr. Smith's family for the last 30 years," she testified that "she had never seen George but once in her life."[53] (George Smith is thus the closest lunatic I have found to the fictional Mrs. Rochester in the attic.) The Smith family's secrecy about George aroused curiosity and suspicion in people, which in turn aggravated the family's nervous concern to hide him. Whether it is true or not, a newspaper article said that "the brother and sister then spread a report that their house was haunted, in order to deter persons from visiting it." Mary Hulme, the servant to the house, recalled that "there was people . . . always jawing her, and telling her to go to Mucklestone Wood to see the madman."[54]

The vicious circle of secrecy and suspicion intensified, and the final catharsis came on 25 January 1826. The action was prompted by an ex-servant girl who had quitted her position with the Smiths. She went into the service of one of the neighboring magistrates, and told him about George's circumstances.[55] Two magistrates of the county of Stafford, Mr. Eld and Rev. Mr. Broughton, accompanying a constable, then came to the house and demanded to see George. In the ensuing confusion, the magistrates forced themselves into the room where George was kept, to find him in a state that they found horrible: a darkened room, with bricks blocking the light from the window; the floor covered with heaps of filth, excrement, oat chaff, and straw; George himself covered with a filthy blanket, lying "coiled up like a greyhound."[56] The magistrates sent for John Garret, the house surgeon to the Staffordshire County Lunatic Asylum, to which George was taken that same evening.[57] Later, the magistrates openly spoke of what they had seen at the house, perhaps with some exaggeration, which led one of the brothers to bring an action against Broughton for propagating calumnies. Broughton responded by prosecuting the family for cruelty to their brother, as well as asking for a commission of lunacy. While these suits were pending, the *Birmingham Journal,* a Whig-Radical newspaper, published two articles that included some totally fictive accounts of cruelty against George practiced by the family. The Smith family brought another legal action for libel, this time against the proprietors of the paper. After a trial that involved contradictory testimonies from the major protagonists and lengthy arguments about the liberty of the press, the Smiths won the case and the proprietors of the *Birmingham Journal* were fined £400.[58]

As far as the libel case is concerned, this is a clear victory for the Smith family. Their vindication was confirmed in another lawsuit related to George's confinement. In *R. v. Smith* (1826), the Smiths were indicted for "unlawfully and maliciously contriving and intending to hurt and injure one George Smith." The attorney for the prosecution stated that the family's way of leaving George without sufficient warmth and clothing (or, according to the legal parlance at that time, "exposure to the inclemency of the weather") was a "gross mal-treatment," which, he claimed, amounted to assault. The counsel for the defendants, on the other hand, insisted that neither actual assault nor the existence of malice had been proven in the family's conduct toward George. The final judgment was made on a legal-technical ground that a brother did not have the legal obligation to maintain another brother and that his failure to give sufficient care did not amount to a crime.[59] On that basis, the Smiths were acquitted. They secured another legal victory.

On the other hand, they were not vindicated on other fronts. Eldon, then the Lord Chancellor, dictated that a commission of lunacy against George ought to be issued, and that the family should bear the cost for the commission that they were about to oppose. Because George died shortly after his removal to the asylum, the commission did not materialize. But the fact that the Lord Chancellor thought a commission necessary suggests that the commission would have had a reasonable chance of success if it had been heard. Moreover, Eldon's ruling became a standard, formulated as "the nearest relations of a supposed lunatic should pay the cost occasioned by their opposition to a petition for a commission of lunacy, presented by strangers to the family."[60] Eldon's ruling put a family keeping a lunatic member at home in a very vulnerable position, for now they had to resist the legal interference of third parties in their domestic psychiatric regime *at their own cost.* Perhaps this duty to bear the cost was the reason why Brent Spencer's mother did not formally oppose the commission but instead chose to be present in court and disrupt the proceedings in various informal ways.

The outcome of the Smith case is best summarized as ambiguity. The justice presiding over the libel case seems to have restricted himself to the question of libel, avoiding any comment on the conduct of either the family or the magistrates.[61] The counsel for the plaintiff (the Smith family) criticized the conduct of the magistrates: "he [the counsel] could fearless[ly] assert their [the magistrates'] conduct on this occasion to have been indiscreet and improper." Blame was due, in his eyes, because there was no law that permitted the magistrate to force himself into a family where a lunatic was kept. The same counsel, however, did not think that the family was entirely blameless: "he was not there to say, that this family had acted wisely in not sending this poor creature to some great asylum, where he might always have had at hand the best medical aid."[62] These statements indicate the ambiguity of the propriety of keeping a lunatic at home, however tender the care he or she might receive from family members: the sister's devotion and virtuous self-sacrifice did not exempt the family from criticism. They also suggest the ambiguity of the public authorities' power to intervene in the self-contained site of relatively well-conducted domestic care for the propertied insane. Even though the magistrates obviously acted in good faith, their conduct caused sharp criticism and they did not obtain a clear legal victory over those who, they thought, had treated a lunatic family member in a "cruel" way.

LUNACY COMMISSIONERS AND THEIR AMBIGUOUS POWER

This chapter has so far examined the relationships among the state, public authorities, and the family, through commission of lunacy cases and the cases of Brent Spencer and George Smith. The best word to describe the situation is *ambiguity.* Wealthy families with insane members were exempt from inspection by public authorities. They were not forced to report to the state about the lunatic. Nor were they forced to seek a commission of lunacy and to give up managing the lunatic's property in a private way. They were, however, in effect encouraged to deal with the lunatic in a formal and legal way by asking for a commission of lunacy. There was no law that forbade the family from keeping the lunatic within their family walls, but if suspicion of abuse and cruelty was raised, their family might be raided by the police or magistrates. Against this background of ambiguity, the Commissioners in Lunacy were created to regulate the confinement of lunatics.

The establishment of the Lunacy Commissioners in 1845 confirmed that the state had a clear role in protecting the interest of lunatics if they were confined in asylums, licensed houses, or mental hospitals (except Bethlem until 1853). Some writers wholeheartedly welcomed this new map of responsibility over lunacy. For them, the ultimate responsibility for the well-being of lunatics was conclusively removed from the patient's family to the state and public authorities, and even more clearly from the proprietors of private asylums. In a series of articles published in leading medical journals in the early 1850s, Henry Monro remarked that "the public" was not only "the most unbiased judges in many matters of great importance connected with the welfare of the insane," but its opinion had "proved itself to be the surest defense to the insane." Monro continued, "The sound sense and good feeling of the *sane public* [was] the best antidote for the morbid sense of the *insane,* and a refuge more to be depended upon than the care of either relatives or medical men."[63] The "care and affection of friends" fell short of the task of securing the greatest welfare for the patient under the burden of the trouble and shock of taking care of the insane. He gave clear priority to public over private interest in matters of lunacy: "[General] philanthropy proved itself able and willing to stand the shock which the more sensitive feelings and the selfish fears of friends quailed before. The public sympathy resembled in this respect a rock in the ocean, which can offer a firm hold to him who is sinking beneath the waves; while private affection exhibited the helplessness of a companion a little stronger than his fellow, who refuses to reach out his hand lest he should be dragged into the abyss which awaits one less happy than himself."[64] This is an important statement, which demonstrates that at least for some interested parties, the creation of the Lunacy Commissioners signaled the dawn of a new age in which the state and the public authorities, not the family and the private agent, were principally responsible for the proper care of lunatics.

It is, however, far from clear that such euphoric endorsements of the power of the state vis-à-vis that of private agencies fully captured reality. Examination of the activities of the Lunacy Commissioners shows that the reverse was quite often the case.[65] After the passage of the 1845 Act, the Lunacy Commissioners used their intimate knowledge of the conditions of some lunatics cared for by their families or "friends" and asked the Lord Chancellor to issue commissions against those whom they thought were ill-treated.[66] They visited, for example, Hester Read, residing with one Mr. Shore in Farmborough, "a retired and straggling village about eight miles from Bath" (an inspection that was, strictly speaking, not in their power to make). The two Lunacy Commissioners found her to be of unsound mind, and asked the Lord Chancellor to issue a commission against her.[67] In the course of their visit, the two Lunacy Commissioners had wanted to secure an interview without the presence of the owner of the house but had experienced great difficulty in doing so: "To this proposal Mr Shore at once objected, alleging that it was a hard and unreasonable thing for strangers to require a man to leave a room in his own house; and eventually he persisted in refusing to retire, although we explained to him the motive of our request and the unfavourable inference which might be drawn from his refusal."[68] It turned out that the commissioners were frustrated in their efforts to find ill-usage: indeed Mrs. Read was of unsound mind, but she had been treated kindly by Shore, and they were unable to demonstrate otherwise, despite their attempts to make her bring any complaints.

In the late 1850s and early 1860s, the commissioners undertook an active investigation of the problem of "single lunatics," those patients who were taken care of at lodgings that took only one lunatic, which lay outside the Lunacy Commissioners' statutory power. Again they met with a mixture of success and failure. On many occasions, they were forced to recognize that their legal powers were limited and that examining the care of single patients was a delicate business. They admitted that "in cases of gross neglect or abuse calling for a special report . . . , we are compelled to trust to the good feeling of the friends of the patient or party with whom he resides to carry out our suggestions, rather than to any direct means which we possess of enforcing them."[69] Their power was limited to issuing warnings to the family. Sometimes the Lunacy Commissioners' advice was taken and removal to an asylum was made. Sometimes the families were not sure about the best way to proceed and a compromise was made, incorporating some of the commissioners' advice.[70] But on many occasions, the commissioners had to swallow bitter defeats. In the case of one female patient held under mechanical restraint (an anathema to the commissioners), they recommended that her husband should remove her to an asylum, but he "expressed himself satisfied with his wife's position and treatment, and declined to remove her." For another female patient whose situation was found particularly unsatisfactory (she was "soaked through with urine"), the commissioners "recommended removal with strongest terms" to her sister and even thought of using legal enforcement. But again they had to withdraw their threats: "We were ultimately very unwillingly induced to sanction her continuing under Mr M's care."[71]

These cases where the Lunacy Commissioners had to concede defeat did not mean, however, that they were completely unsuccessful in achieving their goals. From early on, they adopted the tactic of "blame and shame," rather than "prosecute and punish," perhaps recognizing that their statutory powers were sharply limited on many fronts. Well aware that the newspapers were keen to publish stories recounting the abuses of lunatics in lurid terms, which would effectively embarrass those they targeted, the Lunacy Commissioners made effective use of mass media such as newspapers, in order to bring public outrage to bear on situations the commissioners disapproved of but had no statutory powers to amend. This is exemplified in the case of an inmate's death at Surrey County Asylum in 1856, which had been caused by prolonged use of cold showers. The Lunacy Commissioners initiated a criminal prosecution for manslaughter against Charles Snape, the responsible medical superintendent. Eventually they lost the case, but they appear to have been content with their achievement and they subsequently set forth a regulation to limit the duration of such showers. They thus deprived individual doctors of discretionary power over the treatment of their charges. Their Eleventh Report, published in 1857, stated that they "conceived that their duty as a public body had been sufficiently discharged by the attention drawn to the case; by the public hearing at Bow-Street."[72] The same strategy is evident in their approach to the questions respecting the management of single lunatics. In their Fifteenth Report, the lunacy commissioners published accounts of the single lunatics in Carmarthenshire and Cardiganshire and reported that the number of registered "single lunatics" in the area subsequently increased from 119 to 137. They attributed this increase "to the publicity given to the criminal proceeding" they themselves had instituted the year before for the illegal detention of an insane gentleman without certificate.[73] The Lunacy Commissioners lost the case, but what really mattered from their viewpoint was the negative publicity about keeping unregistered single lunatics. Likewise, their legal actions against those who illegally confined lunatics were regularly reported in the press from the 1860s on.[74]

From these fragmentary pieces of evidence, it appears likely that the Lunacy Commissioners could reasonably expect that their visits, recommendations, and warnings to any family keeping a lunatic at home would serve to destabilize the domestic psychiatric regime. They did not have a clear legal right to forcefully remove a lunatic from the family and place him or her in an asylum under their inspection. Nor did they have power to effect the legislative changes they thought desirable. They could act indirectly, however. By creating all but invisible pressure on the family from outside—perhaps through the intervention of relatives, neighbors, and parish officers, or the use of mass media—they could bring the family into conformity with their plan.[75] The effective use of unofficial power of the press and public opinion fits in well with the revisionist interpretations of early and mid-Victorian governmental inspecting bodies put forward by P. W. J. Bartrip: resources allocated to the new agencies were too modest to allow them to achieve much in terms of enforcement.[76] The Lunacy Commissioners' "power" lay more in creating pressure for conformity by private families through the creative use of the nebulous power of "public opinion," the most visible of which was the power of the press.

The key point of this chapter is the deepening sense of ambiguity surrounding the domestic management of the insane in the mid-nineteenth century. There were no clear guidelines that suggested that it was wrong to keep a lunatic in one's own home, nor any law that licensed public authorities to retrieve a lunatic from his or her own family. A series of Lord Chancellors from the early nineteenth century on had *in effect* encouraged people to have recourse to the legal machinery of commission of lunacy, both by lowering the onus of proof required and by reducing the cost for the procedure. But these shifts did not empower public authorities to deny the discretion of a propertied family over an insane family member. Law tacitly sanctioned, within certain limits, the discretion of well-off families over the treatment of their insane members. Similar sentiment was often expressed by those holding governmental office. In the House of Lords in 1831, Lord Chancellor Brougham himself remarked with respect to the Metropolitan Commissioners in Lunacy that "he thought it would be better to trust to the relatives, wives, husbands, or children of persons unhappily afflicted, than to these Commissioners." On another occasion, Brougham endorsed the view that any initiative seeking a commission of lunacy should be taken by the patient's friends, "correcting a commonly received opinion that the Lord Chancellor is the natural guardian of the insane."[77] In 1827, Robert Peel, then the Home Secretary under whom the Metropolitan Commissioners in Lunacy were to operate, maintained in the Commons that troublesome, rather than stark mad, persons were better kept at their own houses, "it being preferable to leave them in the custody of their relations, than to lock them up in mad-houses."[78] These remarks from the heads of the public offices who were charged with supervising the issues related to lunacy suggest that they were reluctant to disfranchise the lunatic's family as the proper guardian in the matter of the lunatic's care and control, by removing the lunatic to an institution that was visited and inspected by public authorities.

Decisions in the criminal court were no less ambiguous. Cases of neglect, ill-treatment, and abuse of lunatics by their family members continued to appear after the case of George Smith. They did not, however, suggest any clear-cut rule. For example, in 1855, John Rundle was prosecuted for abusing and ill-treating his wife, Amelia, a lunatic, with whom the defendant cohabited.[79] At the Devon Spring Assizes in 1855, the jury found him guilty. Later in the year, however, an appeal was made to the Court of Criminal Appeal, claiming that the statute on which the previous indictment was made (16 and 17 Vict.c.96.s.9) did not apply to the case of a husband neglecting the care of his lunatic wife, because the statute stated the duties of the superintendents or the staff of institutions and those of persons in charge of a "single lunatic." The presiding judge concluded that the letter of the law did not apply to "[domestic] custody of a lunatic," in which family members took care of a lunatic as "a natural duty, as father, husband, or otherwise," and he overturned the previous conviction. The ruling was, however, found not to be applicable in the case of a brother taking care of a lunatic sibling. Samuel Porter was convicted in 1867 at the Cornwall Assizes for willfully neglecting the care of his insane brother, Robert Porter. Next year, an appeal based on the ruling of the Rundle case was made to the Court of Criminal Appeal. This time, the judges concurred that a case of a brother taking care of his insane sibling was covered by the statute, and the conviction was confirmed.[80]

On the other hand, there was by now a gathering cloud of moral ambiguity, illegitimacy, or even a hint of criminality over keeping an insane family member at home. The behavior of the two magistrates in the Smith case exemplified this point. When the magistrates arrived at the house, they treated the family members just as they did criminals: Eld did not allow the brother to go upstairs before he did; Broughton ordered Sarah, who stood in front of the door to George's room, to stand away, and he announced that if she did not, "he would knock her down."[81] The magistrates' representation of the situation during their raid to discover an abused lunatic is a close copy of the celebrated account of the disclosure of the horrible abuses at the York Asylum by Godfrey Higgins.[82] The magistrates were sure that they would discover a horrid scene of neglect, filth, and stench, precisely because the Smiths kept the lunatic behind closed doors. For Eld and Broughton, the rumor of a lunatic secretly kept meant that cruelty and abuse were practiced there. In the mind of the two magistrates, the smell of secrecy seems to have blurred the distinction between an institution, which they had power to inspect, and a private house, which they were not legally allowed to enter.

The association between secrecy and suspicion was thus less legal than cultural, pertaining more to a climate of opinion than to the letter of the law. The nebulous but powerful formulations of this "mood" against psychiatric secrecy, particularly that surrounding private madhouses, were discerned by Edward J. Seymour, when he wrote about a private madhouse in a work published in 1859: "Still the feeling fostered by novel writers (who never, by the way, as far as I know, really depict a lunatic case), the feeling for absolute secrecy which pervades society, the idea that where there is secrecy there is the opportunity for injustices—all these operate on the public mind to decry similar institutions."[83] Almost certainly Seymour was here referring to the public panic caused by the cases of false incarceration in 1858 and a host of sensational novels to which they gave rise.[84] He may even be referring specifically to Wilkie Collins's *Woman in White,* which stirred enormous interest in the last months of 1859 when it was first serialized in *All the Year Round.*[85] Seymour also identified the inevitable clash between private interests and public concerns: the family's need for secrecy in matters of lunacy and the public authorities' demand for accessibility to the places where lunatics were kept. The point is that Seymour, who was an eminent lawyer, framed the suspicion of the practice of hiding lunatics in terms of the atmosphere created by popular novels. The domestic care of the insane was a social practice that was losing its legitimacy: it was intimate, but it hid something, and in hiding it, constituted it as presumably illegitimate. The panic about lunacy in 1858 was an explosion of such suspicion that had been building during the course of first half of the nineteenth century.

In the case of George Smith, the family's secrecy created an unfriendly curiosity and suspicion among neighbors, as well as in the minds of the two magistrates. Moreover, there is fragmentary evidence that suggests that the Smith family themselves felt awkward about the situation. The servant who testified for the Smith family admitted that she had once told a lie and denied the existence of George in the house, because she wanted to curtail people's curiosity.[86] The testimony of both the servant (on behalf of the plaintiff) and the magistrates (for the defendants) revealed that the brother initially did not tell the magistrates in a straightforward way that George was in the house.[87] Any firm protest from the Smith family against the forceful intervention of the magistrates at the moment it occurred was conspicuously absent. Only Sarah requested them to "behave like gentlemen," perhaps feeling justified in doing so by her years of sacrifice and devotion.[88] Probably, in the last analysis, the family itself was not absolutely sure of the propriety of taking care of George behind closed doors and a bricked-up window. To put it another way, the pressure of rumor had already effectively redrawn the boundary between the private and public spheres even for members of the family. They were no longer sure whether their home, with a lunatic in it, was their castle, however tender the care they—or at least Sarah—gave him.[89]

The existence of a lunatic, therefore, made the domestic barrier a porous one for neighbors, for magistrates, and for the family itself. In other words, a lunatic in a family effaced the boundary between the private and public realms, and made the usually closed sphere an ambiguously open or vulnerable one. After the watershed Parliamentary Inquiry into Bethlem and the York Asylum in 1815–16, a series of measures in reform in lunacy created a sense of uneasiness about lunatics kept in secret, either in institutions or in their own homes. Without any solid legislative basis, many people felt a vague sense of impropriety about keeping a lunatic behind closed doors. A question mark was now hovering over a lunatic privately kept in a family.

This ambiguity is best captured in an episode that took place at the conclusion of the commission of lunacy against Andrew Mitchell Campbell in 1842. After returning a verdict of unsound mind, the jury took the unusual step of criticizing the way in which the subject had been treated. The commission itself was a straightforward one, as Campbell suffered from a clear-cut delusion: he was "under the impression that there are wire figures which twitch his face into various contortions, and compel him to swear against his will," as well as believing other people were automata with galvanic wires. The point was that the private madhouse in which he had been confined was in very poor condition, and, when examined, the patient stated that "Whitmore-house is very old, and, from its construction, calculated to deprive people of their reason and make them mad. I was never under any delusion before I went to Whitmore-house." Listening to this statement and Campbell's brother's explanation that he at first had wanted to keep him at a private lodging with two keepers, but that in the end he reluctantly put his brother in a private madhouse "for fear that his motives might be misrepresented,"[90] the jury went to some length in their criticism of the family that had arranged for Campbell to be confined in Whitmore House: "We are of opinion that had Major Campbell not been placed in Whitmore-house his intellect would have been improved since; and we strongly recommend that he be placed under the surveillance of two keepers, as proposed by his brother; and we think that, by proper care, he may yet become a useful member of society, and be competent to attend to his own affairs."[91] This rather extraordinary step of a jury advising the family about how to treat the patient was warmly welcomed by the presiding commissioner. He indicated that he would try to implement the recommendation of the jury, because "there is some authority placed in the hands of commissioners in these cases by the new act."[92] The jury and the commissioner thus felt justified in meddling in the ways in which the family treated its insane member, condemning one means and recommending another. Here one can find public power intervening in the most intimate of family matters. The irony, which epitomized the ambiguity surrounding the questions of lunacy, secrecy, and publicity, was that the jury preferred the seclusion of a private lodging to the more public space of a licensed house: the latter was under the inspection of the Metropolitan Commissioners of Lunacy, whereas the former was a totally closed space. Here, public authority, in the form of the jury at the commission of lunacy, was forcefully stepping into the private sphere, only to tell the family to settle the matter in the most private of ways.

Conclusion

Forsi altri cantarà con miglior plettro.
[Perhaps another will sing with a better voice.]

CERVANTES
Don Quixote

THIS BOOK HAS EXAMINED FAMILIES' strategies for understanding, coping with, and managing insane family members, roughly from 1820 to 1860, a period that coincided with the rise of psychiatry and of the asylum. I have analyzed both the internal dynamics and the external relations of families with insane members. My account has naturally included both the intrafamilial tensions and the intersections of the family and various agencies in the world outside, such as doctors, crowds on the street, and public authorities. In so doing, I hope that I have established the family as the major protagonist in matters related to lunacy during the period in question. In this concluding section, I will briefly review some of my major findings and consider their historiographical implications.

I would like to reiterate here the importance of the economic and financial aspects of the domestic problem of lunacy, in contrast to the emotional aspects, which have been emphasized so far in the historiography on nineteenth-century psychiatry. The emphasis on intimate feeling among family members has provided the basic parameter for the historical discussion of lunacy and the family in the nineteenth century. This line of argument has been taken most notably and successfully by Nancy Tomes, who has been the most sophisticated advocate of the importance of family members' feelings toward one another in the development of American asylum psychiatry in the early nineteenth century. My sources indicate something more prosaic and practical: anxiety about the lunatic's property was the basic motivation for actions taken by the family. This is hardly surprising, because management of property was the very reason why people asked for commissions of lunacy. Abundant expressions of family members' agony over the insanity of their loved ones in my sources confirm their emotional burden. My sources do not refute but rather supplement the argument developed by Tomes and others, by examining another side of the question of lunacy and the family that has been neglected by historians. Families were both an emotional and a financial unit, and both aspects were important in the domestic management of lunatics. Emphasis on one aspect at the expense of the other distorts the picture, as has been pointed out by those historians who have criticized the "sentimentalist" approach to the history of the family. Regrettably, my sources have not allowed me to examine in detail the wealth and the property holdings of the families who asked for commissions of lunacy. I hope, however, that I have demonstrated that the economic aspects of the problem of domestic lunacy were at least as important as its emotional aspects.

As for the emotional aspects, my sources call for a revision of the accepted historiography on one important point. Historians have assumed that the strong emotional ties among members of Victorian families weakened the family's role as the caretaker of lunatics. Because of the heightened expectation of emotional fulfillment and intimate relationship within the family, the argument goes, the family could no longer bear the sight of a strange, disruptive, and completely changed family member. The burden of living with the mentally alienated loved one was too much for newly sentimentalized family members. Again, Tomes is the most eloquent proponent of this line of argument, and there is considerable truth to her thesis. My sources tell another story, however, one that is almost diametrically opposed to Tomes's. New emphasis on domestic emotional solidarity seems to have considerably strengthened the family's ability to understand, and at least initially to cope with, the madness of the family member. In their search for the meanings, manifestations, and reasons of madness, families were assisted by mental sciences that were then in vogue, physiognomy and phrenology being the two most conspicuous examples. It should be noted, however, that the greatest inspiration came from religion. Evangelical Christianity, with its emphasis on domestic emotional solidarity, created a powerful background for forging a certain type of domestic psychiatric culture. Particularly important was the emphasis on the interiority of the individual. Among family members, there should be a true communion of the heart: family relationships should not be staged masques or puppet rituals. Communication should be established between the innermost selves of family members, and their anxieties should be listened to attentively. Agonized, depressed, or withdrawn individuals would "unbosom" themselves if appropriately approached. Orders should not be carried out by means of coercion or the threat—let alone the actual use—of physical punishment. Consent to a more regular pattern of behavior should be given freely and from the bottom of the heart. In short, both in moral treatment psychiatry and in religion-inspired domestic psychiatry, what was significant was the interiority of an individual. Domestic psychiatry thus drew strength from the new emphasis on the inner self, promoted by Evangelical Christianity.

The emphasis on emotional ties strengthened the family's capacity to understand the lunacy of its member. What seems to have weakened the family's capacity to cope with family members' lunacy was the duplicity with which the family managed madness—although the lunacy of a family member should not be exposed, at the same time no sign of coarse coercion inside should be revealed. This game of contradictions put the family in a very difficult position: space for maneuvering was very small indeed. I am aware that I am putting the family in a most unfavorable light. Lest my argument be mistaken, I would like to emphasize that I am not casting cynical doubt on the numerous expressions of families' sympathy for their insane members. To interpret all such statements as an invented hypocritical veneer to hide internal coercion and manipulation is absurd. Families' grief over the madness of their loved ones was beyond doubt genuine and sincere. What I would like to emphasize is that the ideal of the emotional solidarity of a family was at the same time an important asset in the public sphere. Domestic virtues were the basis of public life; happy family lives were no less a public statement than a personal goal. The private and the public spheres were mutually reinforcing, intersecting constructions. It is anachronistic to use the label *hypocrisy* to criticize Rosa Bagster's family, who "fenced" her in with two women, or Lord Shaftesbury, who pretended that he was just sitting down with his epileptic son, or many other families who tried to "hide" their insane relatives. To raise such a criticism is to valorize the ways in which the public and the private intersect in our age and to despise the ways in which the two intersected in the nineteenth century. I have used terms such as *hypocrisy* and *duplicity* to describe factually, rather than to judge morally, the behavior of nineteenth-century families as they tried to cope with the mental illness of family members.

This mutual permeation of the private and the public led to the destabilization of the family with a lunatic within its walls. The intrusion of the public measure into the family raised particularly thorny questions when the alleged lunatic was the head of the household. When an alleged lunatic's wife or her sympathizers attempted to deprive the mad paterfamilias of his civil rights, what was at issue was very grave indeed—the discretion of the head of the household over his realm. The jury in the Davenport case declared his insanity and loss of his rights based purely on his domestic conduct, expressing their belief in the desirability of one form of marriage over another. The implication of such a decision was that a husband who could not conduct a normal family life ran the risk of being declared insane. People measured the sanity of an individual, male or female, by domestic and private codes of behavior, based on heightened expectations of happy family life. Failure to observe certain rules in the private sphere led to the loss of one's civil rights, again reflecting the importance of one's domestic conduct as a basis for one's claim to public status. Because of the considerable importance attached to the family, domestic conduct became something too important to be left to the discretion of private individuals.

Such destabilization during the period under consideration had many causes. Commissions of lunacy became easier to obtain, due to both a lowered burden of proof and lowered cost. The state thus established a channel through which control over a lunatic's person and property was directed into the state machinery of law, without forcefully intervening in family affairs. Magistrates were becoming increasingly keen on the issue of lunacy, perhaps owing to their involvement in the management of county asylums. Some of them must have modeled themselves on the heroic figure of Mr. Higgins of the 1814–15 Parliamentary Inquiry. Two magistrates in Gloucestershire did break into the house of George Smith, on only slight evidence of abuse. The position of Lunacy Commissioner, created in 1845, intensified this moral pressure on the family with an insane member living in its midst. Despite their limited statutory power, Lunacy Commissioners effectively heightened the public's suspicion of secrecy in the matter of lunacy. The cloud of moral ambiguity was slowly but steadily gathering around a lunatic kept in the family. Most important, such ambiguity must have been keenly felt by the very family that had confined an insane member within the family home.

Last, I have attempted to highlight the family's presence in psychiatrists' thinking. My sources present a much more nuanced and complex picture than the one that has been presented by historical studies of numerous incidents of wrongful confinement. Psychiatric practitioners were deeply influenced by the families that were their clients, despite their aspiration to scientific psychiatry and autonomous professional status at the bedside, fervently expressed in the pages of their publications. Opinions expressed by members of the patient's family were taken into account. The family's concern to protect its property or reputation was incorporated into doctors' practice in diagnosing and treating lunatics. Indeed, the family's status as an important agent in matters of lunacy became increasingly well established in the manuals for conduct at the psychiatric bedside and in the concept of moral insanity. At the same time, such service to the family needed to be conducted in a publicly acceptable manner: if the psychiatrist's conduct was found wanting in that aspect, the public punished the practitioner with a vengeance. Psychiatric practitioners tried hard to adapt themselves to this new game of the dual mastership of the family and the public, rather than dominating the game.

APPENDIX

List of the Reports of Commissions of Lunacy in the London 'Times,' 1823-1861

Notes: The Date column lists the date when the first report appeared. The Days column lists the length of the trial. Under Institution, I list the place of residence other than the home of the subject of the commission only when such information is given in the report. ("PMH" stands for private madhouse.) Likewise, the Age column contains an entry only when an age is given in the reports.

Date (Year/Month/Day)	*Days*	*Sex*	*Name*	*Institution*	*Age*
1823/02/10	10	M	Portsmouth, Lord		
1825/08/02	8	M	Frank, Edward		
1825/08/30	1	M	Burroughs, Sackville		
1826/04/08	1	M	Talbot, Rev. Thomas		
1826/08/03	1	F	Eliason, Sarah		
1826/08/07	1	F	Creswell, Lady		
1827/01/23	6	M	King, James		
1827/07/25	1	M	Joddiell, Richard Paul		
1827/07/31	1	F	Marton, Marienne		
1827/11/05	1	M	Homes, William		
1828/06/14	1	M	Tatham, John		
1828/06/27	1	M	Callow, William		

(continued)

Date (Year/Month/Day)	*Days*	*Sex*	*Name*	*Institution*	*Age*
1828/12/12	1	M	Rothwell, Thomas Dutton		
1829/08/14	1	F	Burton, Rachel		
1829/08/24	1	M	Randall, J.L.		
1829/10/01	1	M	Jervis, Hon. Mr.		
1829/12/15	14	M	Davies, Edward	PMH	
1830/02/16	1	M	Howitt, John Jervis		
1830/03/30	1	M	Miles, Richard		
1830/04/01	1	M	Hack, Richard	PMH	
1830/06/29	1	F	Sherard, Lady Charlotte	PMH	
1830/08/18	7	M	Brand, John	PMH	
1830/09/25	1	F	Scott, Agnes		
1830/12/11	1	F	Rennay, Jane		
1831/05/10	1	F	Ellison, Sophia	PMH	
1831/06/20	1	M	Liebenhood, George	PMH?	
1831/06/20	1	F	Liebenhood, Lucy C.	PMH?	
1831/08/26	8	M	Clement, Robert		
1831/09/20	3	M	Knight, George		
1832/01/16	1	M	Hook, T. B.		
1832/04/17	1	M	Blewitt, E. T.		
1832/07/04	13	F	Bagster, Rosa		
1832/11/29	1	F	Hawkins, Ellen	PMH	50
1832/12/05	1	M	Wright, Charles	PMH	
1833/05/10	1	M	Blake, Thomas		
1833/06/04	1	F	Burnell, Elizabeth		
1833/07/23	1	M	Kingston, Earl of	PMH	
1833/08/31	1	M	Rowth, Cuthbert	Cottage	
1833/12/19	1	F	Johnson, Rebecca	PMH	54
1834/04/18	1	M	Robbus, John	PMH	65
1834/04/25	1	M	Quath, Charles F.		
1834/04/25	1	M	Vigors, Mr.		
1834/04/28	1	M	Saumarez, Paul		
1834/04/29	1	F	Sturgis, Charlotte	PMH	
1834/06/12	1	F	Crawford, Jane Eliza		
1834/07/05	1	M	Hope, Adrien		
1834/07/16	1	F	Livesay, Mary		30
1834/07/25	1	M	Gray, ——	PMH	
1834/10/02	1	F	Rowley, Frances	PMH	30

Date (Year/Month/Day)	Days	Sex	Name	Institution	Age
1834/10/02	1	F	Rowley, Isabella		45
1834/11/20	1	M	Mills, James	PMH	
1834/12/01	1	M	Tomlin, John	PMH	
1835/02/16	2	F	Filmer, Lady Esther	Cottage	
1835/05/12	1	F	James, Harriet	PMH	
1835/05/13	1	M	Trapp, John	Cottage	50
1835/06/24	1	M	Wescott, Peter Thomas		
1835/06/30	1	F	West, Louisa	PMH	38
1835/08/01	2	M	Jackson, William		
1835/08/25	2	M	Barker, Edward		83
1835/08/31	1	M	Dixon, Rev. William	PMH	80
1835/10/25	1	M	Benison, John		Elderly
1836/01/12	1	F	Dickinson, Frederica		Young
1836/01/26	1	M	Durand, John Nicholas	PMH	Elderly
1836/02/10	7	F	Fitzmaurice, Hon. Anna M.		
1836/02/20	1	M	Ward, William		
1836/04/01	1	M	Belden, Joseph		
1836/04/01	1	M	Fraser, William	A surgeon's	30
1836/04/06	2	M	Norris, John		50–60
1836/06/29	1	M	Toussaint, Benjamin	PMH	27
1836/08/25	1	M	Forbes, Lord		
1836/08/30	2	M	Lyon, George		36
1836/12/21	1	M	Langham, Sir James		35
1837/01/11	1	M	Warlters, Thomas	PMH	
1837/01/11	1	F	Williams, Ann		85
1837/02/28	1	M	Belsey, Mr.		
1837/03/27	1	M	Barham, John		
1837/05/05	1	F	Cobbett, Elizabeth	PMH	
1837/07/19	1	M	Barnet, Rev. William	PMH	
1837/08/08	1	F	Fennell, Prisella Mary		
1837/08/09	1	F	Solomon, Elizabeth		
1837/09/12	1	M	Alderson, Christopher		
1837/09/19	1	M	Baker, Captain		
1837/11/09	1	M	Bushby, Thomas		
1837/12/01	1	M	Frolick, J. H.		
1838/01/15	1	M	Gould, John		
1838/01/25	1	M	Martin, Rev. Richmond		

(continued)

Date (Year/Month/Day)	*Days*	*Sex*	*Name*	*Institution*	*Age*
1838/02/09	1	F	Edwards, Ann		
1838/02/10	6	M	Davenport, George		
1838/02/17	1	M	Lee, Pink	PMH	
1838/03/08	1	F	Loftus, Miss		
1838/03/12	1	M	Booth, George		29
1838/03/21	1	F	Mullins, Jane	PMH	
1838/03/22	1	M	Tubb, Augustus Bedord	PMH	
1838/04/02	1	M	Shipden, James	PMH	33
1838/06/01	1	M	Gould, John	Asylum	
1838/06/28	2	M	Wynne, George Heneage	PMH	
1838/07/12	2	F	Seymour, Dame Sarah L.		
1838/08/06	1	M	Rivett, Tobias		70
1838/08/09	1	M	Eusden, William	PMH	
1838/08/21	1	F	Sprague, Sarah		
1838/08/23	1	F	Sprout, Isabel	PMH	
1838/11/07	1	F	Ridge, Louisa	PMH	
1839/01/01	10	M	Taylor, John	PMH	87
1839/01/11	1	F	Hewlett, Honor	Workhouse	65
1839/03/09	1	M	Bartlett, William	PMH	
1839/03/26	1	F	Wingfield, Hon. Martha		
1839/03/30	1	F	Chasternay, Sophie de		
1839/04/16	1	M	Wilson, Sir James		
1839/09/02	1	M	Cresswell, Richard E.	PMH	
1839/09/12	1	M	Swindall, Thomas		44
1839/10/21	1	M	King, John Shaw		
1839/10/23	1	M	Ebbing, Mather R.	PMH	
1839/11/14	1	F	Lloyd, Eleanor		
1839/12/10	1	F	Tweedale, Caroline Ann		26
1839/12/12	1	M	Pearce, Henry Robert	PMH	
1840/01/30	1	M	Bryant, Henry		
1840/02/11	2	M	Robinson, John Peter		
1840/04/03	1	F	George, Fanny		57
1840/06/26	1	F	Firth, Charlotte		
1840/07/23	1	M	Donnely, Sir Ross		80
1840/10/01	1	F	Parsons, Frances Mary		
1840/12/18	2	M	Place, Rev. Harry J.	PMH	
1840/10/05	1	M	Stevens, William		64

Date (Year/Month/Day)	*Days*	*Sex*	*Name*	*Institution*	*Age*
1840/11/28	1	M	West, John Gurr		21
1841/01/21	1	M	Manning, Richard Pate	PMH	72
1841/03/08	1	M	Fenwick, William		ca. 50
1841/03/23	1	M	Turner, John		87
1841/03/27	1	F	Jennings, Catherine		49
1841/04/02	1	F	White, Barbara	PMH	52
1841/07/03	1	M	Pinks, William		
1841/09/04	1	M	Ireland, Joseph	PMH	
1841/09/09	1	M	Cohen, Solomon	Hanwell	
1841/09/18	1	M	Newton, William A.	PMH	
1841/11/15	1	F	Fisher, Elizabeth	PMH	
1841/11/25	2	M	Weeks, Richard	PMH	54
1841/11/29	1	M	Morgan, Rev. David	PMH	
1841/12/18	1	M	Carter, Charles	PMH	
1842/01/01	1	M	Bishop of Ossory		
1842/02/03	3	M	Gundry, Daniel		
1842/02/05	1	M	Strong, Murray	PMH	
1842/04/02	1	M	Pearch, James	PMH	
1842/06/11	1	M	Sparrow, Henry Weir		
1842/09/16	1	M	Campbell, Andrew M.		
1842/10/31	1	F	Cottrell, Isabella		
1842/11/12	1	F	Cowderoy, Mary Ann		54
1842/12/10	1	F	Jones, Mary		42
1842/12/13	1	M	Brome, John		35
1842/12/20	1	M	Smith, James		
1842/12/20	1	F	Sturrock, Ann		82
1842/12/23	1	M	de Riemer, George		65
1843/01/10	1	M	Vernon, George	PMH	40–50
1843/04/01	1	F	Hoy, Mary		21
1843/04/26	2	M	Burns, John		
1843/05/05	1	F	Bird, Sarah		76
1843/06/26	1	F	Brown, Mary Barbara		60
1843/07/08	1	F	Cheetham, Jane		
1843/08/02	3	M	Sombre, Dyce		
1843/09/04	1	M	Tillard, W. O.		
1843/12/06	3	F	Hartley, Mary		
1843/12/09	2	M	Hartley, [unknown]		

(continued)

Date (Year/Month/Day)	*Days*	*Sex*	*Name*	*Institution*	*Age*
1843/12/20	1	M	Pearce, Author Legent	Bethlem	
1844/01/16	1	F	Bariatinski, Princess		
1844/01/25	1	M	Thomas, Edward		
1844/01/30	1	M	Wilkins, Joshua R.	PMH	
1844/02/02	1	F	Downer, Maria		
1844/08/19	1	M	Spencer, Brent	Workhouse	37
1844/09/23	2	M	Campbell, Thomas T.		
1844/09/24	1	M	Mayo, H.	PMH	40
1844/11/30	1	M	Porter, George		
1845/03/05	1	M	Watts, George		
1845/03/13	1	M	Austin, William		40
1845/04/24	1	M	Nelson, Mr.		
1845/05/26	1	M	Woodcock, Stephen L.		
1845/06/12	1	M	Tucker, John		65
1845/08/30	1	M	Herford, William Lewis		
1845/09/26	1	M	Clarke, David Thomas		50
1845/11/03	1	F	Caney, Sarah		80+
1845/11/19	1	M	Parry, Richard Read		
1850/04/22	1	F	Wakeman, Maria Theresa		80
1850/05/14	1	M	Bridge, Sealy		77
1850/06/13	1	M	Marsh, Rev. Herbert C.		
1850/08/26	1	M	Hartley, Leonard Laurie		30
1850/10/10	1	M	Tollemache, Arthur H. M.		
1851/03/04	1	M	Loveday, [unknown]		
1851/08/25	1	M	Rusbridger, Thomas		50
1852/01/09	17	F	Cuming, Catherine		
1852/05/25	1	F	Hughes, Hon. Emily		
1852/05/25	1	F	Hughes, Hon. Mary M.		
1853/01/17	1	M	Eldon, Lord		
1853/04/13	1	M	O'Connor, Feargus		
1858/05/21	2	M	Leach, Rev. William J. J.		51
1858/06/09	9	M	Meux, Sir Henry		
1858/07/27	2	F	Turner, Mary Jane		
1858/08/24	5	M	Ruck, Lawrence		40
1859/08/19	5	F	Ewing, Phoebe		
1861/12/17	20	M	Windham, W. F.		

NOTES

ABBREVIATIONS

ARLC	*Annual Report of Lunacy Commissioners*
BPP	*British Parliamentary Papers*
DNB	*Dictionary of National Biography*
GLRO	London Metropolitan Archives
MBB	Frederic Boase, *Modern British Biography*
MSS	manuscripts
ODNB	*Oxford Dictionary of National Biography*
PRO	Public Record Office
RCP Edinburgh	Royal College of Physicians of Edinburgh
RCP London	Royal College of Physicians of London
UCL	University College London Library
WCL	City of Westminster Library and Archives
WIHM	Wellcome Institute for the History of Medicine

INTRODUCTION

1. Andrew Scull, *The Most Solitary of Afflictions: Madness and Society in Britain, 1700–1900* (New Haven, Conn.: Yale University Press, 1993).

2. An important caveat should be made to the thesis of the "rise of the asylum." We still do not know the number of men and women who were "recognized" as

insane during the nineteenth century. For a brief discussion of this problem, see Peter Bartlett and David Wright, "Community Care and Its Antecedents," in *Outside the Walls of the Asylum: The History of Care in Community, 1750–2000,* ed. Peter Bartlett and David Wright (London: Athlone Press, 1999), 1–18.

3. Here one should note that Peter Bartlett has debunked the contemporary myth of the trade-off of lunatics between county asylums and workhouses, which were regarded as two antagonistic institutions. See Peter Bartlett, *The Poor Law of Lunacy: The Administration of Pauper Lunatics in Mid-Nineteenth-Century England* (London: Leicester University Press, 1999).

4. James E. Moran, "Asylum in the Community: Managing the Insane in Antebellum America," *History of Psychiatry* 9 (1998): 217–40. Moran draws on the same type of legal documents as I have in this book.

5. See, for example, Leonore Davidoff, "The Family in Britain," in *The Cambridge Social History of Britain, 1750–1950,* ed. F. M. L. Thompson (Cambridge: Cambridge University Press, 1990), vol. 2: 71–129; and Catherine Hall, "The Sweet Delights of Home," in *From the Fires of Revolution to the Great War,* ed. Michelle Perrot, vol. 4 of *A History of Private Life,* ed. Philippe Ariès and Georges Duby, trans. Arthur Goldhammer (Cambridge, Mass.: Belknap Press of Harvard University Press, 1990), 47–93.

6. For perceptive discussions of the limits and potentials of institutional records, see Bartlett and Wright, "Community Care and Its Antecedents"; and Jonathan Andrews, "Case Notes, Case Histories, and Patients' Experience of Insanity at Gartnaval Royal Asylum, Glasgow, in the Nineteenth Century," *Social History of Medicine* 11 (1998): 255–81. See also my discussion in Akihito Suzuki, "Framing Psychiatric Subjectivity: Doctor, Patient, and Record-Keeping at Bethlem in the Nineteenth Century," in *Insanity, Institutions, and Society, 1800–1914,* ed. Joseph Melling and Bill Forsythe (London: Routledge, 1999), 115–36.

7. For essays examining comparable problems in working-class families, see Jonathan Andrews and Anne Digby, eds., *Sex and Seclusion, Class and Custody: Perspectives on Gender and Class in the History of British and Irish Psychiatry* (Amsterdam: Rodopi, 2004).

8. Bartlett and Wright, "Community Care and Its Antecedents"; Joseph Melling, "Accommodating Madness: New Research in the Social History of Insanity and Institutions," in *Insanity, Institutions, and Society, 1800–1914,* ed. Joseph Melling and Bill Forsythe (London: Routledge, 1999), 1–30.

9. D. H. Tuke, *Chapters in the History of the Insane in the British Isles* (London: Kegan Paul, Trench & Co., 1882).

10. Thomas Szasz, *The Myth of Mental Illness* (London: Granada, 1972); Michel Foucault, *Histoire de la folie à l'âge classique* (Paris: Éditions Gallimard, 1972). See also Arthur Still and Irving Velody, eds., *Rewriting the History of Madness: Studies in Foucault's "Histoire de la folie"* (London: Routledge, 1992).

11. Andrew Scull, *Museums of Madness: The Social Organization of Insanity in Nineteenth-Century England* (1979; reprinted, Harmondsworth: Penguin, 1982).

12. Jose Harris, *Private Lives, Public Spirit: Britain, 1870–1914* (Harmondsworth: Penguin, 1994).

13. Foucault, *Histoire de la folie.* See also Michel Foucault, *Discipline and Punish: The Birth of the Prison,* trans. Alan Sheridan (Harmondsworth: Penguin, 1979).

14. Scull, *Most Solitary of Afflictions;* Andrew Scull, *Social Order/Mental Disorder* (London: Routledge, 1989). For critical discussions of Scull's works, see Bartlett and Wright, eds., *Outside the Walls of the Asylum;* and Melling and Forsythe, eds., *Insanity, Institutions, and Society.*

15. Bartlett, *Poor Law of Lunacy;* Leonard D. Smith, *"Cure, Comfort and Safe Custody": Public Lunatic Asylums in Early Nineteenth-Century England* (London: Leicester University Press & Cassell, 1999).

16. Michael MacDonald, *Mystical Bedlam: Madness, Anxiety, and Healing in Seventeenth-Century England* (Cambridge: Cambridge University Press, 1981).

17. Roy Porter, *Mind-Forg'd Manacles: A History of Madness in England from the Restoration to the Regency* (London: Athlone Press, 1987), 136–47, 187–228. For private madhouses in England in general, see William Ll. Parry-Jones, *The Trade in Lunacy* (London: Routledge and Kegan Paul, 1972).

18. Such instances of overlaps are analyzed in Richard Hunter and Ida Macalpine, *Psychiatry for the Poor: 1851 Colney Hatch Asylum, Friern Hospital 1973* (London: Dawsons, 1974).

19. Andrew Scull, Charlotte MacKenzie, and Nicholas Hervey, *Masters of Bedlam: The Transformation of the Mad-Doctoring Trade* (Princeton, N.J.: Princeton University Press, 1996).

20. Jonathan Andrews and Andrew Scull, *Undertaker of the Mind: John Monro and Mad-Doctoring in Eighteenth-Century England* (Berkeley and Los Angeles: University of California Press, 2001); Jonathan Andrews and Andrew Scull, *Customers and Patrons of the Mad Trade: The Management of Lunacy in Eighteenth-Century London* (Berkeley and Los Angeles: University of California Press, 2003).

21. This direction of investigation has been suggested by Nancy Tomes, "The Anatomy of Madness: New Directions in the History of Psychiatry," *Social Studies of Science* 17 (1987): 358–71.

22. Mark Finnane, *Insanity and the Insane in Post-Famine Ireland* (London: Croom Helm, 1981); John L. Walton, "Lunacy in the Industrial Revolution: A Study of Asylum Admissions in Lancashire, 1845–50," *Journal of Social History* 13 (1979): 1–21.

23. David Wright, "Getting Out of the Asylum: Understanding the Confinement of the Insane in the Nineteenth Century," *Social History of Medicine* 10 (1997): 137–55.

24. David Wright, *Mental Disability in Victorian England: The Earlswood Asylum, 1847–1901* (Oxford: Clarendon Press, 2001).

25. Robert Castel, *The Regulation of Madness: The Origin of Incarceration in France,* trans. W. D. Halls (Oxford: Polity, 1988); Yannick Ripa, *Women and Madness: The Incarceration of Women in Nineteenth-Century France,* trans. Catherine du Peloux Menagé (Cambridge: Polity Press, 1990).

26. Ruth Harris, *Murders and Madness: Medicine, Law, and Society in the Fin de Siècle* (Oxford: Oxford University Press, 1989), 155–242.

27. Patricia E. Prestwich, "Family Strategies and Medical Power: 'Voluntary' Committal in a Parisian Asylum, 1876–1914," *Journal of Social History* 27 (1994): 799–818.

28. Nancy Tomes, *The Art of Asylum-Keeping: Thomas Story Kirkbride and the Origin of American Psychiatry* (1984; reprinted, Philadelphia: University of Pennsylvania Press, 1994).

29. Elizabeth Lunbeck, *The Psychiatric Persuasion: Knowledge, Gender, and Power in Modern America* (Princeton, N.J.: Princeton University Press, 1994).

30. The number of works on the cultural history of madness is vast. Classic works include: Sander Gilman, *Seeing the Insane* (New York: John Wiley & Sons, 1982); Sander Gilman, *Difference and Pathology: Stereotypes of Sexuality, Race, and Madness* (Ithaca, N.Y.: Cornell University Press, 1985); and Elaine Showalter, *The Female Malady: Women, Madness and English Culture, 1830–1980* (London: Virago, 1987).

31. Arthur Kleinman, *The Illness Narratives: Suffering, Healing, and the Human Condition* (New York: Basic Books, 1988), 43–48.

32. Nancy Tomes, "Devils in the Heart: A Nineteenth-Century Perspective on Women and Depression," *Transactions and Studies of the College of Physicians of Philadelphia,* ser. 5, 13 (1991): 363–86.

CHAPTER ONE

1. The reports of the case originally appeared in the *Times* (London), and were reprinted in Anon., *A Genuine Report of the Proceedings on the Portsmouth Case, under a Commission Issued by His Majesty* (London: Duncombe, [1823]). Hereafter, all references to the *Times* mean the London *Times.*

2. John Hanson was also Lord Byron's attorney. For Byron's involvement in the Hanson family and the commissions of lunacy against Lord Portsmouth, see Lord Byron, *Byron's Letters and Journals,* ed. Leslie A. Marchand (London: John Murray, 1973–1980), vol. 1: 40; vol. 3: 248; vol. 4: 123–25, 170, 189, 236–37, 244–45, 254, 258–59, 265, 272; vol. 10: 125.

3. At one time, those concerned with Lord Portsmouth's virility consulted *Aristotle's Masterpiece,* a best-selling guide to sexual pleasure and reproduction throughout the eighteenth century. See Anon., *Genuine Report,* 46. For *Aristotle's*

Masterpiece, see Roy Porter, "'The Secrets of Generation Display'd': *Aristotle's Master-piece* in Eighteenth-Century England," in *'Tis Nature's Fault: Unauthorized Sexuality during the Enlightenment,* ed. Robert Purks Maccubin (Cambridge: Cambridge University Press, 1987), 1–21.

4. As an impotent aristocrat treating lesser beings brutally, he anticipated Lord Chatterley.

5. For the erotic undertone of Lord Portsmouth's search for bleeding, see *Byron's Letters and Journals,* vol. 10: 125. For a later reference to this incident, see *Times,* 2 Aug. 1825, 3c. Especially striking is the association of bloodletting with sexual pleasure, a theme explored in novels of the Marquis de Sade such as *Justine.* See Marquis de Sade, *The Misfortunes of Virtue and Other Early Tales,* ed. David Coward (Oxford: Oxford University Press, 1999). For the association of blood (in the context of flagellation) and erotic feeling, see Julie Peakman, *Mighty Lewd Books: The Development of Pornography in Eighteenth-Century England* (London: Palgrave, 2003), 62–66, 176–81.

6. For the examination of divorce cases and accompanying "criminal conversation" suits, see Lawrence Stone, *The Road to Divorce: England, 1530–1987* (Oxford: Oxford University Press, 1990); and Lawrence Stone, *Broken Lives: Separation and Divorce in England, 1660–1857* (Oxford: Oxford University Press, 1993).

7. For the distinction between *lunacy* and *being of unsound mind,* see chapter 6.

8. Anon., *Genuine Report,* 14.

9. Nicholas Hervey, "Lunacy Commission, 1845–1860, with Special Reference to the Implementation of Policy in Kent and Surrey" (Ph.D. diss., University of Bristol, 1987).

10. Lawrence Stone once compared the historian's craft to that of tabloid journalism and advocated a "case history" approach. Lawrence Stone, *Uncertain Unions: Marriage in England, 1660–1753* (Oxford: Oxford University Press, 1992).

11. Andrew Scull, *The Most Solitary of Afflictions: Madness and Society in Britain, 1700–1900* (New Haven, Conn.: Yale University Press, 1993), 115–32.

12. Ibid., 111.

13. Anon., *Genuine Report,* 36.

14. See, for example, ibid., 24–25, in which the lord was horsewhipped by his wife; and ibid., 38, in which he was slapped in the face by her.

15. The commission of lunacy against Lord Portsmouth in 1823 was actually the second commission asked for him. The first commission was asked in 1814, but it failed. See *Byron's Letters and Journals,* vol. 4: 186, 236–37, and elsewhere.

16. My contextualization of the Queen Caroline affair owes much to Thomas W. Laqueur, "The Queen Caroline Affair: Politics as Art in the Reign of George IV," *Journal of Modern History* 54 (1982): 417–66; Leonore Davidoff and Catherine Hall, *Family Fortunes: Men and Women of the English Middle Class, 1780–1850* (London: Routledge, 1992), 149–55; and Flora Fraser, *The Unruly Queen: The Life of Queen Caroline* (London: Macmillan, 1996).

17. Peter Wagner, *Eros Revived: Erotica of the Enlightenment in England and America* (London: Paladin, 1988); Lynn Hunt, ed., *The Invention of Pornography: Obscenity and the Origins of Modernity, 1500–1800* (New York: Zone Books, 1993); Iain McCalman, *Radical Underworld: Prophets, Revolutionaries, and Pornographers in London, 1795–1840* (Oxford: Clarendon Press, 1993).

18. McCalman, *Radical Underworld.* On a similar situation in France, see Robert Darnton, *The Literary Underground of the Old Regime* (Cambridge, Mass.: Harvard University Press, 1982); Sarah Maza, *Private Lives and Public Affairs: The Causes Célèbres of Prerevolutionary France* (Berkeley and Los Angeles: University of California Press, 1993).

19. McCalman, *Radical Underworld,* 152–231; Laqueur, "Queen Caroline Affair."

20. Davidoff and Hall, *Family Fortunes,* 152. Italics in the original.

21. Ibid.; Amanda Vickery, *The Gentleman's Daughter: Women's Lives in Georgian England* (New Haven, Conn.: Yale University Press, 1998); A. James Hammerton, *Cruelty and Companionship: Conflict in Nineteenth-Century Married Life* (London: Routledge, 1992); John Tosh, *A Man's Place: Masculinity and the Middle-Class Home in Victorian England* (New Haven, Conn.: Yale University Press, 1999); George K. Behlmer, *Friends of the Family: The English Home and Its Guardians, 1850–1940* (Stanford, Calif.: Stanford University Press, 1998).

22. For a general discussion of English laws and lunacy in the nineteenth century, see Peter Bartlett, *The Poor Law of Lunacy: The Administration of Pauper Lunatics in Mid-Nineteenth-Century England* (London: Leicester University Press, 1999), 8–31.

23. The next heir was usually precluded from the committee, "to prevent sinister practices," as Blackstone explained in his *Commentaries,* book 1, chapter 8. William Blackstone, *Commentaries on the Laws of England,* ed. Wayne Morrison (London: Cavendish Publishing, 2001), vol. 1: 231. See also James T. Sabben and J. H. Balfour Browne, *Handbook of Law and Lunacy* (London: J. & A. Churchill, 1872), 55. For the outline of commission *de lunatico inquirendo,* see Joseph Elmer, "Chancery Lunatics," in *A Dictionary of Psychological Medicine,* ed. D. H. Tuke (London: J. & A. Churchill, 1892), vol. 1: 195–201; Richard Neugebauer, "Mental Handicap in Medieval and Early Modern England," in *From Idiocy to Mental Deficiency: Historical Perspectives on People with Learning Disabilities,* ed. David Wright and Anne Digby (London: Routledge, 1996), 22–43; and Michael MacDonald, "Lunatics and the State in Georgian England," *Social History of Medicine* 2 (1989): 299–313. My search of legal materials has been greatly facilitated by Peter Bartlett, "Legal Madness in the Nineteenth Century," *Social History of Medicine* 14 (2001): 107–31.

24. Elmer, "Chancery Lunatics"; Blackstone, *Commentaries,* book 1, chapter 8.

25. Richard Neugebauer, "Mental Illness and Government Policy in Sixteenth- and Seventeenth-Century England" (Ph.D. diss., Columbia University, 1976).

26. MacDonald, "Lunatics and the State." See also "Parker, Thomas" [Earl of Macclesfield] in DNB and ODNB.

27. Cleave More, *The Apology, or Vindication of Sir Cleave More, Bart., upon the Suing Forth of a Commission of Lunacy against Joseph Edmonds, Esquire, Setting Forth the Motives and Reasons for So Doing, with a Short Account of the Several Acts of Lunacy, Proved upon Mr. Edmonds* (London: George Croom, 1711).

28. For the accounts of these cases in the eighteenth century, see Roy Porter, *Mind-Forg'd Manacles,* 148–54; and Jonathan Andrews, "'In Her Vapours . . . [or] Indeed in Her Madness'? Mrs Clerke's Case: An Early Eighteenth-Century Psychiatric Controversy," *History of Psychiatry* 1 (1990): 125–43.

29. The Act's professed purpose was "removing or diminishing the delays and expenses now attending on the execution of Commissions in the nature of writs de lunatico inquirendo." 16 and 17 Vict.c.70.

30. 16 and 17 Vict.c.70.s.7. The title "Masters in Lunacy" was adopted in 1845, replacing the former "Commissioners in Lunacy," to avoid confusion with the office of the same name created by the Lunacy Act of 1845 (8 and 9 Vict.c.100.s.2). See D. H. Tuke, "Commissioners in Lunacy," in *A Dictionary of Psychological Medicine,* ed. D. H. Tuke (London: J. & A. Churchill, 1892), vol. 1: 240.

31. 25 and 26 Vict.c.85.s.4.

32. 25 and 26 Vict.c.86.s.12.

33. 45 and 46 Vict.c.82.s.3.

34. Acts of Parliaments and their Amendments related to lunacy proliferated beginning in the early nineteenth century and complicated the medical, legal, and administrative handling of lunatics. Already by 1859, people wanted Parliament to amalgamate and simplify them. See Danby P. Fry, *The Lunacy Acts: Containing All the Statutes Relating to Private Lunatics, etc.* (London: Knight & Co., 1877).

35. Issues related to the commission of lunacy were stated in parts III and IV of the Act. 53 Vict.c.5.ss.90–129. For the Lunacy Act of 1890, see George Pitt-Lewis, R. Percy Smith, and J. A. Hawke, *The Insane and the Law: A Plain Guide for Medical Men, Solicitors, and Others* (London: J. & A. Churchill, 1895); and Kathleen Jones, *A History of the Mental Health Services* (London: Routledge & Kegan Paul, 1972), 176–81.

36. This meant that one could sign a valid contract even if one was certified as a lunatic. For contemporary allusions to this paradox, see William Griggs, *Lunacy and Liberty: A Letter to the Lord Chancellor, on the Defective State of the Law, As Regards Insane Persons, etc.* (London: W. Griggs, 1832), 12; and *Times,* 2 June 1851, 7f.

37. 53 Vict.c.5.s.116.

38. Ibid.

39. Elmer, "Chancery Lunatics."

40. 8 Edw.7.c.47.s.1; 12 and 13 Geo.5.c.60.

41. Gerald E. Mills and A. H. Ronald W. Poyster, *Management and Administration of Estates in Lunacy* (London: Butterworth & Co., 1927), 19.

42. The data are drawn from the index to commissions of lunacy at PRO IND 1 and index to C211.

43. The figures for 1880 and 1881 (45 Victoria) are missing in the original index because the records for these years were lost during the transfer. The unnaturally low figures in 1853 and 1862 are also suspect, for these were the years that saw the new Lunacy Regulation Act and its Amendment.

44. Lawrence Stone, *The Family, Sex, and Marriage in England, 1500–1800* (Harmondsworth: Penguin, 1979).

45. For female lunatics, descriptions of their marital status usually replace those of their means of income. For only two women, a milliner and an ironmonger, are occupations listed (PRO IND 1/17612 H.43, J.73). For twenty-two women, the reports give their titles ("lady," "dame," "duchess," etc.).

46. The only study that has used some reports of commissions of lunacy is Peter McCandless, "Liberty and Lunacy: The Victorians and Wrongful Confinement," in *Madhouses, Mad-Doctors, and Madmen: The Social History of Psychiatry in the Victorian Era,* ed. Andrew Scull (London: Athlone Press, 1981), 339–62. From 1833 on, two physicians and one lawyer were appointed as visitors to inspect Chancery lunatics. Sir John Charles Bucknill and Sir James Crichton-Brown were among the most prominent. See Andrew Scull, Charlotte MacKenzie, and Nicholas Hervey, "From Disciple to Critic: Sir John Charles Bucknill (1817–1897)," in *Masters of Bedlam: Transformation of the Mad-Doctoring Trade* (Princeton, N.J.: Princeton University Press, 1996), 187–225; and Michael Neve and Trevor Turner, "What the Doctor Thought and Did: Sir James Crichton-Brown (1840–1938)," *Medical History* 39 (1995): 399–432.

47. Scotland had a comparable legal procedure but it came under a different jurisdiction and was considerably different. Its original records have been extensively discussed in R. A. Houston, *Madness and Society in Eighteenth-Century Scotland* (Oxford: Clarendon Press, 2000).

48. PRO IND1 C211.

49. See, for example, PRO C217/55; draft medical statements by Edward Kingford of Sunbery, surgeon, and by Joseph Seaton, for the commission of lunacy of John Mitchinson in 1863, GLRO Acc 1156/70 and 1156/73. See also GLRO P92/SAV/1442–47, another set of papers related to a commission of lunacy against Nathaniel Hardy in 1748. The Wellcome Library holds one set of interesting materials related to the commission of lunacy against Rev. Thomas Gayfere in 1845. See WIHM MSS 6047. See also WIHM MSS 7477/1.

50. This is the case of Rev. Edward Frank, which will be discussed in chapter 5.

51. Namely, the cases of Rev. W. J. J. Leach, Sir Henry Meux, Mary Jane Turner, Lawrence Ruck, Phoebe Ewing, and W. F. Windham. See the appendix.

52. *Times,* 28 Apr. 1834, 6a.

53. *Times,* 29 Apr. 1834, 6c.

54. *Times,* 6 Aug. 1836, 2b. In Brougham's defense of privacy in the Frank case, there seems to be an echo of his attack on the government's prying into the privacy of Queen Caroline in 1820. See Laqueur, "Queen Caroline Affair," 436.

55. Another possible explanation is a probable decline in popular interest in commissions of lunacy in the 1840s. The only (and slim) evidence for this interpretation is a passing remark in the case of John Burns in 1843. In reporting a densely crowded room for the commission, the reporter commented that "many years have elapsed since similar proceedings have excited a more lively interest." *Times,* 26 Apr. 1843.

56. For criminal cases, see, for example, the case of Richard Dunn, *Times,* 11 July 1856, 12d; and the case of William Thomas, *Times,* 5 Apr. 1856, 12b. For an attempt to exclude "the public and the press" from an examination of a lunatic, see *Times,* 13 July 1854, 11e.

57. The case of Lord Portsmouth in 1823, the case of Edward Frank in 1825, and the case of John Brand in 1830.

58. Robert Sharp, *The Diary of Robert Sharp of South Cave: Life in a Yorkshire Village, 1812–1837,* ed. Janice E. Crowther and Peter A. Crowther (Oxford: Oxford University Press, 1997), 240, 377.

59. *Times,* 30 June 1828, 7c; *Times,* 22 Apr. 1836, 7d; *Times,* 9 Jan. 1852, 7f.

60. *Times,* 4 Feb. 1842, 6d–f.

61. *Times,* 14 Nov. 1839, 5f. See also a case in Windsor, "which excited great interest throughout the neighbourhood," reported in the *Times,* 27 Mar. 1841, 7c–d; and a case in Newbury, which "excited considerable interest in the town and neighbourhood," reported in the *Times,* 10 Dec. 1842, 3f.

62. *Times,* 20 Aug. 1825, 3f.

63. *Times,* 6 Aug. 1825, 2b. Occasionally, audiences in the court of commissions of lunacy encountered sexually explicit remarks, which were not printed in the *Times.* Such obscenities may have been a hidden attraction of the tribunal. See, e.g., *Times,* 25 Nov. 1841, 6b: "the remaining part of the answer is too indecent for publication." See also a transcription of a love-letter sent to a princess by Richard Dunn, in *Times,* 11 July 1856, 12d.

64. *Times,* 1 Oct. 1829, 3f–4a.

65. The commission for the Reverend David Morgan in 1841 "excited a painful interest throughout, owing to the excellent reputation which the rev. gentleman bore as a member of the Church of England." *Times,* 29 Nov. 1841, 5c. The case of one Mr. Belsey attracted attention because he was the owner of a castle of some historical interest. *Times,* 28 Feb. 1837, 6d. See also the case of Leonard Laurie in York, whose noisy litigation respecting his property brought him notoriety. *Times,* 26 Aug. 1850, 7f.

66. *Times,* 25 Nov. 1841, 6a. See also *Times,* 2 Dec. 1841, 6a, for a report of the

disputes over the will of Anne Weeks, a person of great eccentricity who had herself been the subject of a commission of lunacy.

67. *Times,* 12 Dec. 1828, 3c. The nature of the delusions seems to have been that he was admired by all the women in London.

68. *Times,* 5 Oct. 1840, 7b.

69. *Times,* 2 Apr. 1841, 6b–c.

70. Leonard Shelford, *A Practical Treatise of the Law Concerning Lunatics, Idiots, and Persons of Unsound Mind* (London: S. Sweet et al., 1847), 125.

71. *Times,* 8 Aug. 1826, 2e.

72. *Times,* 14 Aug. 1829, 4b.

73. The case of William Callow, *Times,* 27 June 1828, 3f; the case of Thomas Talbot, *Times,* 8 Apr. 1826, 3b; the case of Richard Pate Manning, *Times,* 21 Jan. 1841, 3d.

74. *Times,* 17 Feb. 1835, 2f.

75. *Times,* 26 Apr. 1843, 6e–f. The commission turned out, however, to be a simple one and the jury immediately returned a verdict of unsound mind after the examination of Barnes. *Times,* 27 Apr. 1843, 8a.

76. *Times,* 9 Aug. 1838, 3d.

77. *Times,* 21 May 1831, 6c.

78. *Times,* 23 July 1840, 6e–f.

79. *Times,* 18 Dec. 1841, 6b. Likewise, John Brome did not put up any opposition to the commission in his case, assuming a resigned attitude: "It is all right; I have no wish to be present myself, nor do I desire any professional man to attend for me; it is of no use. I am not in good health, and I am sure the jury will do what is right, and come to a right conclusion." *Times,* 13 Dec. 1842, 3b–d.

80. *Times,* 10 Dec. 1839, 7e.

81. *Times,* 20 Jan. 1844, 6f.

82. *Times,* 5 May 1843, 7d.

83. *Times,* 15 Nov. 1841, 6c.

84. *Times,* 10 Dec. 1842, 3f.

85. *Times,* 11 July 1856, 12d.

86. *Times,* 7 Nov. 1838, 6a–b.

87. *Times,* 14 June 1828, 4e.

88. He was a solicitor and loquaciousness may well have been his professional habit.

89. She was a daughter of Sir Henry Oakes, who, after his service in India, became insane and committed suicide. See DNB and ODNB, "Henry Oakes."

90. *Times,* 12 July 1838, 5f–6b.

91. *Times,* 26 July 1838, 3a–c.

92. *Times,* 8 Dec. 1843, 6c.

93. *Times,* 2 Apr. 1841, 6b–c.

94. *Times,* 26 May 1845, 7e.

95. Dr. Allen's dubious practice was severely reproached for its "irregularities" by the Metropolitan Commissioners in Lunacy in their report in 1844. See Metropolitan Commissioners in Lunacy, *Report of the Metropolitan Commissioners in Lunacy to the Lord Chancellor* (London: Bradbury and Evnats, 1844), 36–38.

96. *Times,* 23 Sept. 1844, 7a.

97. For an analysis of the practice of visiting Bedlam, see Jonathan Andrews, Asa Briggs, Roy Porter, Penny Tucker, and Keir Waddington, *The History of Bethlem* (London: Routledge, 1997), 178–99.

98. Roy Porter, *The Social History of Madness* (London: Weidenfeld and Nicolson, 1987); Allan Ingram, ed., *Voices of Madness: Four Pamphlets, 1683–1796* (Stroud, Gloucestershire: Sutton Publishing, 1997).

99. Dale Peterson, ed., *A Mad People's History of Madness* (Pittsburgh: University of Pittsburgh Press, 1982).

100. For an early attempt to record mad delusions, see John Haslam, *Illustrations of Madness* (1810; reprinted with an introduction by Roy Porter, London: Routledge, 1989). Bucknill published a poem written by one Macauley, whose insanity became a subject of trial and whose poem was loaned for publication. See [J. C. Bucknill], "Insane Literature," *Asylum Journal of Mental Science* 3 (1857): 43–80; [J. C. Bucknill], "Review of *The Metaphysicians: Being a Memoir of Franz Carvel, Brushmaker, Written by Himself; and of Harold Fremdling, Esquire, Written and Now Re-published by Francis Drake* (1857)," *Journal of Mental Science* 4 (1858), 249–57. For the fascination of Victorian literature with the voices of madness, see Ekbert Faas, *Retreat into the Mind: Victorian Poetry and the Rise of Psychiatry* (Princeton, N.J.: Princeton University Press, 1988); Helen Small, *Love's Madness: Medicine, the Novel, and Female Insanity, 1800–1865* (Oxford: Oxford University Press, 1996); and Sally Shuttleworth, *Charlotte Brontë and Victorian Psychology* (Cambridge: Cambridge University Press, 1996).

101. See the episode of "A Madman's Manuscript," in *The Pickwick Papers,* which was published in 1836. Charles Dickens, *The Pickwick Papers,* ed. James Kinsley (Oxford: Oxford University Press, 1988), 128–34.

102. Michel Foucault, *Histoire de la sexualité 1: La volonté de savoir* (Paris: Éditions Gallimard, 1976).

CHAPTER TWO

1. Alexander Morison, MSS Reports and Notes of Cases, RCP London, SR/471. Morison's interesting and somewhat anomalous career has been studied by Andrew Scull, Charlotte MacKenzie, and Nicholas Hervey, *Masters of Bedlam: The Transformation of the Mad-Doctoring Trade* (Princeton, N.J.: Princeton University Press, 1996), 123–60.

2. RCP London, SR/471, "The Case of Miss Mary M—— By Her Sister."

3. Ibid.

4. Ibid.

5. Dr. Davidson took her pulse and examined her tongue, but he did not include the result in his letter to Morison.

6. Edward Shorter, *Doctors and Their Patients: A Social History,* 2nd ed. (Brunswick, N.J.: Transaction Publishers, 1991); Barbara Duden, *The Women beneath the Skin: A Doctor's Patients in Eighteenth-Century Germany,* trans. Thomas Dunlap (Cambridge, Mass.: Harvard University Press, 1991); Stanley Joel Reiser, *Medicine and the Reign of Technology* (Cambridge: Cambridge University Press, 1978); N. D. Jewson, "Medical Knowledge and the Patronage System in Eighteenth-Century England," *Sociology* 8 (1974): 369–85; N. D. Jewson, "The Disappearance of the Sick-Man from Medical Cosmology, 1770–1870," *Sociology* 10 (1976): 225–44; Dorothy Porter and Roy Porter, *Patient's Progress: Doctors and Doctoring in Eighteenth-Century England* (Oxford: Polity Press, 1989).

7. Mary E. Fissell, "The Disappearance of the Patient's Narrative and the Invention of Hospital Medicine," in *British Medicine in an Age of Reform,* ed. Roger French and Andrew Wear (London: Routledge, 1991), 92–109.

8. Erwin H. Ackerknecht, "A Plea for a 'Behaviorist' Approach in Writing the History of Medicine," *Journal of the History of Medicine and Allied Sciences* 22 (1967): 211–14. See also John Harley Warner, "Science in Medicine," *Osiris,* 2nd ser., 1(1985): 37–58.

9. For doctors' performance in the context of criminal lunacy, see Joel Peter Eigen, *Witnessing Insanity: Madness and Mad-Doctors in the English Court* (New Haven, Conn.: Yale University Press, 1995).

10. Alexander Morison, MSS Reports and Notes of Cases in the handwriting of Sir Alexander Morison, M.D., RCP London, SR/471.

11. *Times,* 13 July 1832.

12. "Imposing Restraint on Lunatics," *London Medical Gazette* 5 (1829–30): 49–52; "Anderdon v. Burrows," *London Medical Gazette* 6 (1830): 183–87.

13. Peter McCandless, "Dangerous to Themselves and Others: The Victorian Debate over the Prevention of Wrongful Confinement," *Journal of British Studies* 23 (1983): 84–104; Peter McCandless, "Liberty and Lunacy: The Victorians and Wrongful Confinement," in *Madhouses, Mad-Doctors, and Madmen: The Social History of Psychiatry in the Victorian Era,* ed. Andrew Scull (London: Athlone Press, 1981), 339–62. On Victorian critics of wrongful confinement, see Nicholas Hervey, "Advocacy of Folly: The Alleged Lunatics' Friend Society, 1845–63," *Medical History* 30 (1986): 245–75.

14. This aspect of the life of Burrows has been closely studied in Irvine Loudon, *Medical Care and the General Practitioner, 1750–1850* (Oxford: Clarendon Press, 1986).

15. There is no modern biography of Burrows. The most informative is his obituary in *Medical Directory* (1847): 189–93. See also the entries in DNB and ODNB.

16. G. M. Burrows, *Commentaries on the Causes, Forms, Symptoms, and Treatment, Moral and Medical, of Insanity* (London: Thomas and George Underwood, 1828).

17. See Richard Hunter and Ida Macalpine, *Three Hundred Years of Psychiatry, 1535–1860* (1963; reprinted, New York: Carlisle Publishing, 1982), 777–81. For the agenda of early nineteenth-century somaticist professionalization, see Andrew Scull, *The Most Solitary of Afflictions: Madness and Society in Britain, 1700–1900* (New Haven, Conn.: Yale University Press, 1993), 203–24.

18. [G. M. Burrows], "Review of J. G. Spurzheim, *Observations on the Deranged Manifestations of the Mind* (1817)," *London Medical Repository* 8 (1817): 217–39, 305–31, especially 221.

19. G. M. Burrows, *An Inquiry into Certain Errors Relative to Insanity, and Their Consequences: Physical, Moral, and Civil* (London: Thomas and George Underwood, 1820), 234–35.

20. Burrows, *Inquiry,* 7; Burrows, *Commentaries,* 2–3.

21. William F. Bynum, "Rationales for Therapy in British Psychiatry, 1780–1835," in *Madhouses, Mad-Doctors, and Madmen: The Social History of Psychiatry in the Victorian Era,* ed. Andrew Scull (London: Athlone Press, 1981), 35–57.

22. Loudon, *Medical Care and the General Practitioner,* 152–70; G. M. Burrows, *A Statement of Circumstances Connected with the Apothecaries' Act, and Its Administration* (London: J. Callow, 1817).

23. See *London Medical, Surgical, and Pharmaceutical Repository* 1 (1814): 173–74, 261–62. For Lucett, see James Lucett, *A Statement of Facts Relative to the Nature and Cure of Mental Diseases* (London: James Truscott, 1833); Hunter and Macalpine, *Three Hundred Years,* 326; and an article in *Medical and Physical Journal* 30 (1813): 124–28.

24. Bynum, "Rationale for Therapy," 44–46; Scull, *Most Solitary of Afflictions,* 115–22.

25. Burrows, *Commentaries,* 7, 59. It is almost certain that he had Haslam's *Illustrations of Madness* in mind. Burrows was highly critical of Haslam's work. See [G. M. Burrows], "Retrospect of the Progress of Medical Science, Part II," *London Medical Repository* 9 (1818): 89–129, especially 110; [G. M. Burrows], "Review of Haslam, *Medical Jurisprudence* (1818)," *London Medical Repository* 9 (1818): 473–82, especially 473.

26. [G. M. Burrows], "Review of John Mayo, *Remarks on Insanity* (1817), Thomas Forster, *Observations on Insanity* (1817), et al.," *London Medical Repository* 8 (1817): 485–501.

27. Burrows, *Commentaries,* 253. For early nineteenth-century nosography of insanity, see Dora B. Weiner, "Mind and Body in the Clinic: Philippe Pinel, Alexander Crichton, Dominique Esquirol, and the Birth of Psychiatry," in *The Language of Psyche: Mind and Body in Enlightenment Thought,* ed. G. S. Rousseau (Los Angeles: William Clark Memorial Library, 1990), 331–402.

28. Burrows, *Commentaries,* 91, 19.

29. G. M. Burrows, "Some Observations on the Pathology of Insanity: Essay I," *London Medical Repository* 6 (1816): 279–88. For Esquirol's theory of the visceral origin of insanity, see Jan Goldstein, *Console and Classify: The French Psychiatric Profession in the Nineteenth Century* (Cambridge: Cambridge University Press, 1987), 251–52.

30. "A Case of Mania," *London Medical Repository* 6 (1816): 377–79; Charles Hastings, "A Remarkable Coincidence of Anomalous Structure in the Brain of Two Idiots, with an Extraordinary State of Disease of the Viscera," *London Medical Repository* 7 (1817): 74–78; Robert Camell, "Case of Disease of the Brain which Had Been Confounded with Hepatic Disease, with the Dissection, and Some Observations," *London Medical Repository* 7 (1817): 92–98; J. Whitshed, "Case of Phrenitis," *London Medical Repository* 7 (1817): 99–101; William Newnham, "Cases of Sympathetic Affection of the Brain with the Abdominal Viscera, Cured by Purgatives," *London Medical Repository* 7 (1817): 282–85, 459–64.

31. [Burrows], "Review of J. G. Spurzheim."

32. Burrows, *Commentaries,* 281–98.

33. Ibid., 297.

34. For social and cultural layers of meaning of dissection and postmortem, see Ruth Richardson, *Death, Dissection and the Destitute* (1988, reprinted, Harmondsworth: Penguin, 1989).

35. Burrows, *Commentaries,* 374–75, 385.

36. Burrows, "Some Observations on the Pathology of Insanity," 288; Burrows, *Commentaries,* 77; G. M. Burrows, "Bethlem Hospital," *London Medical Repository* 6 (1816): 88. For the situation of pathological anatomy and its use in psychiatry in England and France, see Russell Maulitz, *Morbid Appearances: The Anatomy of Pathology in the Early Nineteenth Century* (Cambridge: Cambridge University Press, 1987); and Goldstein, *Console and Classify,* 251–52.

37. Charlotte MacKenzie, *Psychiatry for the Rich: A History of Ticehurst Private Asylum* (London: Routledge, 1992), 97–127; Scull, *Most Solitary of Afflictions,* 356–60.

38. Burrows, *Commentaries,* 427–30.

39. Ibid., 190.

40. Burrows, *Inquiry,* 41–43.

41. Duden, *Women beneath the Skin,* 62–63; Fissell, "Disappearance of the Patient's Narrative"; Mary E. Fissell, "Readers, Texts, and Contexts: Vernacular Medical Works in Early Modern England," in *The Popularization of Medicine, 1650–1850,* ed. Roy Porter (London: Routledge, 1992), 72–96.

42. The juncture of the two styles of narratives and the invasion of the medical one into the lay one is perceptively discussed in Fissell, "Disappearance of the Patient's Narrative."

43. Burrows, *Commentaries,* 185.

44. Ibid.

45. Ibid., 186.

46. Michel Foucault, *The Birth of the Clinic,* trans. A. M. Sheridan (1973; reprinted, London: Routledge, 1976); Mary E. Fissell, *Patient, Power, and the Poor in Eighteenth-Century Bristol* (Cambridge: Cambridge University Press, 1991), 126–70.

47. Burrows, *Commentaries,* 25. See also Burrows, *Inquiry,* 173–74.

48. The major sources on the Anderdon case that I have consulted are: "Anderdon v. Burrows, M.D., and Two Others," *English Reports,* 4 Car. & P. 210–215; *Times,* 3 Nov. 1829, 3d–e; 5 Nov 1829, 4c; 10 Nov. 1829, 2d; 11 Nov. 1829, 2e; 18 Nov. 1829, 2e; 26 Nov. 1829, 3a; 28 Nov. 1829, 2f; and "Imposing Restraint on Lunatics," 311–314, 349–52, which includes Burrows's "Letter to the Editor of *The Times.*" See also *Times,* 26 Nov. 1829, 3a. The report in the *London Medical Gazette* "Anderdon v. Burrows" includes the law report of the trial held at the Court of King's Bench on 26 April 1830.

49. "Imposing Restraint on Lunatics" and "Anderdon v. Burrows." For a similar case of a wealthy man leading an eccentric life, see the commission of lunacy of Tobias Rivett, who left his own mansion and lived in a labourer's cottage, having "dogs, cats, rabbits and other animals as his companions." *Times,* 6 Aug. 1838, 7d.

50. "Anderdon v. Burrows," 183. An article in the *Morning Chronicle* (3 Nov. 1829) suggests that from his eccentric dress, "many persons concluded that Anderdon was non compos mentis." It seems, however, that those who knew him well never doubted his sanity.

51. *Times,* 3 Nov. 1829, 3e; "Anderdon v. Burrows," 184.

52. "Imposing Restraint on Lunatics," 351; "Anderdon v. Burrows," 185.

53. *Times,* 3 Nov. 1829, 3e; "Anderdon v. Burrows," 184.

54. *Times,* 18 Nov. 1829, 2e. The language employed by Wells and the fact that he was himself a certified lunatic anticipated the Alleged Lunatics' Friend Society, about which see Hervey, "Advocacy of Folly." A more technical criticism was raised in the *Times,* 10 Nov. 1829, 2d, to which Robert Browne, one of the Metropolitan Commissioners in Lunacy, responded, pointing out that Burrows's actions were illegal under 9 Geo IV cap. 41, sects. 29, 30, 32, 40. Burrows wrote to the *Times* in response that James Wells "was found a lunatic, under a commission issued a few years ago, and which is not yet superseded" and expressed his disagreement with Browne. *Times,* 26 Nov. 1829, 3a.

55. "Anderdon v. Burrows," 187.

56. "Imposing Restraint on Lunatics," 314.

57. G. M. Burrows, *A Letter to Sir Henry Halford, Bart., K.C.H.* (London: T. & G. Underwood, 1830), 9–10.

58. The law in 1853 prohibited doctors from signing certificates based only on secondhand information. McCandless, "Liberty and Lunacy," 348.

59. "Imposing Restraint on Lunatics," 351. Curiously, the propriety of the deed of the Anderdon brothers was not explicitly questioned throughout the procedure.

60. Ibid.

61. Burrows, *Letter to Sir Henry Halford,* 18.

62. Morison, MSS Reports, etc., RCP London, SR/471; Affidavits of G. M. Burrows for the case of L. P[hillip].

63. Burrows's sense of national competition with French alienists is most obvious in [G. M. Burrows], "A Reply to Messieurs Esquirol's and Falret's Objections to Dr. Burrows's Comparative Proportions of Suicide in Paris and London," *London Medical Repository* 18 (1822): 460–64.

64. Major sources that I have consulted for the Davies case are: *Times,* 15–29 Dec. 1829; Burrows, *Letter to Sir Henry Halford;* and [Robert Gooch], "Review of G. M. Burrows, *Commentaries* (1828) and G. N. Hill, *Observations on Madness* (1809)," *Quarterly Review* 42 (1830): 350–77. McCandless, "Liberty and Lunacy," 349–50, provides a summary of the case.

65. [Gooch], "Review of Burrows," 354–55. The authorship of this review article is somewhat ambiguous. The author of "Attacks on Dr. Burrows," *London Medical Gazette* 6(1830): 84–86, suggests that it was partly written by Robert Gooch, who was motivated by personal hostility to Burrows, and partly by another.

66. [Gooch], "Review of Burrows," 355–56.

67. The mother was reported to have said in June, "I'll make you repent this before the end of the year." Ibid., 356.

68. The attorney was Francis Hobler, who later became a solicitor and principal clerk at the Mansion House Police Court and a figure well-known in London as a cracker of jokes, receiving a short mention by Dickens in his *Sketches by Boz* in 1835. Charles Dickens, *Sketches by Boz,* ed. Dennis Walder (Harmondsworth: Penguin, 1995), 18, 585.

69. Burrows, *Letter to Sir Henry Halford,* 8.

70. Frances Harres, *Henry Brougham* (London: Jonathan Cape, 1957), 162–80. Later Burrows and his sympathizers complained of machinations driven by the "party spirit" of journalists and especially the *Times.* See Burrows, *Letter to Sir Henry Halford,* 19, 34; Andrew Combe, "Commissions of Lunacy—Mad Doctors—London Press," *London Medical Gazette* 5 (1829–30): 719–21; and "Attacks on Dr. Burrows."

71. Brougham was experienced in acting against commissions of lunacy and on behalf of alleged lunatics. See *Times,* 2–10 Aug. 1825, the commission of lunacy against the Rev. Edward Frank, in which Burrows had served as a medical witness, testifying for Frank's sanity. *Times,* 8 Aug. 1825, 3a.

72. For the role of Brougham in the Queen Caroline affair, which made him extremely popular, see Robert Stewart, *Henry Brougham, 1778–1868: His Public*

Career (London: Bodley Head, 1985), 140–59; Flora Fraser, *The Unruly Queen: The Life of Queen Caroline* (London: Macmillan, 1996).

73. *Times*, 24 Dec. 1829, 1f–2c.

74. For the contest of Eldon and Brougham, see Stewart, *Henry Brougham*. For the life of Wetherell, see DNB and ODNB. Burrows dedicated his *Inquiry* to Lord Eldon "with his lordship's permission," which may have fueled Brougham's antagonism to Burrows.

75. *Times*, 21 Dec. 1829, 1c–2a.

76. *Times*, 24 Dec. 1829.

77. *Times*, 19 Dec. 1829. Brougham's team showed that Benjamin Hands, another medical witness, had not conducted any medical inspection of their client. *Times*, 17 Dec. 1829.

78. *Times*, 18 Dec. 1829.

79. Joel Peter Eigen, "Delusion in the Courtroom: The Role of Partial Insanity in Early Forensic Testimony," *Medical History* 35 (1991): 25–49. For Davies's eccentricities, see especially Burrows's and Haslam's testimonies in the *Times*, 21 and 22 Dec. 1829.

80. *Times*, 19 Dec. 1829, 1e–2b.

81. *Times*, 21 Dec. 1829, 1c–2a.

82. *Times*, 28 Dec. 1829, 3b–d.

83. Lucett, *Statement of Facts Relative to the Nature and Cure of Mental Diseases*, 7–8.

84. William Griggs, *Lunacy and Liberty. A Letter to the Lord Chancellor . . .* (London: W. Griggs, 1832), 13.

85. Thomas Little, *Mad-Houses! Sketch of the Seduction and Treatment, Il-legal and Non-Medical, of Miss Stabback* (London: J. J. Stockdale, [1831]), preface. For a similar publication by political radicals on abuses in private madhouses, see [John Mitford], *A Description of the Crimes and Horrors in the Interior of Warburton's Private Mad-House at Hoxton, Commonly Called Whitmore House* (London: Benbow, [1826]). See Iain McCalman, *Radical Underworld: Prophets, Revolutionaries, and Pornographers in London, 1795–1840* (Oxford: Clarendon Press, 1993), 206.

86. [Gooch], "Review of Burrows," 362. The author of "Attacks on Dr. Burrows," however, maintained that this particularly venomous new term could not come from Gooch's pen.

87. *Times*, 1 Apr. 1830, 3c.

88. Burrows, *Letter to Sir Henry Halford*, 21–23. For the place of anonymous threatening letters in the history of radicalism, see E. P. Thompson, "The Crime of Anonymity," in *Albion's Fatal Tree: Crime and Society in Eighteenth-Century England*, ed. Douglas Hay et al. (Harmondsworth: Penguin, 1977), 255–344.

89. For the hitherto unexplored radical political undercurrent of the criticism against psychiatry and its abuse, see McCalman, *Radical Underworld*, 206. For

the medical politics of the early and mid-nineteenth century, see Adrian Desmond, *The Politics of Evolution: Morphology, Medicine, and Reform in Radical London* (Chicago: University of Chicago Press, 1989).

90. Clapham Retreat was licensed for receiving about thirty private patients. Metropolitan Commissioners of Lunacy found it "in excellent order" when they visited it in July 1829 and April 1830. Annual Report of the Metropolitan Commissioners of Lunacy, 1830, PRO HO 44/51.

91. Manuscript letter of George Man Burrows to Henry Brougham, 20 Oct. 1831, University College London, Brougham papers, 35, 585. Burrows had asked for Brougham's patronage for his son about a year before, but Brougham had declined. The first letter does not survive. In a further irony, Burrows's elder son, George, delivered his first lectures in forensic medicine at St. Bartholomew's Hospital in 1831 and had to talk to students about the "nature of the commission de lunatico inquirendo" and "certificates of insanity." George Burrows, *Introductory Lecture of a Course on Forensic Medicine, Delivered in the Anatomical Theatre of St. Bartholomew's Hospital* (London: J. Mallet, [1831]), 32.

92. Burrows, *Letter to Sir Henry Halford,* 20.

93. *Times,* 24 Dec. 1829, 1f–2c.

94. For a contemporary reference to the Davies case, see Robert Sharp, *The Diary of Robert Sharp of South Cave: Life in a Yorkshire Village, 1812–1837,* ed. Janice E. Crowther and Peter A. Crowther (Oxford: Oxford University Press, 1997), 240

95. See A. L. Wigan, *A New View of Insanity: The Duality of the Mind* (London: Longman, Brown, Green, and Longmans, 1844), 277.

96. The chapter on diagnosis in Bucknill and Tuke's *Manual* was reprinted in the *Journal of Mental Science,* which was edited by Bucknill at that time, with the name of Bucknill as the single author. J. C. Bucknill, "The Diagnosis of Insanity," *Asylum Journal of Mental Science* 2 (1856): 229–45, 432–45; 3 (1857): 141–85.

97. J. C. Bucknill and Daniel H. Tuke, *A Manual of Psychological Medicine* (Philadelphia: Blancard and Lea, 1858), 267.

98. Ibid.

99. Ibid., 275.

100. Ibid., 277–89.

101. For the formulation of diagnostic process and the incorporation of the interview with the patient into medicine in general, see P. C. A. Louis, *Memoir on the Proper Method of Examining a Patient, and of Arriving at Facts of a General Nature,* trans. Henry I. Bowditch, M.D (N.p.: n.p., n.d.).

102. Jewson, "Disappearance of the Sick-Man"; Fissell, "Disappearance of the Patient's Narrative."

103. David Wright, "The Certification of Insanity in Nineteenth-Century England and Wales," *History of Psychiatry* 9 (1998): 267–90.

CHAPTER THREE

1. Leonore Davidoff, "The Family in Britain," in *The Cambridge Social History of Britain, 1750–1950,* ed. F. M. L. Thompson (Cambridge: Cambridge University Press, 1990), vol. 2: 71–129, especially 73, 79.

2. Jose Harris, *Private Lives, Public Spirit: Britain, 1870–1914* (Harmondsworth: Penguin, 1994), 69, 96–122.

3. *Times,* 8 Aug. 1835, 6b–c. Emphasis added.

4. *Times,* 1 Apr. 1830, 3c.

5. For this new legal definition of madness, see chapter 6.

6. John Haslam, *A Letter to the Right Honorable the Lord Chancellor, on the Nature and Interpretation of Unsoundness of Mind, and Imbecility of Intellect* (London: R. Hunter, 1823), 9–10, 16.

7. "Letter to Dr. Burrows," *Lancet* 2 (1829–30): 251–52.

8. "Review of G. M. Burrows, *A Letter to Sir Henry Halford* (1830)," *London Medical and Physical Journal* 63 (1830): 427–34, especially 427.

9. The *London Medical Gazette* gave sanction to this act, writing: "This is as it should be, and a few such refusals would bring the gentlemen of the long robe to their senses on this point." *London Medical Gazette* 6 (1830): 217.

10. *Lancet* 1 (1829–30): 477; [Thomas Wakley], "Review of Burrows, *Commentaries* (1828)," *Lancet* 2 (1829–30): 136–40. Although Wakley was often brutally sarcastic, this particular venomous (and effective) remark may have been motivated by Wakley's close relationship with Brougham, who acted as his counsel in a trial in 1825. See S. Squire Sprigge, *The Life and Times of Thomas Wakley* (1899; reprinted, New York: Robert E. Krieger Publishing Company, 1974), 117–26.

11. "Law versus Physic," *London Medical Gazette* 5 (1829–30): 439–42, 474–76, 501–4.

12. *Medical Examiner* 1 (2 Jan. 1830): 232–33.

13. On issues related with criminal responsibility, see Roger Smith, *Trial by Medicine: Insanity and Responsibility in Victorian Trials* (Edinburgh: Edinburgh University Press, 1981).

14. "An Attempt to Simplify and Explain the Diagnostics of Insanity, with More Immediate Reference to Commissions of Lunacy," MSS RCP London 1045/25. The authorship of this document is unclear. Although it is unknown exactly when the document was written and deposited at the Royal College of Physicians, one can reasonably assume the date to be in late 1830 or early 1831 because we know that this paper was consulted by several Fellows in February 1831.

15. The use of psychology by the anonymous paper seems to signal that the "psychological turn" of the Collegiate physicians, which appears to have taken

place in the late 1820s, extended to the area of forensic psychiatric diagnosis. See Henry Halford, *Essays and Orations, Read and Delivered at the Royal College of Physicians,* 3rd ed. (London: John Murray, 1842); Thomas Mayo, *A Letter to the Reverend Thomas Rennell Concerning His Remarks on Scepticism: From a Graduate in Medicine, of the University of Oxford* (London: Thomas and George Underwood, [1819]); and Thomas Mayo, *Elements of the Pathology of the Human Mind* (London: John Murray, 1838).

16. "An Attempt to Simplify and Explain the Diagnostics of Insanity," 12.

17. Ibid., 14.

18. Even when a doctor failed to persuade the jury, something should be done: "Many instances of distress shew that something ought to be done when the commission does not issue, not only for the present protection of the party, but it may be also for maintaining the rightful demand of his honours and his estate." Ibid., 14–15.

19. Halford, *Essays and Orations,* essay IV, "Popular and Classical Illustrations of Insanity," 49–59.

20. Ibid., 52–53.

21. Irvine Loudon, *Medical Care and the General Practitioner, 1750–1850* (Oxford: Clarendon Press, 1986); Anne Digby, *Making a Medical Living: Doctors and Patients in the English Market for Medicine, 1720–1911* (Cambridge: Cambridge University Press, 1994); M. Jeanne Peterson, *The Medical Profession in Mid-Victorian London* (Berkeley and Los Angeles: University of California Press, 1978).

22. On the shift from the genteel London culture to the serious professionalism imported from Scottish universities, see Marilyn Butler, "Culture's Medium: The Role of the Review," in *The Cambridge Companion to British Romanticism,* ed. Stuart Curran (Cambridge: Cambridge University Press, 1993), 120–47.

23. "An Attempt to Simplify and Explain the Diagnostics of Insanity," 7–8. Alienists' claim to expertise often lay in their ability to pull the right strings so as to reveal the latent delusions of apparently sane people. See, e.g., John Haslam, *Illustrations of Madness: Exhibiting a Singular Case of Insanity . . .* (1810: reprinted with an introduction by Roy Porter, London: Routledge, 1989).

24. The cunning of a lunatic to conceal his or her delusion and the ability of an interested party to "tutor" him or her to do so were frequently discussed. Tuthill, Burrows, and Haslam raised the issue in the Davies case, referring to the case of James Tilly Matthews. *Times,* 19 Dec. 1829, 1e–2b; 21 Dec. 1829, 1c–2a; 22 Dec. 1829, 3b–3c.

25. Hunter, Macalpine, and Scull are certainly right in seeing *Indications* as the realization of Conolly's concern to develop an institutional basis for clinical psychiatry, as expressed in his University College London inaugural lecture in 1828. The most direct concern of the book was, however, no doubt the crisis faced by

medical men in this field in the wake of the Anderdon and Davies cases. See Richard Hunter and Ida Macalpine, "Introduction," to *An Enquiry Concerning the Indications of Insanity,* by John Conolly (1830; reprinted, London: Dawsons, 1964); and Andrew Scull, Charlotte MacKenzie, and Nicholas Hervey, *Masters of Bedlam: The Transformation of the Mad-Doctoring Trade* (Princeton, N.J.: Princeton University Press, 1996), 52–56.

26. Conolly, *Enquiry Concerning the Indications of Insanity,* 9.

27. "Dr Conolly on Insanity," *London Medical Gazette* 6 (1830): 727–28. The vituperative review appeared in *Lancet* 2 (1829–30): 646–52, 695–96. Conolly's protest was reprinted in *Lancet* 2 (1829–30): 795–96. Wakley and Conolly then edited rival periodicals, namely, *Lancet* and *London Medical Repository.*

28. Conolly, *Enquiry Concerning the Indications of Insanity,* 361–477; "Dr Conolly on Insanity"; Hunter and Macalpine, "Introduction" to *Enquiry Concerning the Indications of Insanity,* 34.

29. "Dr Conolly on Insanity."

30. Conolly, *Enquiry Concerning the Indications of Insanity,* 139–40.

31. Ibid., 364–65. Judging from the sentiment expressed here, it was perhaps the young Conolly himself who wrote to the *Times* in 1822 under the signature of "J.C." that a physician should be "at once the guardian, the advocate, and medical attendant of the deranged." *Times,* 27 Nov. 1822, 2e. As Brougham did in the Davies case, the short letter insisted that physicians should not own their own madhouses, for "in so doing, they sink the dignity of their profession, and thus probably lose that sensibility so essential to a successful exercise of their professional talents."

32. Hunter and Macalpine, "Introduction" to *Enquiry Concerning the Indications of Insanity,* 15.

33. John W. Yolton, *John Locke and the Way of Ideas* (Oxford: Clarendon Press, 1956).

34. Conolly, *Enquiry Concerning the Indications of Insanity,* 164–69.

35. Henry Maudsley, "Memoir of the Late John Conolly," *Journal of Mental Science* 12 (1866): 151–74, especially 164–74. Another important University College London connection in this context may be George Birkbeck, the founder of the London Mechanics' Institute, who pleaded for the sanity of James Matthews in 1810. See Haslam, *Illustrations of Madness,* 5–9.

36. Conolly, *Enquiry Concerning the Indications of Insanity,* 476–77.

37. Ibid., 363.

38. Ibid., 364, 383–86, 412–13.

39. Ibid., 373.

40. Ibid., 361.

41. Ibid., 368.

42. Ibid., 365–68.

43. Ibid., 377.

44. Hunter and Macalpine, "Introduction" to *Enquiry Concerning the Indications of Insanity*, 33–35, clearly exaggerates the success of the book.

45. The major sources that I have used for the commission of lunacy against John Brand are: Charles Dunne, *Brand's Lunacy Case: A Full Report of the Most Interesting and Extraordinary Investigation; Including Copious Animadversions on the Principal Actors in This Drama* (London: sold by John Wilson, 1830); and *Times*, 8 Aug.–2 Sept. 1830.

46. Dunne, *Brand's Lunacy Case*, 30.

47. Ibid., 55–56.

48. Charles Dunne, *The Appellatory, or the Complaint of a Subject to His King against Ministerial Tyranny and Oppression* (London: for the author, [1829]), 10; Charles Dunne, *Parliamentary Impeachment of Sir William Draper Best, Knt., Chief Justice of the Commons Pleas* (London: by the author, n.d.), "Preface."

49. Charles Dunne, *The Chiurgical Candidate: Or, Reflections on Education* (London: Samuel Highley, 1808).

50. Dunne, *Parliamentary Impeachment*, 4.

51. Ibid., 5–7.

52. Ibid., 11.

53. Charles Dunne, *The Star Chamber, or a Panorama of the Moral Assassins of the Metropolis* (London: by the author, 1825).

54. Dunne, *Brand's Lunacy Case*, 5, 81.

55. Ibid., 6–7.

56. Ibid., 58.

57. Ibid., 101. His confessed model here was Wakley's medicalization of the coroner. See Sprigge, *Life and Times of Thomas Wakley*, 353–403.

58. Dunne, *Brand's Lunacy Case*, 30.

59. Ibid., 53, 56.

60. Ibid., 55. Although in a much more reserved way, some doctors used some bodily symptoms as an evidence for or against insanity of the person in question. See, for instance, Alexander Morison, MSS Reports and Notes of Cases, RCP London, SR/471, Burrows's testimony in the commission of lunacy against L. Phillip, in which Burrows presented the injury on the spine of Mr. Phillip as supportive evidence.

61. Dunne, *Brand's Lunacy Case*, 57.

62. Jan Goldstein, *Console and Classify: The French Psychiatric Profession in the Nineteenth Century* (Cambridge: Cambridge University Press, 1987), 152–96.

63. Akihito Suzuki, "Dualism and the Transformation of Psychiatric Language in the Seventeenth and Eighteenth Centuries," *History of Science* 33 (1995): 417–47; Benjamin Rush, *Two Essays on the Mind*, ed. Eric T. Carlson (New York: Brunner/Mazel, 1972).

64. Hannah Augstein, "J. C. Prichard's Concept of Moral Insanity: A Medical Theory of the Corruption of Human Nature," *Medical History* 40 (1996):

311–43; John Addington Symonds, *Some Accounts of the Life, Writings, and Character of the Late James Cowles Prichard* (N.p: n.p, 1849).

65. Augstein, "J. C. Prichard's Concept." See also James Cowles Prichard, "J. C. Prichard and the Concept of 'Moral Insanity,'" ed. German Berrios, *History of Psychiatry* 10 (1999): 111–26.

66. *Times,* 23 July 1833, 6a–b.

67. James Cowles Prichard, *A Treatise on Insanity and Other Disorders Affecting the Mind* (London: Sherwood, Gilbert, and Piper, 1835), 353.

68. Ibid., 383.

69. For the use of moral insanity in the criminal context, see Smith, *Trial by Medicine.*

70. Prichard, *Treatise on Insanity,* 23–24.

71. Smith, *Trial by Medicine,* 38–39. See also D. H. Tuke, "Moral Insanity," in *A Dictionary of Psychological Medicine,* ed. D. H. Tuke (London: J. & A. Churchill, 1892), vol. 2: 813–16.

72. *Times,* 4 Aug. 1825, 2d.

73. *Times,* 17 Dec. 1829, 3c.

74. *Times,* 19 Dec. 1829, 5c. However, to defeat such an argument was child's play for the lawyers. The lawyer asked the medical witness, Sir George Tuthill: "Then do I understand you to say that every man who quarrels with his mother is mad?" to which Tuthill meekly answered in the negative.

75. Moreover, as Nancy Tomes has pointed out in the American context, antipathy or indifference toward family members or "perverted feelings," rather than clear-cut delusions, were commonly cited symptoms of insanity. Nancy Tomes, *The Art of Asylum-Keeping: Thomas Story Kirkbride and the Origin of American Psychiatry* (1984: reprinted, Philadelphia: University of Pennsylvania Press, 1994), 100–101. See also her discussion of moral insanity in ibid., 120–21.

76. Symonds, *Some Accounts,* 44–45.

77. Prichard, *Treatise on Insanity,* 50. On Symonds and Prichard, see D. H. Tuke, *Prichard and Symonds: In Special Relation to Mental Science with Chapters on Moral Insanity* (London: J. A. Churchill, 1891), 52.

78. A. L. Wigan, *A New View of Insanity: The Duality of the Mind* (London: Longman, Brown, Green, and Longmans, 1844), 279–80.

79. Peter McCandless, "Dangerous to Themselves and Others: The Victorian Debate over the Prevention of Wrongful Confinement," *Journal of British Studies* 23 (1983): 84–104; Peter McCandless, "Liberty and Lunacy: The Victorians and Wrongful Confinement," in *Madhouses, Mad-Doctors, and Madmen: The Social History of Psychiatry in the Victorian Era,* ed. Andrew Scull (London: Athlone Press, 1981), 339–62; Helen Small, *Love's Madness: Medicine, the Novel, and Female Insanity, 1800–1865* (Oxford: Oxford University Press, 1996), 179–220. Small points out the importance of the Burrows case, but she misunderstands the type of legal procedure in which Burrows was involved and states that

he "was brought before the Metropolitan Commissioners in Lunacy." Small, *Love's Madness,* 184.

80. Tomes, *Art of Asylum-Keeping,* 118–28.

81. For Parkinson's involvement in Daintree's case, see Shirley Roberts, *James Parkinson: From Apothecary to General Practitioner* (London: Royal Society of Medicine, 1997), 81–86; *Statesman,* 31 Oct. 1810; and William H. McMenemey, "James Parkinson, 1755–1824: A Biographical Essay," in *James Parkinson (1755–1824),* ed. MacDonald Critchley, with the collaboration of William H. McMenemey et al. (London: Macmillan, 1955), 1–144, especially 103–14.

82. Scull, MacKenzie, and Hervey, *Masters of Bedlam,* 75–76.

83. For the *Nottidge v. Ripley* case, see J. J. Schwieso, "Religious Fanaticism and Wrongful Confinement in Victorian England: The Affair of Louisa Nottidge," *Social History of Medicine* 9 (1996): 159–74. For the case of Ruck, see chapter 5 in this volume and Scull, MacKenzie, and Hervey, *Masters of Bedlam,* 75–76.

CHAPTER FOUR

1. Charlotte MacKenzie, *Psychiatry for the Rich: A History of Ticehurst Private Asylum* (London: Routledge, 1992), 97–127; Nancy Tomes, *The Art of Asylum-Keeping: Thomas Story Kirkbride and the Origin of American Psychiatry* (1984; reprinted, Philadelphia: University of Pennsylvania Press, 1994), 90–128.

2. MacKenzie, *Psychiatry for the Rich,* 102.

3. In his *Domestic Medicine,* one of the most successful works of that genre, William Buchan wrote about madness: "There is no great occasion to be solicitous about the definition of a disease which every body knows." William Buchan, *Domestic Medicine: Or the Family Physician* (Edinburgh: Balfour et al., 1769), 516. See also John Trusler, *The Physical Friend: Pointing Out the Symptoms of Every Distemper Incident to Man* (London: for the author, 1776), 51; and Charles Perry, *A Treatise of Diseases in General* (London: T. Woodward et al., 1741), vol. 1: 53. As for Buchan's strategy to instruct rather than impose, see Charles E. Rosenberg, "Medical Text and Social Context: Explaining William Buchan's Domestic Medicine," *Bulletin of the History of Medicine* 57 (1983): 22–42.

4. For a selection of many key texts in this field, see Jenny Bourne Taylor and Sally Shuttleworth ed., *Embodied Selves: An Anthology of Psychological Texts, 1830–1890* (Oxford: Oxford University Press, 1998).

5. Roger Cooter, *The Cultural Meaning of Popular Science: Phrenology and the Organization of Consent in Nineteenth-Century Britain* (Cambridge: Cambridge University Press, 1984).

6. Alison Winter, *Mesmerized: Powers of Mind in Victorian Britain* (Chicago: University of Chicago Press, 1998).

7. Sally Shuttleworth, *Charlotte Brontë and Victorian Psychology* (Cambridge: Cambridge University Press, 1996).

8. Mary Cowling, *The Artist as Anthropologist: The Representation of Type and Character in Victorian Art* (Cambridge: Cambridge University Press, 1989).

9. The eyes in particular became the focus of attention. See, for example, *Times,* 18 Dec. 1840, 3b.

10. On the relationship between science and literature, see Gillian Beer, "Science and Literature," in *Companion to the History of Modern Science,* ed. R. C. Olby et al. (London: Routledge, 1990), 783–98.

11. See, among other sources, Dorothy Porter and Roy Porter, *Patient's Progress: Doctors and Doctoring in Eighteenth-Century England* (Oxford: Polity Press, 1989); Roy Porter, ed., *Patients and Practitioners: Lay Perceptions of Medicine in Pre-Industrial Society* (Cambridge: Cambridge University Press, 1985); Barbara Duden, *The Women beneath the Skin: A Doctor's Patients in Eighteenth-Century Germany,* trans. Thomas Dunlap (Cambridge, Mass.: Harvard University Press, 1991); Mary E. Fissell, *Patient, Power, and the Poor in Eighteenth-Century Bristol* (Cambridge: Cambridge University Press, 1991); and Mary E. Fissell, "The Disappearance of the Patient's Narrative and the Invention of Hospital Medicine," in *British Medicine in an Age of Reform,* ed. Roger French and Andrew Wear (London: Routledge, 1991), 92–109.

12. Michael MacDonald, *Mystical Bedlam: Madness, Anxiety, and Healing in Seventeenth-Century England* (Cambridge: Cambridge University Press, 1981), 126–28, 165.

13. The three-volume letter-books of Middleton are held in the City of Westminster Library WBA 796, with an index compiled by G. F. Osborn in 1978. These are referred to as WCL HNMLB, with volume and page numbers.

14. For the notion of everyday practice, see Pierre Bourdieu, *Outline of a Theory of Practice,* trans. Richard Nice (Cambridge: Cambridge University Press, 1977).

15. The outline of Middleton's life given here is drawn from Osbourn's introduction to the letter-books. WCL Index to the letter-books of Hastings Nathaniel Middleton, 26 Aug. 1816–1821 (hereafter Index to HNMLB).

16. H. N. Middleton to Anne Frances Middleton, 26 Aug. 1816, WCL HNMLB, vol. 1: 1–2; Index to HNMLB.

17. Middleton to Mrs. Atkinson, 5 Oct. 1816, WCL HNMLB, vol. 1: 69, 75.

18. Middleton to Miss Lee, 13 Oct. 1816, WCL HNMLB, vol. 1: 88.

19. Middleton to Miss Gale, 25 Oct. 1816, WCL HNMLB, vol. 1: 97.

20. Ibid., 97–98.

21. For a perceptive analysis of narrative structures of nineteenth-century psychiatric case histories, see Helen Small, "'In the Guise of Science': Literature and the Rhetoric of 19th-Century English Psychiatry," *History of the Human Sciences* 7 (1994): 27–55.

22. Middleton to Miss Gale, 25 Oct. 1816, WCL HNMLB, vol. 1: 95.

23. Ibid., 97.

24. Ibid., 95–96. As for his earlier hope, see Middleton to Miss Gale, 9 Oct. 1816, WCL HNMLB, vol. 1: 82–83. However, before he saw his mother he expressed his pessimism about mental disease in general in his letters to Mrs. Atkinson, 5 Oct. 1816, WCL HNMLB, vol. 1: 75, and to Mr. Charles Green, 11 Oct. 1816, WCL HNMLB, vol. 1: 86.

25. Middleton to Mrs. Atkinson, 26 Oct. 1816, WCL HNMLB, vol. 1: 107. Emphasis in the original.

26. Middleton to Mrs. Cator, 29 Oct. 1815, WCL HNMLB, vol. 1: 111.

27. Middleton to Miss Gale, 20 Nov. 1816, WCL HNMLB, vol. 1: 119–20.

28. Middleton to Mrs. Charles Herbert, 18 Jan. 1820, WCL HNMLB, vol. 1: 244. See also Middleton to Mrs. Watson, 12 Oct. 1820, WCL HNMLB, vol. 1: 296.

29. Middleton to Mrs. Edward Jerningham, 12 Jan. 1820, WCL HNMLB, vol. 1: 242–43. Emphasis in the original. See also Middleton to Mrs. Watson, 10 Nov. 1819, WCL HNMLB, vol. 1: 218–19.

30. Middleton to Edward Jernigham, 10 Mar. 1821, WCL HNMLB, vol. 2: 17–19.

31. Middleton to Mr. Charles Green, 11 Oct. 1816, WCL HNMLB, vol. 1: 85–86. See also Middleton to Mrs. Cator, 17 Oct. 1816, WCL HNMLB, vol. 1: 93–94; Middleton to Miss Gale, 25 Oct. 1816, WCL HNMLB, vol. 1: 98; Middleton to Mrs. Cator, 29 Oct. 1816, WCL HNMLB, vol. 1: 112–13; Middleton to Mr. Henry Johnson Middleton, 10 Feb. 1820, WCL HNMLB, vol. 1: 249–50.

32. Middleton to Miss Gale, 25 Oct. 1816, WCL HNMLB, vol. 1: 99.

33. Middleton to Mrs. Cator, 29 Oct. 1816, WCL HNMLB, vol. 1: 112.

34. Lawrence Stone, *The Family, Sex, and Marriage in England, 1500–1800* (Harmondsworth: Penguin, 1979); Lawrence Stone, *The Road to Divorce: England, 1530–1987* (Oxford: Oxford University Press, 1990).

35. Middleton to Miss Gale, 25 Oct. 1816, WCL HNMLB, vol. 1: 99.

36. Middleton to Mrs. Edward Jerningham, 12 Jan. 1820, WCL HNMLB, vol. 1: 241. In the same letter, he mentioned that the experiment was based on "erroneous opinion."

37. When he received two thousand pounds from his mother after the failure of the bank, he expressed surprise and wrote to his aunt, "A few more such traits, and I shall be tempted to read my recantation." Middleton to Mrs. Green, 29 Sept. 1816, WCL HNMLB, vol. 1: 62.

38. Middleton to Mrs. Atkinson, 26 Oct. 1816, WCL HNMLB, vol. 1: 108–9.

39. Middleton to Miss Gale, 25 Oct. 1816, WCL HNMLB, vol. 1: 99–100. The belief that one's personality was a seed of insanity was a cliché in the nineteenth century. See, for example, *Times,* 10 Feb. 1838, 5d.

40. Middleton to Miss Gale, 9 Oct. 1816, WCL HNMLB, vol. 1: 79.

41. Middleton to Miss Gale, 25 Oct. 1816, WCL HNMLB, vol. 1: 94.

42. Middleton to Miss Gale, 9 Oct. 1816, WCL HNMLB, vol. 1: 78–79. Emphasis added.

43. Middleton to Mrs. Atkinson, 26 Oct. 1816, WCL HNMLB, vol. 1: 107.

44. Middleton to Miss Gale, 9 Oct. 1816, WCL HNMLB, vol. 1: 82.

45. Middleton to Mrs. Atkinson, 26 Oct. 1816, WCL HNMLB, vol. 1: 109–10.

46. Middleton to Miss Gale, 9 Oct. 1816, WCL HNMLB, vol. 1: 82.

47. Middleton to his mother, 15 Oct. 1816, WCL HNMLB, vol. 1: 90–91.

48. Middleton to Miss Gale, 25 Oct. 1816, WCL HNMLB, vol. 1: 98.

49. Middleton to Mrs. Cator, 29 Oct. 1816, WCL HNMLB, vol. 1, 113–14.

50. Ibid., 114. John Perceval criticized exactly this kind of self-serving logic of his family, whom he had trusted at the beginning of his disease. John Perceval, *Perceval's Narrative: A Patient's Account of His Psychosis, 1830–1832,* ed. Gregory Bateson (Stanford, Calif.: Stanford University Press, 1961), 74, 138, and elsewhere.

51. George Battiscombe, *Shaftesbury: A Biography of the Seventh Earl, 1801–1885* (London: Constable, 1974), 208–9, 240, and elsewhere. Shaftesbury was aware that epilepsy was closely associated with madness. He once wrote: "[Fits] are treated as madness, and madness constitutes a right, as it were, to treat people as vermin." See Geoffrey B. A. M. Finlayson, *The Seventh Earl of Shaftesbury, 1801–1885* (London: Eyre Methuen, 1981), 335–36. An advertisement of a French asylum is found in the pamphlet *Retreat at Vanves, Near Paris, for the Reception and Recovery of Ladies and Gentlemen Afflicted with Disorders of the Mind* (N.p.: n.p., [1841]). The asylum was under the direction of "Drs. Voisin et Falret." The only copy I know of the advertisement is held at the Wellcome Library.

52. Thomas Campbell, *Life and Letters of Thomas Campbell,* ed. William Beattie (London: Edward Moxon, 1859), vol. 2: 403–6.

53. J. C. Bucknill and Daniel H. Tuke, *A Manual of Psychological Medicine* (Philadelphia: Blancard and Lea, 1858), 269–70.

54. "Memorandum upon Madame Dupontes, in order to light the celebrated British Doctors Physicians concerning the Cause of Her Malady," a letter inserted in GLRO H12/CH/B/11/1/B.

55. *Times,* 27 June 1828, 3f.

56. *Times,* 13 Dec. 1842, 3c.

57. Colney Hatch Asylum, Male Casebook, GLRO H12/CH/B13/6/15.

58. William Makepeace Thackeray, *The Letters and Private Papers of William Makepeace Thackeray,* ed. Gordon N. Ray (London: Oxford University Press, 1945), vol. 1: 473. For the progress of the malady and Thackeray's search for a cure, see Gordon N. Ray, *Thackeray: The Uses of Adversity, 1811–1846* (London: Oxford University Press, 1955), 250–77. See also the perceptive discussion in Helen Small, *Love's Madness: Medicine, the Novel, and Female Insanity, 1800–1865* (Oxford: Oxford University Press, 1996), 178–81.

59. *Times,* 23 Jan. 1827, 3c.

60. *The Times,* 12 Dec. 1839, 6c–d. James Seddall stated that he entered the

service of Mr. Blood for the purpose of attending upon Mr. Pearce, "whom I understood to be of weak mind."

61. *Times,* 13 Dec. 1842, 3b–d.

62. Henry Blyth, *Caro—The Fatal Passion: The Life of Lady Caroline Lamb* (London: Rupert Hart-Davis, 1972), 214. Emphasis in the original.

63. Anon., *A Genuine Report of the Proceedings on the Portsmouth Case, under a Commission Issued by His Majesty* (London: Duncombe, [1823]), 7–9.

64. *Times,* 1 Oct. 1829, 3f–4a.

65. As for Lady Portsmouth, she even played the role of a doctor: it was explicitly stated that she dispensed "medical aid."

66. Portsmouth, *Genuine Report of the Portsmouth Case,* 15.

67. Ibid., 8. Emphasis added. It should be noted that many doctors in the early nineteenth century assumed the position of personal physician for aristocratic clients, often serving them from inside the latter's households, particularly when they traveled abroad. Among alienists, Alexander Morison had been engaged in such a practice. See Andrew Scull, Charlotte MacKenzie, and Nicholas Hervey, *Masters of Bedlam: The Transformation of the Mad-Doctoring Trade* (Princeton, N.J.: Princeton University Press, 1996), 123–60. For a similar arrangement for a traveling doctor, see Venetia Murray, *High Society in the Regency Period, 1788–1830* (Harmondsworth: Penguin, 1999), 74–75.

68. This is the case of Rosa Bagster, which will be examined in detail in chapter 5.

69. Nicholas Hervey, "Lunacy Commission, 1845–1860, with Special Reference to the Implementation of Policy in Kent and Surrey" (Ph.D. diss., University of Bristol, 1987), 237–38, discusses problems arising from this kind of practice.

70. Pamela Horn, *The Rise and Fall of the Victorian Servant* (Stroud: Alan Sutton Publishing, 1990); Bridget Hill, *Servants: English Domestics in the Eighteenth Century* (Oxford: Clarendon Press, 1996).

71. In 1830, only eleven out of forty-two licensed houses in the metropolis were licensed to accept more than thirty patients, and as many as ten houses were meant for fewer than ten patients. Annual Report of the Metropolitan Commissioners of Lunacy, 1830. PRO HO 44/51.

72. Ida Macalpine and Richard Hunter, *George III and the Mad-Business* (London: Pimlico, 1991), 104; Arthur D. Morris, *The Hoxton Madhouses* (N.p.: Goodwin Books, 1958).

73. *Times,* 8 Aug. 1826, 2e.

74. *Times,* 2 Apr. 1841, 6c, the case of Barbara White.

75. WIHM MSS Autograph Letter 349775. A Letter by Arabella Norford to the First Earl of Powis, dated 30 Oct. 1826.

76. Ibid.

77. Ibid.

78. Thirteenth ARLC, BPP 1859 XIV, 83.

79. Stone, *Family, Sex, and Marriage in England;* Keith Wrightson, *English Society, 1580–1680* (1982; reprinted, London: Routledge, 1993); Leonore Davidoff, "The Family in Britain," in *The Cambridge Social History of Britain, 1750–1950,* ed. F. M. L. Thompson (Cambridge: Cambridge University Press, 1990), vol. 2: 71–129.

80. Eric Hobsbawm, *The Age of Revolution: Europe, 1789–1848* (London: Abacus, 1992); Davidoff, "Family in Britain"; Catherine Hall, "The Sweet Delights of Home," in *From the Fires of Revolution to the Great War,* ed. Michelle Perrot, vol. 4. of *A History of Private Life,* ed. Philippe Ariès and Georges Duby, trans. Arthur Goldhammer (Cambridge, Mass.: Belknap Press of Harvard University Press, 1990), 47–93.

81. Hall, "Sweet Delights of Home."

82. The interview, however, turned out to be unsuccessful. *Times,* 12 July 1838, 5f–6b; 26 July 1838, 3a–c.

83. Henry Halford, "On the Treatment of Insanity," read at the Royal College of Physicians, 28 Jan. 1833. RCP London, MSS D/2902.

84. Leonore Davidoff and Catherine Hall, *Family Fortunes: Men and Women of the English Middle Class, 1780–1850* (London: Routledge, 1992), 215–19.

85. The origin of moral treatment and its impact on the emerging discipline of psychiatry have been one of the foci of recent historical study of psychiatry. See, e.g., Andrew Scull, "Moral Treatment Reconsidered: Some Sociological Comments on an Episode in the History of British Psychiatry," in *Madhouses, Mad-Doctors, and Madmen: The Social History of Psychiatry in the Victorian Era,* ed. Andrew Scull (London: Athlone Press, 1981), 105–18; William F. Bynum, "Rationales for Therapy in British Psychiatry, 1780–1835," in *Madhouses, Mad-Doctors, and Madmen,* 35–57; Foucault, *Histoire de la folie à l'âge classique,* 2nd edition (Paris: Éditions Gallimard, 1972), 483–530; Roy Porter, *Mind-Forg'd Manacles: A History of Madness in England from the Restoration to the Regency* (London: Athlone Press, 1987), 206–28; Anne Digby, *Madness, Morality, and Medicine: A Study of the York Retreat, 1796–1914* (Cambridge: Cambridge University Press, 1985), 33–86; and Jan Goldstein, "Psychiatry" in *Companion Encyclopedia of the History of Medicine,* ed. W. F. Bynum and Roy Porter (London: Routledge, 1993), vol. 2: 1350–72.

86. Andrew Scull, *The Most Solitary of Afflictions: Madness and Society in Britain, 1700–1900* (New Haven, Conn.: Yale University Press, 1993), 115–74.

87. Foucault, *Histoire de la folie,* 483–530; Scull, "Moral Treatment Reconsidered."

88. Goldstein, "Psychiatry"; Jan Goldstein, *Console and Classify: The French Psychiatric Profession in the Nineteenth Century* (Cambridge: Cambridge University Press, 1987).

89. For an analysis of works of those late-eighteenth-century pioneers of psychological management, see Porter, *Mind-Forg'd Manacles,* 206–28.

90. Andrew Scull, "Domestication of Madness," *Medical History* 27 (1983): 233–48.

91. Tomes, *Art of Asylum-Keeping,* 113–28.

CHAPTER FIVE

1. For international comparative analyses of psychiatric confinement, see Roy Porter and David Wright, eds., *The Confinement of the Insane: International Perspectives, 1800–1965* (Cambridge: Cambridge University Press, 2003).

2. Carolyne Elizabeth le Neve and Hannah Ann le Neve, who had lived together with Augustus Adolphus le Neve, were so scared of him that they had drawn up a special contract with Frederick Candle, a surgeon in Southwark, in order to keep Augustus in custody and never "permit him to go to the houses where the said Carolyne Elizabeth le Neve and Hannah Ann le Neve shall then be or to molest annoy or disturb them." GLRO O/84/1, "Agreement between C. E. le Neve and H. A. le Neve and Mrs H. Yeats and Others," dated 24 Aug. 1842. The document contains an interesting detail about the power of habeas corpus to discharge a certified lunatic from custody.

3. See, for instance, H. C. Erik Midelfort, *A History of Madness in Sixteenth-Century Germany* (Stanford, Calif.: Stanford University Press, 1999), 277–384.

4. Lawrence Stone, *The Family, Sex, and Marriage in England, 1500–1800* (Harmondsworth: Penguin, 1979),164–68; Susan Moller Okin, "Patriarchy and Married Women's Property in England: Questions on Some Current Views," *Eighteenth-Century Studies* 17 (1983–84): 121–38.

5. Leonore Davidoff and Catherine Hall, *Family Fortunes: Men and Women of the English Middle Class, 1780–1850* (London: Routledge, 1992), 319; Amanda Vickery, *The Gentleman's Daughter: Women's Lives in Georgian England* (New Haven, Conn.: Yale University Press, 1998); Amanda Vickery, "Golden Age to Separate Spheres? A Review of the Categories and Chronology of English Women's History," *Historical Journal* 36 (1993): 383–414.

6. "Commissioner: Did he put you to pain then? / Miss Bagster: (A pause, and in a low tone, she said), Yes, Sir." *Times,* 11 July 1832, 3c.

7. *Times,* 14 July 1832, 4a. In his diary, Robert Sharp expressed doubt about the reasoning of the medical witnesses after reading their testimonies in the newspaper. See Robert Sharp, *The Diary of Robert Sharp of South Cave: Life in a Yorkshire Village, 1812–1837,* ed. Janice E. Crowther and Peter A. Crowther (Oxford: Oxford University Press, 1997), 377.

8. For Crowder's life, see R. C. Fell, *Passages from the Private and Official Life of the Late Alderman Kelly* (London: Groombridge & Sons, 1856), 188–94. See also Alfred B. Beaven, *The Aldermen of the City of London* (London: Eden Fisher & Company, 1908), vol. 1: 152.

9. For the mother's elopement, see *Times,* 5 July 1832, 5f; 6 July 1832, 3f.

10. *Times,* 7 July 1832, 3d.

11. For the summary of her life, see *Times,* 4 July 1832, 6b–c.

12. Toward the end of his life, Crowder reluctantly gave sanction to get "some proper person" to take care of Rosa. He was aware that it meant that "it would end in a strait waistcoat." *Times,* 5 July 1832, 5d.

13. *Times,* 6 July 1832, 3f.

14. *Times,* 5 July 1832, 5f.

15. *Times,* 14 July 1832, 6b. See also Peter Laurie's testimony in *Times,* 7 July 1832, 3d.

16. *Times,* 13 July 1832, 3d.

17. *Times,* 4 July 1832, 6b; 5 July 1832, 6a; 10 July 1832, 4a–b. One of the eager suitors was one Mr. Jupp, an employee of the family solicitor, who made a romantic advance by throwing his miniature into the carriage while Rosa was out riding. *Times,* 5 July 1832, 5e.

18. *Times,* 5 July 1832, 5d.

19. *Times,* 4 July 1832, 6c.

20. *Times,* 5 July 1832, 5e; 13 July 1832, 3a.

21. Her violent behavior was detailed mainly by her governesses, in *Times,* 4 July 1832, 6b–c; 5 July 1832, 5d.

22. *Times,* 6 July 1832, 3f–4b.

23. *Times,* 14 July 1832, 6b; 5 July 1832, 5e. Mr. Jupp died soon after he was rejected.

24. *Times,* 12 July 1832, 5e.

25. Seen in this light, their mentioning of Alderman Kelly as a suitable husband for Rosa may not have been just a bluff.

26. *Times,* 5 July 1832, 5e; 11 July 1832, 2e–f; 12 July 1832, 5e.

27. *Times,* 12 July 1832, 5e; 14 July 1832, 6b.

28. For marriage at Gretna Green, see Lawrence Stone, *The Road to Divorce: England, 1530–1987* (Oxford: Oxford University Press, 1990), 130–35.

29. *Times* 7 July 1832, 3d. For modeling one's romantic behavior after characters in fiction, see Vickery, *Gentleman's Daughter,* 70–71.

30. *Times,* 13 July 1832, 3f.

31. *Times,* 23 Oct. 1839, 6d.

32. Anon., *A Genuine Report of the Proceedings on the Portsmouth Case, under a Commission Issued by His Majesty* (London: Duncombe, [1823]), 15, 36.

33. *Times,* 29 July 1830, 4c. The subject was a sister of the fifth Earl of Harborough (1797–1859) and was put in James Stilwell's Moorcroft-House in Hillingdon.

34. *Times,* 4 Jan. 1839, 3f.

35. *Times,* 4 July 1832, 6b–c.

36. *Times,* 2 Apr. 1841, 6b–c. Likewise, when John Nicholas Durand ordered six watches, each of which cost between thirty-five and forty-five guineas, under

the delusion that he possessed an immense property of £20,000,000, they were not delivered, because the accompanying clerk informed the watch-seller of his disease. *Times,* 26 Jan. 1836, 7a–b.

37. *Times,* 7 Nov. 1837, 6a–b. See also the case of Edward Thomas, *Times,* 25 Jan. 1844, 8a.

38. *Times,* 5 Jan. 1839, 2f.

39. *Times,* 1 Jan. 1839, 2f; 3 Jan. 1839, 7a.

40. *Times,* 1 Apr. 1843, 6d.

41. *Times,* 16 Jan. 1844, 5d–e. The letter reads: "Dear Mr. Newman,—Since I have had the pleasure of seeing you I have thought of a pleasant scheme. I think I should like to go to Walmer [Weimer?]. I dare say Mrs. Brooks will let me go with you any day, and I should like to have a child very much."

42. For the nature of marriage as "the most important of means of property transaction," see Stone, *Road to Divorce,* 6.

43. *Times,* 4 July 1832, 6c; 5 July 1832, 5d.

44. The picture, emerging from my samples, of entrenchment in the domestic sphere is thus considerably different from that suggested by James E. Moran, who emphasizes the importance of community-based response in managing lunatics outside the asylum. This is virtually absent in my sources. This difference may result from the difference in our respective samples: Moran draws on cases mainly from modestly wealthy people from agricultural areas, whereas my sources have a strong bias toward the very wealthy sector of the metropolis. See James Moran, "Asylum in the Community: Managing the Insane in Antebellum America," *History of Psychiatry* 9 (1998): 217–40.

45. *Times,* 11 Feb. 1840, 7b–c. The commissions against Robinson and Clement were both sought by the heirs and were opposed by those who had been in charge of the lunatics. Similar cases were the commission against Edward Barker in 1835 and John Taylor in 1839. See *Times,* 29 Aug. 1835, 3f; 31 Aug. 1835, 3d; 1–14 Jan. 1839.

46. *Times,* 11 Feb. 1840, 7c.

47. *Times,* 17 Feb. 1840, 3b.

48. *Times,* 26 Aug. 1831, 3f; 27 Aug. 1831, 4a; 29 Aug. 1831, 6a.

49. *Times,* 27 Aug. 1831, 4a.

50. *Times,* 1 Sept. 1831, 4b.

51. *Times,* 17 Jan. 1853, 4f.

52. George Edward Cokayne, *The Complete Peerage of England, Scotland, Ireland, Great Britain and the United Kingdom: Extant, Extinct, or Dormant* (London: St. Catherine Press, 1926), vol. 5: 38–40. Eldon's wife died in 1852, and he was declared insane the next year.

53. R. A. Houston, *Madness and Society in Eighteenth-Century Scotland* (Oxford: Clarendon Press, 2000), 139.

54. *Times,* 29 Aug. 1831, 6e; 1 Sept. 1831, 4b.

55. For the importance of religious gatherings as a public space and the ambiguity of gender distinction, see Davidoff and Hall, *Family Fortunes,* 107–48.
56. *Times,* 9 Sept. 1841, 6d.
57. *Times,* 16 Jan. 1844, 5d–e.
58. *Times,* 16 Sept. 1842, 6f.
59. *Times,* 5 July 1832, 5d–e.
60. *Times,* 13 Dec. 1842, 3b.
61. *Times,* 8 Aug. 1823, 2e.
62. *Times,* 16 Jan. 1844, 5d.
63. *Times,* 27 Mar. 1841, 7d.
64. *Times,* 3 Feb. 1842, 6a–c.
65. *Times,* 4 Feb. 1842, 6d.
66. *Times,* 3 Nov. 1845, 8a. See also the case of Mary Barbara Budger Brown, *Times,* 26 June 1843, 6d.
67. *Times,* 19 Sept. 1837, 4d.
68. For the practice of the public's visit to Bedlam and its discontinuation, see Jonathan Andrews, Asa Briggs, Roy Porter, Penny Tucker, and Keir Waddington, *The History of Bethlem* (London: Routledge, 1997), 178–99.
69. Classic works of the political and cultural dynamics of the crowd include: George Rudé, *The Crowd in History* (1964: reprinted, London: Serif, 1995); and E. P. Thompson, "The Moral Economy of the English Crowd in the Eighteenth Century," *Past and Present* 50 (1971): 76–136.
70. G. M. Burrows, *A Letter to Sir Henry Halford, Bart, K.C.H* (London: T. and G. Underwood, 1830), 9–10.
71. Ibid., 10.
72. *The Mysteries of the Madhouse: Or Annals of Bedlam by a Discharged Officer of Twenty Years' Experience* (London: S. Chauntler, 1847), 11–12.
73. *Times,* 9 May 1867, 10f.
74. "[Maurice] fell yesterday in the Park and I trembled lest a vast crowd should be gathered. Sent away the children and sat by his side as though we were only lying on the grass, and by degrees he recovered and walked home." This passage is cited in Charlotte MacKenzie, *Psychiatry for the Rich: A History of Ticehurst Private Asylum* (London: Routledge, 1992), 101–2.
75. D. A. Miller, *The Novel and the Police* (Berkeley and Los Angeles: University of California Press, 1988).
76. For Victorian hypocrisy, see Walter E. Houghton, *The Victorian Frame of Mind, 1830–1870* (New Haven, Conn.: Yale University Press, 1957), 394–430.
77. Norbert Elias, *The Civilizing Process,* trans. Edmund Jephcott (New York: Urizen Books, 1978).
78. Nancy Tomes, *The Art of Asylum-Keeping: Thomas Story Kirkbride and the Origin of American Psychiatry* (1984: reprinted, Philadelphia: University of Pennsylvania Press, 1994), 127.

79. Tomes has pointed out the importance of privacy for the patrons of Philadelphia Hospital. Ibid., 114.

80. The background of this disjointed marriage was complex. The clergyman had made insulting comments about his wife's alleged frigidity: "[She] is, she adds, as he always said of her, a cold constitution in that way." *Times,* 4 Aug. 1825, 2d.

81. *Times,* 2 Aug. 1825, 3b–3c; 3 Aug. 1825, 2d–3b.

82. For the legal mechanism of separation and divorce, see Stone, *Road to Divorce.*

83. *Times,* 3 Aug. 1825, 2e–f.

84. *Times,* 2 Aug. 1825, 3b.

85. *Times,* 10 Feb. 1838, 5d.

86. *Times,* 16 Feb. 1838, 6e; 26 Feb. 1838, 6a–d.

87. Serjeant Bompas, the counsel in support of the commission, described him as laboring "under a delusion of benevolence." *Times,* 10 Feb. 1838, 5d–e.

88. *Times,* 10 Feb. 1838, 5e.

89. He also intended to give away his carriage and horses to a coachman because "his carriage was an abomination." *Times,* 10 Feb. 1838, 5e–f.

90. *Times,* 10 Feb. 1838, 5e; 16 Feb. 1838, 6d.

91. *Times,* 16 Feb. 1838, 6e.

92. Ibid.

93. Ibid.

94. A. James Hammerton, *Cruelty and Companionship: Conflict in Nineteenth-Century Married Life* (London: Routledge, 1992), 94–102.

95. The behavior of Davenport fell, however, far short of justifying divorce on the basis of the husband's cruelty against his wife. For marital cruelty, see Stone, *Road to Divorce,* 198–206; A. James Hammerton, "Victorian Marriage and the Law of Matrimonial Cruelty," *Victorian Studies* 33 (1990): 267–92; and Hammerton, *Cruelty and Companionship,* 102–33. For physical cruelty to a wife, see the case of Daniel Gundry, who tortured his wife in sadistic ways. *Times,* 3 Feb. 1842, 6a–c.

96. Almost certainly the wife wanted a divorce, for the commission against Daniel Gundry was requested by his wife, who had been living separately from him. *Times,* 3 Feb. 1842, 6a–c.

97. *Times,* 24–28 Aug. 1858.

98. *Times,* 24 Aug. 1856, 10b–c.

99. *Times,* 25 Aug. 1858, 6a.

100. *Times,* 28 Aug. 1858, 11b.

101. Ibid.

102. The amendment in the 1853 Act forbade the charge of lunacy to be "carried back" prior to the date of inquiry, in the absence of special instructions from the Lord Chancellor. See *Times,* 24 Aug. 1858, 10b; 28 Aug. 1858, 11b; Joseph Elmer, *The Lunacy Regulation Act (1853)* (London: V. & R. Stevens and G. S. Norton, 1853), 8. For confusions arising from such an attempt, and a jury's even-

tual inability to set a clear date on which lunacy had commenced, see the case of Sir Henry Meux, *Times,* 9–18 June 1858, particularly 18 June, 5e.

103. *Times,* 18 Sept. 1841, 7f.

104. *Times,* 20 Dec. 1842, 6b; 9 Mar. 1839, 7e–f.

105. *Times,* 24 Sept. 1844, 6f.

106. *Times,* 23 Jan. 1827, 3c.

107. John Tosh, *A Man's Place: Masculinity and the Middle-Class Home in Victorian England.* (New Haven, Conn.: Yale University Press, 1999), 1.

108. See Geoff Baldwin, "Individual and Self in the Late Renaissance," *Historical Journal* 44 (2001): 341–64.

109. The classic work in this field remains Elaine Showalter, *The Female Malady: Women, Madness and English Culture, 1830–1980* (London: Virago, 1987). Important works include: Jane E. Kromm, "The Feminization of Madness in Visual Representation," *Feminist Studies* 20 (1994): 507–36; and Nancy Tomes, "Feminist Histories of Psychiatry," in *Discovering the History of Psychiatry,* ed. Mark S. Micale and Roy Porter (Oxford: Oxford University Press, 1994), 348–83.

110. For a skilful and perceptive assessment of the vast scholarship on hysteria, see Mark S. Micale, *Approaching Hysteria: Disease and Its Interpretations* (Princeton, N.J.: Princeton University Press, 1995).

111. Mark Micale, "Charcot and the Idea of Hysteria in the Male: Gender, Mental Science, and Medical Diagnosis in Late Nineteenth-Century France," *Medical History* 34 (1990): 363–411, especially 406.

112. For female domestic behavior in a slightly later period, see Carol Dyhouse, "Mothers and Daughters in the Middle-Class Home, c.1870–1914," in *Labour and Love: Women's Experience of Home and Family, 1850–1940,* ed. Jane Lewis (Oxford: Basil Blackwell, 1986), 26–47.

113. *Times,* 6 Dec. 1843, 5d–e.

114. See, for example, evidence proffered against Loveday, a farmer and mill-owner of Gloucester: "neglect of business, cutting down an orchard while bearing fruit, forcing matrimonial proposals upon two women, discontinuing his attendance at market, selling a mill at half its value." *Times,* 4 Mar. 1851, 7d.

115. *Times,* 8 Aug. 1826, 2e.

116. Tomes, "Feminist Histories of Psychiatry."

117. Davidoff and Hall, *Family Fortunes;* Vickery, *Gentleman's Daughter;* Linda Colley, *Britons: Forging the Nation* (New Haven, Conn.: Yale University Press, 1992), 237–81.

CHAPTER SIX

1. *Times,* 6 Apr. 1836, 1d.
2. *Times,* 1 Apr. 1836, 4e.
3. *Times,* 23 Jan. 1827, 3c.

4. Robert Castel, *The Regulation of Madness: The Origin of Incarceration in France,* trans. W. D. Halls (Cambridge: Polity Press, 1988). For a feminist application of Castel's thesis, see Yannick Ripa, *Women and Madness: The Incarceration of Women in Nineteenth-Century France,* trans. Catherine du Peloux Menagé (Cambridge: Polity Press, 1990). For a criticism of the classic Marxist interpretation on which Castel's analysis is based, see Jacques Donzelot, *The Policing of Families,* trans. Robert Hurley (London: Hutchinson, 1979).

5. *Times,* 18 Nov. 1829, 2e. Louisa Lowe, *The Bastilles of England, or, the Lunacy Law at Work* (London: Crookenden and Co., 1883). See also B. A. Morel, "The Present State and Future Prospects of Psychological Medicine," *Journal of Mental Science* 10 (1864–65): 338–42.

6. A similar example was the 1839 case of Thomas Swindall. The case was petitioned by the brother of the supposed lunatic to nullify his marriage with a woman of whom his family did not approve and to invalidate the settlement of his property. The commission was successful. *Times,* 12 Sept. 1839, 6a–d.

7. Such overlapping of, and conflict and convergence between, different authorities over the matter of pauper lunatics are perceptively discussed in Peter Bartlett, *The Poor Law of Lunacy: The Administration of Pauper Lunatics in Mid-Nineteenth-Century England* (London: Leicester University Press, 1999). For the powers and limits of Lunacy Commissioners, see Nicholas Hervey, "Lunacy Commission, 1845–1860, with Special Reference to the Implementation of Policy in Kent and Surrey," (Ph.D. diss., University of Bristol, 1987).

8. Joel Peter Eigen, *Witnessing Insanity: Madness and Mad-Doctors in the English Court* (New Haven, Conn.: Yale University Press, 1995); Roger Smith, *Trial by Medicine: Insanity and Responsibility in Victorian Trials* (Edinburgh: Edinburgh University Press, 1981); J. C. Bucknill, *Unsoundness of Mind in Relation to Criminal Acts: An Essay to Which the First Sugden Prize Was This Year Awarded* (Philadelphia: T. & J. W. Johnson & Co., 1856).

9. For brief histories of the notion of the commission of lunacy and how a commission should proceed, see, among others, Anthony Highmore, *A Treatise on the Law of Idiocy and Lunacy* (London: J. Butterworth & J. Cooke, 1807); Joseph Elmer, *An Outline of the Practice in Lunacy, under Commissions in the Nature of Writs de Lunatico Inquirendo* (London: V. & R. Stevens and G. S. Norton, 1844); Leonard Shelford, *A Practical Treatise of the Law concerning Lunatics, Idiots, and Persons of Unsound Mind* (London: S. Sweet et al., 1847), 9–35, 116–42.

10. Lord Donegal's case, 2 Ves. Sen. 408.

11. Ibid. Hardwicke's statement is quoted in Shelford, *Practical Treatise,* 104. See also Hardwicke's similar interpretation in a commission of lunacy against William Barnsley in 1744, in Ex Parte Barnsley, 3 Atk. 168.

12. *Ridgeway v. Darwin,* 8 Ves. 65–66.

13. Ibid.

14. It should be noted as well that Hardwicke admitted the existence of such

cases, but he tried to achieve the protection by other means than expanding the scope of the commission. See Ex Parte Barnsley, 3 Atk. 168.

15. Ex Parte Cranmer, 12 Ves. Jun. 445–56.

16. Ibid.

17. Highmore, *Treatise on the Law of Idiocy and Lunacy,* xii–xiii.

18. Shelford, *Practical Treatise,* 5. See also John Haslam, *A Letter to the Right Honorable the Lord Chancellor, on the Nature and Interpretation of Mind, and Interpretation of Unsoundness of Mind, and Imbecility of Intellect* (London: R. Hunter, 1823), 9–10.

19. For the debauchery of Regency aristocrats and criticism of it, see Iain McCalman, *Radical Underworld: Prophets, Revolutionaries, and Pornographers in London, 1795–1840* (Oxford: Clarendon Press, 1993).

20. *Times,* 8 Aug. 1825, 2f–3b.

21. *Times,* 1 Aug. 1825, 3b–c.

22. *Times,* 2 Aug. 1825, 3b; 9 Aug. 1825, 2f.

23. *Times,* 6 Aug. 1825, 2b–3a. Both Brougham and Blackstone contrasted Roman law with English law, which prioritized "the liberty of using their own property as they please" above the prevention of prodigal wasting of one's estate. See William Blackstone, *Commentaries on the Laws of England,* ed. Wayne Morrison (London: Cavendish Publishing, 2001), vol. 1: 231–32.

24. *Hansard's Parliamentary Debates,* 3rd ser., 1 (1831): 1344.

25. For the life of Eldon, see R. A. Mellikan, *John Scott, Lord Eldon, 1751–1838: The Duty of Loyalty* (Cambridge: Cambridge University Press, 1999).

26. *Hansard's Parliamentary Debates,* 2nd ser., 22 (1830): 1148–54; *Hansard's Parliamentary Debates,* 2nd ser., 23 (1830): 547–48. See also *Times,* 28 Dec. 1829, 3b–d.

27. 3 and 4 W.IV, c.36. Under this Act, the Lord Chancellor could appoint one or more commissioners to hear a case, instead of the three or more commissioners that had previously been required. Section 2 of this Act empowered the Lord Chancellor to appoint two physicians and one barrister to visit the so-called Chancery lunatics. See also *Hansard's Parliamentary Debates,* 3rd ser., 1 (1831): 1840–43; *Hansard's Parliamentary Debates,* 3rd ser., 2 (1831): 838–42; and *Hansard's Parliamentary Debates,* 3rd ser., 15 (1833): 550–58. For still more ambitious plans of Brougham, see *Hansard's Parliamentary Debates,* 3rd ser., 2 (1831): 915–29; *Hansard's Parliamentary Debates,* 3rd ser., 6 (1831): 448–49; and *Hansard's Parliamentary Debates,* 3rd ser., 7 (1831): 603–5, 877–79.

28. *Times,* 14 Jan. 1839, 5f.

29. "An Act to Alter and Amend the Practice and Course of Proceeding under Commissions in the Nature of Writs *De Lunatico Inquirendo,*" 5 and 6 Vict. c.84. See also *Hansard's Parliamentary Debates,* 3rd ser., 61 (1842): 203–8.

30. "Act for the Regulation of Proceedings under Commissions of Lunacy," 16 and 17 Vict. c.70.

31. Elmer, *Outline of the Practice in Lunacy,* 5; Joseph Elmer, *The Lunacy Regulation Act (1853)* (London: V. & R. Stevens and G. S. Norton, 1853), 7.

32. John Millar, *Hints on Insanity* (London: Henry Renshow, 1859), 64–65.

33. Some of these figures were reported in the *Times.* See, e.g., *Times,* 10 June 1856, 6b.

34. *Times,* 9 Sept. 1841, 6d.

35. *Times,* 19 Aug. 1844, 6f.

36. For a nuanced and balanced overview of the question, see Oliver MacDonagh, *Early Victorian Government, 1830–1870* (London: Weidenfeld and Nicolson, 1977).

37. K. Theodore Hoppen, *The Mid-Victorian Generation: 1846–1886* (Oxford: Oxford University Press, 1998), 91–124.

38. Nicholas Hervey, "Lunacy Commission"; Andrew Scull, *The Most Solitary of Afflictions: Madness and Society in Britain, 1700–1900* (New Haven, Conn.: Yale University Press, 1993), 115–74. See, however, Bartlett, *Poor Law of Lunacy,* for a sophisticated revision of the one-sided emphasis on initiatives of the state and the Lunacy Commissioners.

39. David Wright, "The Certification of Insanity in Nineteenth-Century England and Wales," *History of Psychiatry* 9 (1998): 267–90, quotation on 290.

40. Scull, *Most Solitary of Afflictions,* 83–87, 115–74. For an in-depth study of Evangelicalism, see Boyd Hilton, *The Age of Atonement: The Influence of Evangelicalism on Social and Economic Thought, 1785–1865* (Oxford: Oxford University Press, 1988).

41. Two important exceptions are: Hervey, "Lunacy Commission"; and Bartlett, *Poor Law of Lunacy,* 20–26.

42. Pat Thane, "Government and Society in England and Wales, 1750–1914," in *Cambridge Social History of Britain, 1750–1950,* ed. F. M. L. Thompson (Cambridge: Cambridge University Press, 1990), vol. 3: 1–61, quotation on 1.

43. Moreover, Brougham's bill was not created single-handedly. Although the details are unknown, the bill Brougham put to Parliament had been considered for three years. See *Times,* 29 July 1833, 6a.

44. *Times,* 15 March 1841, 6b.

45. *Times,* 19 Aug. 1844, 6f. The commission was unopposed, but Spencer's mother was present at the examination and repeatedly interrupted the examination, which prompted remonstrance from the commissioner.

46. Highmore, *Treatise on the Law of Idiocy and Lunacy,* 193.

47. 16 and 17 Vict.c.97.s.68. Although the Act itself related chiefly to provisions for pauper lunatics, it was understood that this particular section applied to nonpauper lunatics as well. See Danby P. Fry, *The Lunacy Acts: Containing All the Statues Relating to Private Lunatics, etc.* (London: Knight & Co., 1877), 80. Lunatics committed to asylums on the basis of this section represented a significant minority of the institutionalized population. Peter Bartlett's study showed

that about 13 percent of the total admissions to Leicester and Rutland County Lunatic Asylum from 1861 to 1865 fell into the categories of "wandering at large," "not under proper care and control," or "cruelly treated or neglected." See Bartlett, *Poor Law of Lunacy*, 153.

48. The Queen against Harriet Eleanor Pelham, *English Reports*, 8 Q.B. 959.

49. *Times*, 7 Aug. 1826, 3a; 11 Aug. 1826, 3a.

50. *Times*, 7 Aug. 1826, 3a, 3d.

51. Ibid., 3a, 3c–d.

52. Ibid., 3a–b. The room where George was kept was, however, reported to be the best room on the first floor of the house.

53. Ibid., 3c.

54. Ibid., 3b, 3d.

55. Ibid., 3b, an extract from the *Birmingham Journal*, 11 Feb. 1826.

56. *Times*, 11 Aug. 1825, 3b–3c, the testimony of Eld and Broughton.

57. Although George seems to have been relatively calm and well at the asylum, he soon died there. George's immediate death raises some doubt about the propriety of his removal to the asylum.

58. *Times*, 12 Aug. 1826, 3c. At the beginning of the trial, it was predicted that several other actions would depend on the result of the trial *Smith v. Hodget.*

59. *Rex v. William Smith, Thomas Smith, and Sarah Smith.* 2 Car. and P.449.

60. In re Smith, 1 Russ 348.

61. Justice Burrough stated in his summary that the newspaper should be "most guarded against unwarrantable attacks upon private character." *Times*, 12 Aug. 1826, 3c.

62. *Times*, 7 Aug. 1826, 3a; 11 Aug. 1826, 3d.

63. Henry Monro, *Articles on Reform in Private Asylums* (London: John Churchill, 1852), 1–2. They had already appeared in various medical journals, such as *Psychological Journal*, *Medical Gazette*, and *Lancet*, in 1851–52.

64. Ibid., 3.

65. For a discussion of Lunacy Commissioners' attempts to regulate "single patients," see Hervey, "Lunacy Commission," 242–62.

66. For the relationship between the Lunacy Commissioners and the Lord Chancellor, see ibid., 294–301.

67. PRO MH 51/29.

68. PRO MH 51/29.

69. Fourteenth ARLC, BPP, 1860, XXXIV, 70. For the role of Gaskell in these energetic investigations, see Andrew Scull, Charlotte Mackenzie, and Nicholas Hervey, *Masters of Bedlam: The Transformation of the Mad-Doctoring Trade* (Princeton, N.J.: Princeton University Press, 1996), 174–83.

70. Thirteenth ARLC, BPP, 1859 XIV, 78–80. The cases of Mr. B, Mr. G., Miss D., Hon. Mr. W., and Miss G.

71. Fourteenth ARLC, BPP, 1860, XXXIV, 71–73.

72. Eleventh ARLC, BPP, 1857, XVI, 24–40. For a discussion of this case, see Akihito Suzuki, "Psychiatric Therapeutics and the 'Public' in England in the Eighteenth and Nineteenth Centuries," *Harvard Review of Psychiatry* 10 (2002): 123–26. As the editor of the *Asylum Journal of Mental Science*, Bucknill wrote bitterly about the increased attention to the case due to an unusual move of the venue of the trial from Surrey to Central London. This move may have been a strategic one, calculated by the Commissioners to maximize publicity for the case.

73. Fifteenth ARLC, BPP, 1861, XXVII, 68.

74. *Times*, 9 Nov. 1866, 11d; 21 Nov. 1867, 9e; 25 Nov. 1867, 10c; 30 Nov. 1867, 11e; 6 Dec. 1867, 9e; 7 Dec. 1867, 11f; 14 Dec. 1867, 9f; 10 Mar. 1869, 11e.

75. In 1865, a relieving officer of the parish of St. Mary, Newington, initiated an investigation into two lunatics kept in a private lodging in a wretched state by their brother. This case soon drew the attention of the Lunacy Commissioners, who advised the parish how to proceed. *Times*, 20 May 1865, 11f; 27 May 1865, 11f.

76. P. W. J. Bartrip, "British Government Inspection, 1832–1875: Some Observations," *Historical Journal* 25 (1982): 605–26. Abstracts and notices of the ARLC appeared regularly in the *Times*. See, for example, 25 Nov. 1850, 4f; 23 June 1855, 12f; 25 Aug. 1857, 11c. For a similar view of the power of Lunacy Commissioners vis-à-vis local authorities and Poor Law Commissioners, see Bill Forsythe, Joseph Melling, and Richard Adair, "Politics of Lunacy: Central State Regulation and the Devon Pauper Lunatic Asylum, 1845–1914," in *Insanity, Institutions, and Society, 1800–1914*, ed. Joseph Melling and Bill Forsythe (London: Routledge, 1999), 68–92. For a different view of Lunacy Commissioners, see Bartlett, *Poor Law of Lunacy*, 24–25, 197–237.

77. J. E. D. Esquirol, *Observations on the Illusions of the Insane, and on the Medico-Legal Question of Their Confinement*, trans. William Liddell (London: Renshaw and Rush, 1833), 87.

78. *Hansard's Parliamentary Debates*, 3rd ser., 7 (1831): 878; *Hansard's Parliamentary Debates*, 2nd ser., 18 (1828): 584.

79. *English Reports*, Dears. 482.

80. *Law Journal*, new series, vol. 33, Mag. Cases, 126–28.

81. *Times*, 7 Aug. 1826, 3c; 11 Aug. 1826, 3b.

82. It is significant that Higgins was a magistrate (of West Riding, Yorkshire), with whom Eld and Broughton could easily identify themselves.

83. Edward J. Seymour, *A Letter to the Right Honourable the Earl of Shaftesbury etc. etc. etc. on the Laws Which Regulate Private Lunatic Asylums, with a Comparative View of the Process "De Lunatic Inquirendo" and the Law of Interdiction in France* (London: Longman, Brown, Green, Longmans, & Roberts, 1859), 18.

84. For Seymore's endorsement of privacy and domestic atmosphere in the care of lunatics, see Hervey, "Lunacy Commission," 248. For the panic in 1858–

59 and its literary exploitation, see Peter McCandless, "Liberty and Lunacy: The Victorians and Wrongful Confinement," in *Madhouses, Mad-Doctors, and Madmen: The Social History of Psychiatry in the Victorian Era,* ed. Andrew Scull (London: Athlone Press, 1981), 339–62; Helen Small, *Love's Madness: Medicine, the Novel, and Female Insanity, 1800–1865* (Oxford: Oxford University Press, 1996), 179–220; and Jenny Bourne Taylor, *In the Secret Theatre of Home: Wilkie Collins, Sensation Narrative, and Nineteenth-Century Psychology* (London: Routledge, 1988).

85. See Matthew Sweet, "Introduction" to *The Woman in White,* by Wilkie Collins (London: Penguin Books, 1999), xiii–xxxiv.

86. *Times,* 7 Aug. 1826, 3d.

87. *Times,* 7 Aug. 1826, 3c; 11 Aug. 1826, 3b. Of course, the two accounts of the scene are very different. Almost certainly the magistrates' version exaggerated the alarm and hesitation of the family, while the servant's account exaggerated the integrity of the family.

88. *Times,* 11 Aug. 1826, 3b.

89. For the intrusion of middle-class agencies into the working-class family in the late nineteenth and early twentieth centuries, see George K. Behlmer, *Friends of the Family: The English Home and Its Guardians, 1850–1940* (Stanford, Calif.: Stanford University Press, 1998).

90. *Times,* 16 Sept. 1842, 6f.

91. Ibid., 6f.

92. The commissioner probably referred to section 3 of the 1842 Act (5 and 6 Vict.c.82.s.2), which empowered commissioners to perform the duties in lunacy that had been done by Masters in Chancery.

BIBLIOGRAPHY

PRIMARY SOURCES

Archives

City of Westminster Library and Archives
London Metropolitan Archives
Public Record Office
Royal College of Physicians of Edinburgh
Royal College of Physicians of London
University College London Library
Wellcome Institute for the History of Medicine

Governmental and Parliamentary Publications

British Parliamentary Papers
Hansard's Parliamentary Debates

Law Reports

English Reports
Law Journal

Biographical References

Boase, Frederic. *Modern British Biography.* 6 vols. Truro: for the author, 1892–1921.

Cokayne, George Edward. *The Complete Peerage of England, Scotland, Ireland, Great Britain and the United Kingdom: Extant, Extinct, or Dormant.* London: St. Catherine Press, 1926.

Dictionary of National Biography

Oxford Dictionary of National Biography

Contemporary Books and Articles

"Anderdon v. Burrows." *London Medical Gazette* 6 (1830): 83–87.

Anon. *A Genuine Report of the Proceedings on the Portsmouth Case, under a Commission Issued by His Majesty.* London: Duncombe, [1823].

"Attacks on Dr. Burrows." *London Medical Gazette* 6 (1830): 84–86.

Beaven, Alfred B. *The Aldermen of the City of London.* 2 vols. London: Eden Fisher & Company, 1908.

Blackstone, William. *Commentaries on the Laws of England.* Edited with an introduction by Wayne Morrison. London: Cavendish Publishing, 2001.

Buchan, William. *Domestic Medicine: Or the Family Physician.* Edinburgh: Balfour et al., 1769.

Bucknill, J. C. "The Diagnosis of Insanity." *Asylum Journal of Mental Science* 2 (1856): 229–45, 432–45; 3 (1857): 141–85.

[——]. "Insane Literature." *Asylum Journal of Mental Science* 3 (1857): 43–80.

[——]. "Review of *The Metaphysicians: Being a Memoir of Franz Carvel, Brushmaker, Written by Himself; and of Harold Fremdling, Esquire, Written and Now Re-published by Francis Drake* (1857)." *Journal of Mental Science* 4 (1858): 249–57.

——. *Unsoundness of Mind in Relation to Criminal Acts: An Essay to Which the First Sugden Prize Was This Year Awarded.* Philadelphia: T. & J. W. Johnson & Co., 1856.

Bucknill, J. C., and Daniel H. Tuke. *A Manual of Psychological Medicine.* Philadelphia: Blancard and Lea, 1858.

Burrows, G. M. "Bethlem Hospital." *London Medical Repository* 6 (1816): 88.

——. *Commentaries on the Causes, Forms, Symptoms, and Treatment, Moral and Medical, of Insanity.* London: Thomas and George Underwood, 1828.

——. *An Inquiry into Certain Errors Relative to Insanity, and Their Consequences: Physical, Moral, and Civil.* London: Thomas and George Underwood, 1820.

——. "Letter to the Editor of *The Times.*" *Times* [London], 26 Nov. 1829, 3a.

——. *A Letter to Sir Henry Halford, Bart, K.C.H.* London: T. and G. Underwood, 1830.

———. "A Reply to Messieurs Esquirol's and Falret's Objections to Dr. Burrows's Comparative Proportions of Suicide in Paris and London." *London Medical Repository* 18 (1822): 460–64.

[———]. "Retrospect of the Progress of Medical Science, Part II." *London Medical Repository* 9 (1818): 89–129.

[———]. "Review of Haslam, *Medical Jurisprudence* (1818)." *London Medical Repository* 9 (1818): 473–82.

[———]. "Review of J. G. Spurzheim, *Observations on the Deranged Manifestations of the Mind* (1817)." *London Medical Repository* 8 (1817): 217–39, 305–31.

[———]. "Review of John Mayo, *Remarks on Insanity* (1817), Thomas Forster, *Observations on Insanity* (1817), et al." *London Medical Repository* 8 (1817): 485–501.

[———]. "Some Observations on the Pathology of Insanity: Essay I." *London Medical Repository* 6 (1816): 279–88.

———. *A Statement of Circumstances Connected with the Apothecaries' Act, and Its Administration.* London: J. Callow, 1817.

Burrows, George. *Introductory Lecture of a Course on Forensic Medicine, Delivered in the Anatomical Theatre of St. Bartholomew's Hospital.* London: J. Mallet, [1831].

Byron, Lord. *Byron's Letters and Journals.* Edited by Leslie A. Marchand. 13 vols. London: John Murray, 1973–80.

Camell, Robert. "Case of Disease of the Brain which Had Been Confounded with Hepatic Disease, with the Dissection, and Some Observations." *London Medical Repository* 7 (1817): 92–98.

Campbell, Thomas. *Life and Letters of Thomas Campbell.* Edited by William Beattie. 3 vols. London: Edward Moxon, 1859.

"A Case of Mania." *London Medical Repository* 6 (1816): 377–79.

Collins, Wilkie. *The Woman in White.* Edited by Matthew Sweet. London: Penguin Books, 1999.

Combe, Andrew. "Commissions of Lunacy—Mad Doctors—London Press." *London Medical Gazette* 5 (1829–30): 719–21.

Conolly, John. *An Enquiry Concerning the Indications of Insanity.* 1830; reprinted, London: Dawsons, 1964.

Dickens, Charles. *The Pickwick Papers.* Edited by James Kinsley. Oxford: Oxford University Press, 1988.

———. *Sketches by Boz.* Edited by Dennis Walder. Harmondsworth: Penguin, 1995.

"Dr Conolly on Insanity." *London Medical Gazette* 6 (1830): 727–28.

Dunne, Charles. *The Appellatory, or the Complaint of a Subject to His King against Ministerial Tyranny and Oppression.* London: for the author, [1829].

———. *Brand's Lunacy Case: A Full Report of the Most Interesting and Extraordinary Investigation; Including Copious Animadversions on the Principal Actors in This Drama.* London: sold by John Wilson, 1830.

———. *The Chiurgical Candidate: Or, Reflections on Education.* London: Samuel Highley, 1808.
———. *Parliamentary Impeachment of Sir William Draper Best, Knt., Chief Justice of the Commons Pleas.* London: by the author, n.d.
———. *The Star Chamber, or a Panorama of the Moral Assassins of the Metropolis.* London: by the author, 1825.
Elmer, Joseph. "Chancery Lunatics." In *A Dictionary of Psychological Medicine,* edited by D. H. Tuke, vol. 1: 195–201. London: J. & A. Churchill, 1892.
———. *The Lunacy Regulation Act (1853).* London: V. & R. Stevens and G. S. Norton, 1853.
———. *An Outline of the Practice in Lunacy, under Commissions in the Nature of Writs de Lunatico Inquirendo.* London: V. & R. Stevens and G. S. Norton, 1844.
Esquirol, J. E. D. *Observations on the Illusions of the Insane, and on the Medico-Legal Question of Their Confinement.* Translated by William Liddell. London: Renshaw and Rush, 1833.
Fell, R. C. *Passages from the Private and Official Life of the Late Alderman Kelly.* London: Groombridge & Sons, 1856.
Fry, Danby P. *The Lunacy Acts: Containing All the Statutes Relating to Private Lunatics, etc.* London: Knight & Co., 1877.
[Gooch, Robert]. "Review of G. M. Burrows, *Commentaries* (1828) and G. N. Hill, *Observations on Madness* (1809)." *Quarterly Review* 42 (1830): 350–77.
Griggs, William. *Lunacy and Liberty: A Letter to the Lord Chancellor, on the Defective State of the Law, As Regards Insane Persons, etc.* London: W. Griggs, 1832.
Halford, Henry. *Essays and Orations, Read and Delivered at the Royal College of Physicians.* 3rd ed. London: John Murray, 1842.
Haslam, John. *Illustrations of Madness.* 1810; reprinted with an introduction by Roy Porter, London: Routledge, 1989.
———. *A Letter to the Right Honourable the Lord Chancellor, on the Nature and Interpretation of Unsoundness of Mind, and Imbecility of Intellect.* London: R. Hunter, 1823.
Hastings, Charles. "A Remarkable Coincidence of Anomalous Structure in the Brain of Two Idiots, with an Extraordinary State of Disease of the Viscera." *London Medical Repository* 7 (1817): 74–78.
Highmore, Anthony. *A Treatise on the Law of Idiocy and Lunacy.* London: J. Butterworth & J. Cooke, 1807.
Hunter, Richard, and Ida Macalpine, eds. *Three Hundred Years of Psychiatry, 1535–1860.* 1963; reprinted, New York: Carlisle Publishing, 1982.
"Imposing Restraint on Lunatics." *London Medical Gazette* 5 (1829–30): 311–14, 349–52.
Ingram, Allan, ed. *Voices of Madness: Four Pamphlets, 1683–1796.* Stroud, Gloucestershire: Sutton Publishing, 1997.

"Law versus Physic." *London Medical Gazette* 5 (1829–30): 439–42, 474–76, 501–4.

"Letter to Dr. Burrows." *Lancet* 2 (1829–30): 251–52.

Little, Thomas. *Mad-Houses! Sketch of the Seduction and Treatment, Il-legal and Non-Medical, of Miss Stabback.* London: J. J. Stockdale, [1831].

Louis, P. C. A. *Memoir on the Proper Method of Examining a Patient, and of Arriving at Facts of a General Nature.* Translated by Henry I. Bowditch, M.D. N.p.: n.p., n.d.

Lowe, Louisa. *The Bastilles of England, or, the Lunacy Law at Work.* London: Crookenden and Co., 1883.

Lucett, James. *A Statement of Facts Relative to the Nature and Cure of Mental Diseases.* London: James Truscott, 1833.

Maudsley, Henry. "Memoir of the Late John Conolly." *Journal of Mental Science* 12 (1866): 151–74.

Mayo, Thomas. *Elements of the Pathology of the Human Mind.* London: John Murray, 1838.

———. *A Letter to the Reverend Thomas Rennell Concerning His Remarks on Scepticism: From a Graduate in Medicine, of the University of Oxford.* London: Thomas and George Underwood, [1819].

Metropolitan Commissioners in Lunacy. *Report of the Metropolitan Commissioners in Lunacy to the Lord Chancellor.* London: Bradbury and Evnats, 1844.

Millar, John. *Hints on Insanity.* London: Henry Renshow, 1859.

Mills, Gerald E., and A. H. Ronald W. Poyster. *Management and Administration of Estates in Lunacy.* London: Butterworth & Co., 1927.

[Mitford, John]. *A Description of the Crimes and Horrors in the Interior of Warburton's Private Mad-House at Hoxton, Commonly Called Whitmore House.* London: Benbow, [1826].

Monro, Henry. *Articles on Reform in Private Asylums.* London: John Churchill, 1852.

More, Cleave. *The Apology, or Vindication of Sir Cleave More, Bart., upon the Suing Forth of a Commission of Lunacy against Joseph Edmonds, Esquire.* London: George Croom, 1711.

Morel, B. A. "The Present State and Future Prospects of Psychological Medicine." *Journal of Mental Science* 10 (1864–65): 338–42.

The Mysteries of the Madhouse: Or Annals of Bedlam by a Discharged Officer of Twenty Years' Experience. London: S. Chauntler, 1847.

Newnham, William. "Cases of Sympathetic Affection of the Brain with the Abdominal Viscera, Cured by Purgatives." *London Medical Repository* 7 (1817): 282–85, 459–64.

"Obituary: George Man Burrows." *Medical Directory* (1847): 189–93.

Perceval, John. *Perceval's Narrative: A Patient's Account of His Psychosis, 1830–1832.* Edited by Gregory Bateson. Stanford, Calif.: Stanford University Press, 1961.

Perry, Charles. *A Treatise of Diseases in General.* 2 vols. London: T. Woodward et al., 1741.

Peterson, Dale, ed. *A Mad People's History of Madness.* Pittsburgh: University of Pittsburgh Press, 1982.

Pitt-Lewis, George, R. Percy Smith, and J. A. Hawke. *The Insane and the Law: A Plain Guide for Medical Men, Solicitors, and Others.* London: J. & A. Churchill, 1895.

Prichard, James Cowles. "J. C. Prichard and the Concept of 'Moral Insanity.'" Edited by German Berrios. *History of Psychiatry* 10 (1999): 111–26.

———. *A Treatise on Insanity and Other Disorders Affecting the Mind.* London: Sherwood, Gilbert, and Piper, 1835.

Retreat at Vanves, Near Paris, for the Reception and Recovery of Ladies and Gentlemen Afflicted with Disorders of the Mind. N.p.: n.p., [1841].

"Review of G. M. Burrows, *A Letter to Sir Henry Halford* (1830)." *London Medical and Physical Journal* 63 (1830): 427–34.

Rush, Benjamin. *Two Essays on the Mind.* Edited by Eric T. Carlson. New York: Brunner/Mazel, 1972.

Sabben, James T., and J. H. Balfour Browne. *Handbook of Law and Lunacy.* London: J. & A. Churchill, 1872.

Sade, Marquis de. *The Misfortunes of Virtue and Other Early Tales.* Edited by David Coward. Oxford: Oxford University Press, 1999.

Seymour, Edward J. *A Letter to the Right Honourable the Earl of Shaftesbury etc. etc. etc. on the Laws Which Regulate Private Lunatic Asylums, with a Comparative View of the Process "De Lunatico Inquirendo" and the Law of Interdiction in France.* London: Longman, Brown, Green, Longmans, & Roberts, 1859.

Sharp, Robert. *The Diary of Robert Sharp of South Cave: Life in a Yorkshire Village, 1812–1837.* Edited by Janice E. Crowther and Peter A. Crowther. Oxford: Oxford University Press, 1997.

Shelford, Leonard. *A Practical Treatise of the Law Concerning Lunatics, Idiots, and Persons of Unsound Mind.* London: S. Sweet et al., 1847.

Symonds, John Addington. *Some Accounts of the Life, Writings, and Character of the Late James Cowles Prichard.* N.p.: n.p., 1849.

Thackeray, William Makepeace. *The Letters and Private Papers of William Makepeace Thackeray.* Edited by Gordon N. Ray. 4 vols. London: Oxford University Press, 1945.

Trusler, John. *The Physical Friend: Pointing Out the Symptoms of Every Distemper Incident to Man.* London: for the author, 1776.

Tuke, D. H. *Chapters in the History of the Insane in the British Isles.* London: Kegan Paul, Trench & Co., 1882.

———. "Commissioners in Lunacy." In *A Dictionary of Psychological Medicine,* edited by D. H. Tuke, vol. 1: 240. London: J. & A. Churchill, 1892.

———. "Moral Insanity." In *A Dictionary of Psychological Medicine,* edited by D. H. Tuke, vol. 2: 813–16. London: J. & A. Churchill, 1892.
———. *Prichard and Symonds: In Special Relation to Mental Science with Chapters on Moral Insanity.* London: J. A. Churchill, 1891.
[Wakley, Thomas]. "Review of Burrows, *Commentaries* (1828)." *Lancet* 2 (1829–30): 136–40.
Whitshed, J. "Case of Phrenitis." *London Medical Repository* 7 (1817): 99–101.
Wigan, A. L. *A New View of Insanity: The Duality of the Mind.* London: Longman, Brown, Green, and Longmans, 1844.

SECONDARY SOURCES

Ackerknecht, Erwin H. "A Plea for a 'Behaviorist' Approach in Writing the History of Medicine." *Journal of the History of Medicine and Allied Sciences* 22 (1967): 211–14.
Andrews, Jonathan. "Case Notes, Case Histories, and Patients' Experience of Insanity at Gartnaval Royal Asylum, Glasgow, in the Nineteenth Century." *Social History of Medicine* 11 (1998): 255–81.
———. "'In Her Vapours . . . [or] Indeed in Her Madness'? Mrs Clerke's Case: An Early Eighteenth-Century Psychiatric Controversy." *History of Psychiatry* 1 (1990): 125–43.
Andrews, Jonathan, Asa Briggs, Roy Porter, Penny Tucker, and Keir Waddington. *The History of Bethlem.* London: Routledge, 1997.
Andrews, Jonathan, and Anne Digby, eds. *Sex and Seclusion, Class and Custody: Perspectives on Gender and Class in the History of British and Irish Psychiatry.* Amsterdam: Rodopi, 2004.
Andrews, Jonathan, and Andrew Scull. *Customers and Patrons of the Mad Trade: The Management of Lunacy in Eighteenth-Century London.* Berkeley and Los Angeles: University of California Press, 2003.
———. *Undertaker of the Mind: John Monro and Mad-Doctoring in Eighteenth-Century England.* Berkeley and Los Angeles: University of California Press, 2001.
Augstein, Hannah. "J. C. Prichard's Concept of Moral Insanity: A Medical Theory of the Corruption of Human Nature." *Medical History* 40 (1996), 311–43.
Baldwin, Geoff. "Individual and Self in the Late Renaissance." *Historical Journal* 44 (2001): 341–64.
Bartlett, Peter. "Legal Madness in the Nineteenth Century." *Social History of Medicine* 14 (2001): 107–31.
———. *The Poor Law of Lunacy: The Administration of Pauper Lunatics in Mid-Nineteenth-Century England.* London: Leicester University Press, 1999.
Bartlett, Peter, and David Wright. "Community Care and Its Antecedents." In

Outside the Walls of the Asylum: The History of Care in Community, 1750–2000, edited by Peter Bartlett and David Wright, 1–18. London: Athlone Press, 1999.

———, eds. *Outside the Walls of the Asylum: The History of Care in Community, 1750–2000.* London: Athlone Press, 1999.

Bartrip, P. W. J. "British Government Inspection, 1832–1875: Some Observations." *Historical Journal* 25 (1982): 605–26.

Battiscombe, George. *Shaftesbury: A Biography of the Seventh Earl, 1801–1885.* London: Constable, 1974.

Beer, Gillian. "Science and Literature." In *Companion to the History of Modern Science,* edited by R. C. Olby et al., 783–98. London: Routledge, 1990.

Behlmer, George K. *Friends of the Family: The English Home and Its Guardians, 1850–1940.* Stanford, Calif.: Stanford University Press, 1998.

Blyth, Henry. *Caro—The Fatal Passion: The Life of Lady Caroline Lamb.* London: Rupert Hart-Davis, 1972.

Bourdieu, Pierre. *Outline of a Theory of Practice.* Translated by Richard Nice. Cambridge: Cambridge University Press, 1977.

Butler, Marilyn. "Culture's Medium: The Role of the Review." In *The Cambridge Companion to British Romanticism,* edited by Stuart Curran, 120–47. Cambridge: Cambridge University Press, 1993.

Bynum, William F. "Rationales for Therapy in British Psychiatry, 1780–1835." In *Madhouses, Mad-Doctors, and Madmen: The Social History of Psychiatry in the Victorian Era,* edited by Andrew Scull, 35–57. London: Athlone Press, 1981.

Castel, Robert. *The Regulation of Madness: The Origin of Incarceration in France.* Translated by W. D. Halls. Oxford: Polity, 1988.

Colley, Linda. *Britons: Forging the Nation.* New Haven, Conn.: Yale University Press, 1992.

Cooter, Roger. *The Cultural Meaning of Popular Science: Phrenology and the Organization of Consent in Nineteenth-Century Britain.* Cambridge: Cambridge University Press, 1984.

Cowling, Mary. *The Artist as Anthropologist: The Representation of Type and Character in Victorian Art.* Cambridge: Cambridge University Press, 1989.

Darnton, Robert. *The Literary Underground of the Old Regime.* Cambridge, Mass.: Harvard University Press, 1982.

Davidoff, Leonore. "The Family in Britain." In *The Cambridge Social History of Britain, 1750–1950,* edited by F. M. L. Thompson, vol. 2: 71–129. Cambridge: Cambridge University Press, 1990.

Davidoff, Leonore, and Catherine Hall. *Family Fortunes: Men and Women of the English Middle Class, 1780–1850.* London: Routledge, 1992.

Desmond, Adrian. *The Politics of Evolution: Morphology, Medicine, and Reform in Radical London.* Chicago: University of Chicago Press, 1989.

Digby, Anne. *Madness, Morality, and Medicine: A Study of the York Retreat, 1796–1914.* Cambridge: Cambridge University Press, 1985.

———. *Making a Medical Living: Doctors and Patients in the English Market for Medicine, 1720–1911.* Cambridge: Cambridge University Press, 1994.

Donzelot, Jacques. *The Policing of Families.* Translated by Robert Hurley. London: Hutchinson, 1979.

Duden, Barbara. *The Women beneath the Skin: A Doctor's Patients in Eighteenth-Century Germany.* Translated by Thomas Dunlap. Cambridge, Mass.: Harvard University Press, 1991.

Dyhouse, Carol. "Mothers and Daughters in the Middle-Class Home, c. 1870–1914." In *Labour and Love: Women's Experience of Home and Family, 1850–1940*, edited by Jane Lewis, 26–47. Oxford: Basil Blackwell, 1986.

Eigen, Joel Peter. "Delusion in the Courtroom: The Role of Partial Insanity in Early Forensic Testimony." *Medical History* 35 (1991): 25–49.

———. *Witnessing Insanity: Madness and Mad-Doctors in the English Court.* New Haven, Conn.: Yale University Press, 1995.

Elias, Norbert. *The Civilizing Process.* Translated by Edmund Jephcott. 2 vols. New York: Urizen Books, 1978.

Faas, Ekbert. *Retreat into the Mind: Victorian Poetry and the Rise of Psychiatry.* Princeton, N.J.: Princeton University Press, 1988.

Finlayson, Geoffrey B. A. M. *The Seventh Earl of Shaftesbury, 1801–1885.* London: Eyre Methuen, 1981.

Finnane, Mark. *Insanity and the Insane in Post-Famine Ireland.* London: Croom Helm, 1981.

Fissell, Mary E. "The Disappearance of the Patient's Narrative and the Invention of Hospital Medicine." In *British Medicine in an Age of Reform,* edited by Roger French and Andrew Wear, 92–109. London: Routledge, 1991.

———. *Patient, Power, and the Poor in Eighteenth-Century Bristol.* Cambridge: Cambridge University Press, 1991.

———. "Readers, Texts, and Contexts: Vernacular Medical Works in Early Modern England." In *The Popularization of Medicine, 1650–1850,* edited by Roy Porter, 72–96. London: Routledge, 1992.

Forsythe, Bill, Joseph Melling, and Richard Adair. "Politics of Lunacy: Central State Regulation and the Devon Pauper Lunatic Asylum, 1845–1914." In *Insanity, Institutions, and Society, 1800–1914,* edited by Joseph Melling and Bill Forsythe, 68–92. London: Routledge, 1999.

Foucault, Michel. *The Birth of the Clinic.* Translated by A. M. Sheridan. 1973; reprinted, London: Routledge, 1976.

———. *Discipline and Punish: The Birth of the Prison.* Translated by Alan Sheridan. Harmondsworth: Penguin, 1979.

———. *Histoire de la folie à l'âge classique.* 2nd ed. Paris: Éditions Gallimard, 1972.

———. *Histoire de la sexualité 1: La volonté de savoir.* Paris: Éditions Gallimard, 1976.

Fraser, Flora. *The Unruly Queen: The Life of Queen Caroline*. London: Macmillan, 1996.

Gilman, Sander. *Difference and Pathology: Stereotypes of Sexuality, Race, and Madness.* Ithaca, N.Y.: Cornell University Press, 1985.

———. *Seeing the Insane.* New York: John Wiley & Sons, 1982.

Goldstein, Jan. *Console and Classify: The French Psychiatric Profession in the Nineteenth Century.* Cambridge: Cambridge University Press, 1987.

———. "Psychiatry." In *Companion Encyclopedia of the History of Medicine,* edited by W. F. Bynum and Roy Porter, vol. 2: 1350–72. London: Routledge, 1993.

Hall, Catherine. "The Sweet Delights of Home." In *From the Fires of Revolution to the Great War,* edited by Michelle Perrot, 47–93. Vol. 4 of *A History of Private Life,* edited by Philippe Ariès and Georges Duby, translated by Arthur Goldhammer. Cambridge, Mass.: Belknap Press of Harvard University Press, 1990.

Hammerton, A. James. *Cruelty and Companionship: Conflict in Nineteenth-Century Married Life.* London: Routledge, 1992.

———. "Victorian Marriage and the Law of Matrimonial Cruelty." *Victorian Studies* 33 (1990): 267–92.

Harres, Frances. *Henry Brougham.* London: Jonathan Cape, 1957.

Harris, Jose. *Private Lives, Public Spirit: Britain, 1870–1914.* Harmondsworth: Penguin, 1994.

Harris, Ruth. *Murders and Madness: Medicine, Law, and Society in the Fin de Siècle.* Oxford: Oxford University Press, 1989.

Hervey, Nicholas. "Advocacy of Folly: The Alleged Lunatics' Friend Society, 1845–63." *Medical History* 30 (1986): 245–75.

———. "Lunacy Commission, 1845–1860, with Special Reference to the Implementation of Policy in Kent and Surrey." Ph.D. diss., University of Bristol, 1987.

Hill, Bridget. *Servants: English Domestics in the Eighteenth Century.* Oxford: Clarendon Press, 1996.

Hilton, Boyd. *The Age of Atonement: The Influence of Evangelicalism on Social and Economic Thought, 1785–1865.* Oxford: Oxford University Press, 1988.

Hobsbawm, Eric. *The Age of Revolution: Europe, 1789–1848.* London: Abacus, 1992.

Hoppen, K. Theodore. *The Mid-Victorian Generation: 1846–1886.* Oxford: Oxford University Press, 1998.

Horn, Pamela. *The Rise and Fall of the Victorian Servant.* Stroud: Alan Sutton Publishing, 1990.

Houghton, Walter E. *The Victorian Frame of Mind, 1830–1870.* New Haven, Conn.: Yale University Press, 1957.

Houston, R. A. *Madness and Society in Eighteenth-Century Scotland.* Oxford: Clarendon Press, 2000.

Hunt, Lynn, ed. *The Invention of Pornography: Obscenity and the Origins of Modernity, 1500–1800.* New York: Zone Books, 1993.
Hunter, Richard, and Ida Macalpine. "Introduction." In *An Enquiry Concerning the Indications of Insanity,* by John Conolly, 1–35. 1830; reprinted, London: Dawsons, 1964.
———. *Psychiatry for the Poor: 1851 Colney Hatch Asylum, Friern Hospital 1973.* London: Dawsons, 1974.
Jewson, N. D. "The Disappearance of the Sick-Man from Medical Cosmology, 1770–1870." *Sociology* 10 (1976), 225–44.
———. "Medical Knowledge and the Patronage System in Eighteenth-Century England." *Sociology* 8 (1974): 369–85.
Jones, Kathleen. *A History of the Mental Health Services.* London: Routledge & Kegan Paul, 1972.
Kleinman, Arthur. *The Illness Narratives: Suffering, Healing, and the Human Condition.* New York: Basic Books, 1988.
Kromm, Jane E. "The Feminization of Madness in Visual Representation." *Feminist Studies* 20 (1994): 507–36.
Laqueur, Thomas W. "The Queen Caroline Affair: Politics as Art in the Reign of George IV." *Journal of Modern History* 54 (1982): 417–66.
Loudon, Irvine. *Medical Care and the General Practitioner, 1750–1850.* Oxford: Clarendon Press, 1986.
Lunbeck, Elizabeth. *The Psychiatric Persuasion: Knowledge, Gender, and Power in Modern America.* Princeton, N.J.: Princeton University Press, 1994.
Macalpine, Ida, and Richard Hunter. *George III and the Mad-Business.* London: Pimlico, 1991.
MacDonagh, Oliver. *Early Victorian Government, 1830–1870.* London: Weidenfeld and Nicolson, 1977.
MacDonald, Michael. "Lunatics and the State in Georgian England." *Social History of Medicine* 2 (1989): 299–313.
———. *Mystical Bedlam: Madness, Anxiety, and Healing in Seventeenth-Century England.* Cambridge: Cambridge University Press, 1981.
MacKenzie, Charlotte. *Psychiatry for the Rich: A History of Ticehurst Private Asylum.* London: Routledge, 1992.
Maulitz, Russell. *Morbid Appearances: The Anatomy of Pathology in the Early Nineteenth Century.* Cambridge: Cambridge University Press, 1987.
Maza, Sarah. *Private Lives and Public Affairs: The Causes Célèbres of Prerevolutionary France.* Berkeley and Los Angeles: University of California Press, 1993.
McCalman, Iain. *Radical Underworld: Prophets, Revolutionaries, and Pornographers in London, 1795–1840.* Oxford: Clarendon Press, 1993.
McCandless, Peter. "Dangerous to Themselves and Others: The Victorian Debate over the Prevention of Wrongful Confinement." *Journal of British Studies* 23 (1983): 84–104.

———. "Liberty and Lunacy: The Victorians and Wrongful Confinement." In *Madhouses, Mad-Doctors, and Madmen: The Social History of Psychiatry in the Victorian Era,* edited by Andrew Scull, 339–62. London: Athlone Press, 1981.

McMenemey, William H. "James Parkinson, 1755–1824: A Biographical Essay." In *James Parkinson (1755–1824),* edited by MacDonald Critchley, with the collaboration of William H. McMenemey et al., 1–144. London: Macmillan, 1955.

Mellikan, R. A. *John Scott, Lord Eldon, 1751–1838: The Duty of Loyalty.* Cambridge: Cambridge University Press, 1999.

Melling, Joseph. "Accommodating Madness: New Research in the Social History of Insanity and Institutions." In *Insanity, Institutions, and Society, 1800–1914,* edited by Joseph Melling and Bill Forsythe, 1–30. London: Routledge, 1999.

Melling, Joseph, and Bill Forsythe, eds. *Insanity, Institutions, and Society, 1800–1914.* London: Routledge, 1999.

Micale, Mark S. *Approaching Hysteria: Disease and Its Interpretations.* Princeton, N.J.: Princeton University Press, 1995.

———. "Charcot and the Idea of Hysteria in the Male: Gender, Mental Science, and Medical Diagnosis in Late Nineteenth-Century France." *Medical History* 34 (1990): 363–411.

Midelfort, H. C. Erik. *A History of Madness in Sixteenth-Century Germany.* Stanford, Calif.: Stanford University Press, 1999.

Miller, D. A. *The Novel and the Police.* Berkeley and Los Angeles: University of California Press, 1988.

Moran, James E. "Asylum in the Community: Managing the Insane in Antebellum America." *History of Psychiatry* 9 (1998): 217–40.

Morris, Arthur D. *The Hoxton Madhouses.* N.p.: Goodwin Books, 1958.

Murray, Venetia. *High Society in the Regency Period, 1788–1830.* Harmondsworth: Penguin, 1999.

Neugebauer, Richard. "Mental Handicap in Medieval and Early Modern England." In *From Idiocy to Mental Deficiency: Historical Perspectives on People with Learning Disabilities,* edited by David Wright and Anne Digby, 22–43. London: Routledge, 1996.

———. "Mental Illness and Government Policy in Sixteenth- and Seventeenth-Century England." Ph.D. diss., Columbia University, 1976.

Neve, Michael Trevor Turner. "What the Doctor Thought and Did: Sir James Crichton-Brown (1840–1938)." *Medical History* 39 (1995): 399–432.

Okin, Susan Moller. "Patriarchy and Married Women's Property in England: Questions on Some Current Views." *Eighteenth-Century Studies* 17 (1983–84): 121–38.

Parry-Jones, William Ll. *The Trade in Lunacy.* London: Routledge and Kegan Paul, 1972.

Peakman, Julie. *Mighty Lewd Books: The Development of Pornography in Eighteenth-Century England.* London: Palgrave, 2003.
Peterson, M. Jeanne. *The Medical Profession in Mid-Victorian London.* Berkeley and Los Angeles: University of California Press, 1978.
Porter, Dorothy, and Roy Porter. *Patient's Progress: Doctors and Doctoring in Eighteenth-Century England.* Oxford: Polity Press, 1989.
Porter, Roy. "Madness and Its Institutions." In *Medicine in Society: Historical Essays,* edited by Andrew Wear, 277–301. Cambridge: Cambridge University Press, 1992.
———. *Mind-Forg'd Manacles: A History of Madness in England from the Restoration to the Regency.* London: Athlone Press, 1987.
———, ed. *Patients and Practitioners: Lay Perceptions of Medicine in Pre-Industrial Society.* Cambridge: Cambridge University Press, 1985.
———. "'The Secrets of Generation Display'd': *Aristotle's Master-piece* in Eighteenth-Century England." In *'Tis Nature's Fault: Unauthorized Sexuality during the Enlightenment,* edited by Robert Purks Maccubin, 1–21. Cambridge: Cambridge University Press, 1987.
———. *The Social History of Madness.* London: Weidenfeld and Nicolson, 1987.
Porter, Roy, and David Wright, eds. *The Confinement of the Insane: International Perspectives, 1800–1965.* Cambridge: Cambridge University Press, 2003.
Prestwich, Patricia E. "Family Strategies and Medical Power: 'Voluntary' Committal in a Parisian Asylum, 1876–1914." *Journal of Social History* 27 (1994): 799–818.
Ray, Gordon N. *Thackeray: The Uses of Adversity, 1811–1846.* London: Oxford University Press, 1955.
Reiser, Stanley Joel. *Medicine and the Reign of Technology.* Cambridge: Cambridge University Press, 1978.
Richardson, Ruth. *Death, Dissection and the Destitute.* 1988; reprinted, Harmondsworth: Penguin, 1989.
Ripa, Yannick. *Women and Madness: The Incarceration of Women in Nineteenth-Century France.* Translated by Catherine du Peloux Menagé. Cambridge: Polity Press, 1990.
Roberts, Shirley. *James Parkinson: From Apothecary to General Practitioner.* London: Royal Society of Medicine, 1997.
Rosenberg, Charles E. "Medical Text and Social Context: Explaining William Buchan's Domestic Medicine." *Bulletin of the History of Medicine* 57 (1983): 22–42.
Rudé, George. *The Crowd in History.* 1964; reprinted, London: Serif, 1995.
Schwieso, J. J. "Religious Fanaticism and Wrongful Confinement in Victorian England: The Affair of Louisa Nottidge." *Social History of Medicine* 9 (1996): 159–74.
Scull, Andrew. "Domestication of Madness." *Medical History* 27 (1983): 233–48.

——. "Moral Treatment Reconsidered: Some Sociological Comments on an Episode in the History of British Psychiatry." In *Madhouses, Mad-Doctors, and Madmen: The Social History of Psychiatry in the Victorian Era,* edited by Andrew Scull, 105–18. London: Athlone Press, 1981.

——. *The Most Solitary of Afflictions: Madness and Society in Britain, 1700–1900.* New Haven, Conn.: Yale University Press, 1993.

——. *Museums of Madness: The Social Organization of Insanity in Nineteenth-Century England.* 1979; reprinted, Harmondsworth: Penguin, 1982.

——. *Social Order/Mental Disorder.* London: Routledge, 1989.

Scull, Andrew, Charlotte MacKenzie, and Nicholas Hervey. "From Disciple to Critic: Sir John Charles Bucknill (1817–1897)." In *Masters of Bedlam: The Transformation of the Mad-Doctoring Trade,* 187–225. Princeton, N.J.: Princeton University Press, 1996.

——, eds. *Masters of Bedlam: The Transformation of the Mad-Doctoring Trade.* Princeton, N.J.: Princeton University Press, 1996.

Shorter, Edward. *Doctors and Their Patients: A Social History.* 2nd edition. Brunswick, N.J.: Transaction Publishers, 1991.

Showalter, Elaine. *The Female Malady: Women, Madness and English Culture, 1830–1980.* London: Virago, 1987.

Shuttleworth, Sally. *Charlotte Brontë and Victorian Psychology.* Cambridge: Cambridge University Press, 1996.

Small, Helen. "'In the Guise of Science': Literature and the Rhetoric of 19th-Century English Psychiatry." *History of the Human Sciences* 7 (1994): 27–55.

——. *Love's Madness: Medicine, the Novel, and Female Insanity, 1800–1865.* Oxford: Oxford University Press, 1996.

Smith, Leonard D. *"Cure, Comfort and Safe Custody": Public Lunatic Asylums in Early Nineteenth-Century England.* London: Leicester University Press & Cassell, 1999.

Smith, Roger. *Trial by Medicine: Insanity and Responsibility in Victorian Trials.* Edinburgh: Edinburgh University Press, 1981.

Sprigge, S. Squire. *The Life and Times of Thomas Wakley.* 1899; reprinted, New York: Robert E. Krieger Publishing Company, 1974.

Stewart, Robert. *Henry Brougham, 1778–1868: His Public Career.* London: Bodley Head, 1985.

Still, Arthur, and Irving Velody, eds. *Rewriting the History of Madness: Studies in Foucault's "Histoire de la folie."* London: Routledge, 1992.

Stone, Lawrence. *Broken Lives: Separation and Divorce in England, 1660–1857.* Oxford: Oxford University Press, 1993.

——. *The Family, Sex, and Marriage in England, 1500–1800.* Harmondsworth: Penguin, 1979.

——. *The Road to Divorce: England, 1530–1987.* Oxford: Oxford University Press, 1990.

———. *Uncertain Unions: Marriage in England, 1660–1753.* Oxford: Oxford University Press, 1992.
Suzuki, Akihito. "Dualism and the Transformation of Psychiatric Language in the Seventeenth and Eighteenth Centuries." *History of Science* 33 (1995): 417–47.
———. "Family, the State and the Insane in Japan, 1900–1945." In *Psychiatric Confinement in International Perspective,* edited by Roy Porter and David Wright, 193–225. Cambridge: Cambridge University Press, 2003.
———. "Framing Psychiatric Subjectivity: Doctor, Patient, and Record-Keeping at Bethlem in the Nineteenth Century." In *Insanity, Institutions, and Society, 1800–1914,* edited by Joseph Melling and Bill Forsythe, 115–36. London: Routledge, 1999.
———. "Household and the Care of Lunatics in Eighteenth-Century London." In *The Locus of Care: Families, Communities, and Institutions in History,* edited by Richard Smith and Peregrine Horden, 153–75. London: Routledge, 1997.
———. "Politics and Ideology of Non-Restraint: The Case of the Hanwell Asylum." *Medical History* 39 (1995): 1–17.
———. "Psychiatric Therapeutics and the 'Public' in England in the Eighteenth and Nineteenth Centuries." *Harvard Review of Psychiatry* 10 (2002): 123–26.
Szasz, Thomas. *The Myth of Mental Illness.* London: Granada, 1972.
Taylor, Jenny Bourne. *In the Secret Theatre of Home: Wilkie Collins, Sensation Narrative, and Nineteenth-Century Psychology.* London: Routledge, 1988.
Taylor, Jenny Bourne, and Sally Shuttleworth, eds. *Embodied Selves: An Anthology of Psychological Texts, 1830–1890.* Oxford: Oxford University Press, 1998.
Thane, Pat. "Government and Society in England and Wales, 1750–1914." In *Cambridge Social History of Britain, 1750–1950,* edited by F. M. L. Thompson, vol. 3: 1–61. Cambridge: Cambridge University Press, 1990.
Thompson, E. P. "The Crime of Anonymity." In *Albion's Fatal Tree: Crime and Society in Eighteenth-Century England,* edited by Douglas Hay et al., 255–344. Harmondsworth: Penguin, 1977.
———. "The Moral Economy of the English Crowd in the Eighteenth Century." *Past and Present* 50 (1971): 76–136.
Tomes, Nancy. "The Anatomy of Madness: New Directions in the History of Psychiatry." *Social Studies of Science* 17 (1987): 358–71.
———. *The Art of Asylum-Keeping: Thomas Story Kirkbride and the Origin of American Psychiatry.* 1984; reprinted, Philadelphia: University of Pennsylvania Press, 1994.
———. "Devils in the Heart: A Nineteenth-Century Perspective on Women and Depression." *Transactions and Studies of the College of Physicians of Philadelphia,* ser. 5, 13 (1991): 363–86.
———. "Feminist Histories of Psychiatry." In *Discovering the History of Psychiatry,* edited by Mark S. Micale and Roy Porter, 348–83. Oxford: Oxford University Press, 1994.

Tosh, John. *A Man's Place: Masculinity and the Middle-Class Home in Victorian England.* New Haven, Conn.: Yale University Press, 1999.

Vickery, Amanda. *The Gentleman's Daughter: Women's Lives in Georgian England.* New Haven, Conn.: Yale University Press, 1998.

———. "Golden Age to Separate Spheres? A Review of the Categories and Chronology of English Women's History." *Historical Journal* 36 (1993): 383–414.

Wagner, Peter. *Eros Revived: Erotica of the Enlightenment in England and America.* London: Paladin, 1988.

Walton, John L. "Lunacy in the Industrial Revolution: A Study of Asylum Admissions in Lancashire, 1845–50." *Journal of Social History* 13 (1979): 1–21.

Warner, John Harley. "Science in Medicine." *Osiris,* 2nd ser., 1 (1985): 37–58.

Weiner, Dora B. "Mind and Body in the Clinic: Philippe Pinel, Alexander Crichton, Dominique Esquirol, and the Birth of Psychiatry." In *The Language of Psyche: Mind and Body in Enlightenment Thought,* edited by G. S. Rousseau, 331–402. Los Angeles: William Clark Memorial Library, 1990.

Winter, Alison. *Mesmerized: Powers of Mind in Victorian Britain.* Chicago: University of Chicago Press, 1998.

Wright, David. "The Certification of Insanity in Nineteenth-Century England and Wales." *History of Psychiatry* 9 (1998): 267–90.

———. "Getting Out of the Asylum: Understanding the Confinement of the Insane in the Nineteenth Century." *Social History of Medicine* 10 (1997): 137–55.

———. *Mental Disability in Victorian England: The Earlswood Asylum, 1847–1901.* Oxford: Clarendon Press, 2001.

Wrightson, Keith. *English Society, 1580–1680.* 1982; reprinted, London: Routledge, 1993.

Yolton, John W. *John Locke and the Way of Ideas.* Oxford: Clarendon Press, 1956.

INDEX

Text: 11.25/13.5 Adobe Garamond
Display: Adobe Garamond
Compositor: BookMatters, Berkeley
Printer and binder: Friesens Corporation
Indexer: Kevin Millham

Lightning Source UK Ltd.
Milton Keynes UK
UKOW04f0708120615

253385UK00002B/113/P